TERRA
NORTHWEST

Sherman and Mabel Smith Pettyjohn Distinguished Lecture Series publications.

John W. Reps, *Panoramas of Promise: Pacific Northwest Cities and Towns on Nineteenth-Century Lithographs* (1984).

David H. Stratton and George A. Frykman, eds., *The Changing Pacific Northwest: Interpreting Its Past* (1988).

William H. Goetzmann, *Looking at the Land of Promise: Pioneer Images of the Pacific Northwest* (1988).

David H. Stratton, ed., *Spokane & the Inland Empire: An Interior Pacific Northwest Anthology* (1991).

David H. Stratton, ed., *Washington Comes of Age: The State in the National Experience* (1992).

Paul W. Hirt, ed., *Terra Pacifica: People and Place in the Northwest States and Western Canada* (1998).

David H. Stratton, ed., *Spokane & the Inland Empire: An Interior Pacific Northwest Anthology*, Revised Edition (2005).

David H. Stratton, ed., *Terra Northwest: Interpreting People and Place* (2007).

TERRA
NORTHWEST

INTERPRETING PEOPLE AND PLACE

EDITED BY DAVID H. STRATTON

Washington State University Press
Pullman, Washington

Washington State University Press
PO Box 645910
Pullman, Washington 99164-5910
Phone: 800-354-7360
Fax: 509-335-8568
E-mail: wsupress@wsu.edu
Web site: wsupress.wsu.edu

Library of Congress Cataloging-in-Publication Data

Terra Northwest : interpreting people and place / edited by David H. Stratton.
   p. cm.
  "Sherman and Mabel Smith Pettyjohn Distinguished Lectures Series publications."
  ISBN 978-0-87422-291-3 (alk. paper)
  1. Northwest, Pacific—History. 2. Northwest, Pacific—History, Local. 3. Northwest,
Pacific—Social conditions. 4. Social ecology—Northwest, Pacific. I. Stratton, David H.
(David Hodges), 1927-
  F851.T315 2007
  979.0072—dc22

Fine Quality Books from the Pacific Northwest

To the memory of
Margaret H. Pettyjohn *and* Herman J. Deutsch

Contents

Introduction

David H. Stratton

ALTHOUGH NOT PLANNED AS SUCH, *Terra Northwest* inevitably became a tribute to two influential figures in the study and writing of Pacific Northwest history. Margaret Pettyjohn and Herman J. Deutsch had undoubtedly met earlier, but their involvement in the celebratory events commemorating the Centennial of Washington's creation as a territory (1853) caused their paths to cross again.

Miss Pettyjohn (d. 1978) of Walla Walla, was the daughter of Sherman and Mabel Smith Pettyjohn, pioneer farming settlers in the Prescott area. She had what can only be described as a "passion" for local history, having absorbed much of it through family experiences and the tales of other homesteaders. A graduate of Whitman College where she relished historical studies, she later gave a great deal of her time and support to organizations devoted to that cause.[1]

Professor Deutsch, who joined the faculty of the State College of Washington in Pullman (now Washington State University) in 1926, and retired in 1962, had broad scholarly interests, but became an especially vigorous promoter of the research, teaching, and public appreciation of this region's history. A meticulous scholar and exemplary teacher, he was renowned for memorizing the names of every student in his large classes, and for unerringly recalling those names in chance meetings years later. With a near missionary zeal, he shared his enthusiasm for the Pacific Northwest in public meetings and professional conferences alike, painstakingly encouraging all of those interested in regional studies. In the last publication before his death in 1979, he emphasized the need for "democratic history" that accomplished much the same objective as this anthology; "a common meeting ground" where personal identity is realized "by self-discovery" leading to an "orientation" with the rest of humankind.[2]

The Washington Territorial Centennial celebration culminated on statehood day, November 11, 1953. During the year, the "Washington Story" had been told through school plays, special newspaper editions, radio and television shows, a commemorative postal stamp, and other venues. Professor Deutsch took a leading role in the statewide program, sponsored by the

Washington State Historical Society, while the various counties organized local observances.[3]

At one of these centennial gatherings, according to legendary lore, Margaret Pettyjohn mentioned to Professor Deutsch that she intended to include in her will a generous bequest to the University of Washington for the promotion of regional history. A spirited booster of his own institution, whether of its academic programs or Cougar sports, Deutsch reminded Miss Pettyjohn of the faculty research, participation of graduate students, and well-recognized interest in the field at the State College in Pullman. He also pointed out a similar involvement at the University of Idaho in Moscow. Later, Dennis J. Morrison, assistant to the president, reinforced WSU's case by reminding Miss Pettyjohn of Professor Deutsch's scholarly work. In her will, made in 1963, there were three equal bequests for Pacific Northwest history to the University of Washington, Washington State University, and the University of Idaho. The total of all three endowments exceeded $1 million.[4]

When these funds became available to the WSU Department of History in 1979, a major portion was used to establish and sustain the Pettyjohn Distinguished Lecture Series, which served as a memorial to Margaret Pettyjohn's parents, Sherman and Mabel Smith Pettyjohn. Although the series itself now has been discontinued, the majority of the essays included in this volume, highlighting people and place in the Pacific Northwest, originated as Pettyjohn lectures or events associated with them.

The Washington State University Press has previously published, in various volumes, the lectures presented over the years in the Pettyjohn Series—the essays included here for *Terra Northwest* were chosen as outstanding examples.[5] Two new essays also have been added to this volume—Susan Armitage's provocative challenge to bring broader perspectives into our textbooks, and Mark Moreno's revealing insights into some aspects of the importance of the region's Hispanic population. The two new contributions especially exemplify this anthology's theme of "Interpreting People and Place."

For instance, Armitage refers to guidance from a statement by Donald Worster of the University of Kansas, himself a past Pettyjohn lecturer: "What the regional historian should first want to know is how a people or peoples acquired a place and, then, how they perceived and tried to make use of it." Moreno's essay helps fulfil the editorial plea in a previous volume of this series: "Of all the topics deserving scholarly study, the social, political, and cultural impact of a burgeoning Hispanic element in the Inland Northwest should be near the top of the list."[6]

As in the past, the strong support and encouragement of Director Mary B. Read and Editor-in-Chief Glen W. Lindeman at the WSU Press have made the publication of this anthology a reality. It is also especially appropriate here to recognize the crucial role of the late Raymond Muse, WSU History chair (1956-1979), in the final stages of securing the Pettyjohn bequest for the department. In addition, V. Lane Rawlins, who recently retired as WSU President, has paid close attention to the WSU Press and supported its overall publication program, often reading and offering evaluative comments on newly released books. Sally Savage, Vice President for University Relations, likewise has enthusiastically supported and has successfully acquired resources for the WSU Press.

Notes

1. Sherman and Mabel Smith Pettyjohn Memorial Endowment File, Department of History, Washington State University, Pullman.
2. Herman J. Deutsch, "Pacific Northwest History in Some World Perspectives," *Pacific Northwest Quarterly* 64 (January 1973):6–7. For Deutsch's professional career, see my tribute, "Herman J. Deutsch, 1897–1979," ibid. 71 (October 1980):183–84.
3. *Walla Walla Union-Bulletin*, February 22, March 2, and November 11, 1953. For an example of Deutsch's participation in the territorial centennial and of the celebration's program generally, see C.S. Kingston and Herman J. Deutsch, eds., *Grassroot Cuttings: Sources of the History of the Territory of Washington* (Longview, Washington: Longview Daily News, 1954). This short volume bears the inscription, "Published in Recognition of the Washington Territorial Centennial, 1953, under the auspices of the Centennial History Committee." It contains 48 brief historical articles by Deutsch and other authors intended for publication in newspapers and for other publicity uses. See also, Guide to "Grassroots [sic] Cuttings of Territorial Days" Project, typescripts, ca. 1953, cage 4886, Manuscripts, Archives, and Special Collections, Washington State University, Pullman; and, as an example of local observances, *Years Ago* (Rockford, Washington: Standard-Register, 1953).
4. Dennis J. Morrison to David H. Stratton, May 18, 1979, copy of "Last Will and Testament of Margaret H. Pettyjohn," October 9, 1963, and WSU News Service release, August 29, 1979, in Pettyjohn Memorial Endowment File.
5. Nine of the essays included in *Terra Northwest* are from three Pettyjohn Series books, now out-of-print—David H. Stratton and George A. Frykman, eds., *The Changing Pacific Northwest: Interpreting Its Past* (Pullman: WSU Press, 1988); David H. Stratton, ed., *Washington Comes of Age: The State in the National Experience* (Pullman: WSU Press, 1992); and Paul W. Hirt, ed., *Terra Pacifica: People and Place in the Northwest States and Western Canada* (Pullman: WSU Press, 1998).
6. Donald Worster, "New West, True West: Interpreting the Region's History," *Western Historical Quarterly* 18 (March 1987):149; the plea for scholarly recognition of the Hispanic population is in my introduction to the Pettyjohn Series book, *Spokane & the Inland Empire: An Interior Pacific Northwest Anthology*, rev. ed. (Pullman: WSU Press, 2005), 12.

Section One

Place

I

The Spanish Moment in the Pacific Northwest [1]

David J. Weber

I N 1929, ON A HILLTOP in Vancouver along a stretch of scenic coast called Spanish Banks, the Canadian government placed a plaque that read in part:

> Near this place, Captain George Vancouver on the 22nd June 1792 met the *Sutil* and *Mexicana* under Captains Galiano and Valdes—the last Spanish exploring expedition in what is now the BC [British Columbia] coast. The commanders exchanged information, established mutual confidence, and continued exploration together. It was dawn for Britain, but twilight for Spain.

More than a half-century later, in 1984, King Juan Carlos and Queen Sophia of Spain spent several days in Vancouver. In anticipation of their visit, the Historic Sites and Monuments Board of Canada removed the plaque and replaced it with a new one designed to give no offense to Iberian sensibilities. The Board had thoughtfully removed the words "dawn for Britain, but twilight for Spain."[2]

This story would surprise many Americans, but not because it illustrates the way in which present-day agendas reshape our understanding of the past. Americans more likely would be surprised at the notion that Spaniards once were present in the area. As one scholar recently put it: "Today's general public remains little aware of Spain's once significant presence along the coastlines and near the shores of modern Oregon, Washington, British Columbia, and Alaska."[3]

Spaniards did, of course, reach the Pacific Northwest, preceding all other European powers in exploring the coastlines of Oregon, Washington, and British Columbia. Spanish subjects, many of them Mexican-born, also planted the first non-Indian settlements in the region—short-lived posts on Vancouver Island and in Washington at the entrance to the Strait of Juan de Fuca. The Spanish empire, then, extended to the Pacific Northwest both in theory and in practice. Spain claimed that coast—as well, for that matter, sole navigation rights to the vast Eastern Pacific, both north and south of the Equator—by right of Papal donation (1493), and a long list of subsequent discoveries, international agreements, and first occupancies.

At first blush, Spain's momentary presence in the Pacific Northwest may seem unworthy of attention. Spain, after all, is no longer around. Indeed, by the time Americans reached the Northwest Coast in consequential numbers, England was the United States' chief competitor, not Spain. Why then, concern ourselves with a nation that lost? That question was posed clearly by a reviewer of my book appearing in 1992—a study of Spain's activities in all of North America.

"Usually," Nicholas Lemann wrote in the *Atlantic Monthly*, "the history of an undertaking is written only if it went well." Lemann did not think Spain's story went well at all. "As a colonial power in what is now the United States, Spain was a complete failure," Lemann wrote. "Spain's substantial efforts," he added, "never amounted to anything." He liked my book, but thought my narrative failed because Spain failed and thereby prevented me from arranging historical events along, what he called, "a rising arc of portentousness."[4]

Spain clearly failed to win contests with England, France, Russia, and the United States for control of North America, but failing to win is not tantamount to "complete failure." It is interesting and instructive to see how Spain played the game—what it did, and how and why it lost. Indeed, few stories, be they of nations or individuals, follow "a rising arc of portentousness." Sooner or later, all lose the game somewhere.

When Americans contemplate Spanish activity in what is now the United States—if they contemplate it at all—it is the 16th-century "age of exploration" that comes most readily to mind. Americans who are unlikely to know the name of any Spaniard in the New World in the 17th or 18th centuries recognize the names of 16th-century *conquistadores,* whom they associate with high adventure—Ponce de León, Francisco Vázquez de Coronado, and Hernando de Soto. And scholars, no less drawn to high adventure than the general public, have devoted a disproportionate amount of writing and research to that age of exploration.[5]

While *conquistadores* swarmed across much of the southern parts of the continent in the 16th century, the Pacific Northwest lay just beyond their horizon, shielded by stormy seas, contrary currents, and chance. Spanish mariners did, however, reach the southern border of Oregon. Sailing for the viceroy of New Spain, as Mexico had come to be called, Juan Rodríguez Cabrillo[6] set out from the Pacific port of Navidad in June 1542 with three small ships and orders to explore northward. Viceroy Antonio de Mendoza had instructed Cabrillo to seek evidence of rich Indian cities, and to find the passage through the continent that Spaniards imagined must exist and even knew by name—the Strait of Anian. Cabrillo's orders also required him to follow the coast all the way to China; Spanish officials imagined the two continents were joined at their northern extremities.

As the European discoverer of San Diego harbor and other points along the shoreline of what is now Southern California, Cabrillo is well remembered, but the journey went beyond Southern California. A veteran conquistador from Andalusia, who had survived battles against well-trained Aztec armies while fighting alongside Hernán Cortés, Cabrillo slipped on a rock on Santa Catalina Island and died from his injury shortly after the New Year in 1543.

The chief pilot, Bartolomé Ferrer, then took command and pointed the expedition's three small ships north. Near the present-day California-Oregon boundary, at 42° latitude, a shortage of supplies and a tempest "with a sea so high that [the sailors] became crazed," forced Ferrer to abandon plans to continue to China.[7] He turned back to Mexico. They probably had reached the high water mark of purposeful Spanish exploration on the Pacific coast for the next two centuries—unless one believes the controversial account of Juan de Fuca's visit to the strait that bears his name.[8]

Although Cabrillo and Ferrer failed to locate the Strait of Anian or find rich civilizations, they did explore some 1,200 miles of coastline, and established a Spanish claim to the Pacific coast of North America that no European power challenged seriously for over two centuries. They also made exceptional navigational notes, added to the growing doubt that a North American waterway connected the Atlantic and Pacific, and contributed evidence that Asia and North America were not joined, but might be two separate continents.

The Cabrillo-Ferrer voyage of 1542–1543 occurred just three decades after the first Spaniard touched foot on the shores of what would become the United States—i.e., when Ponce de León reached Florida in 1513. Between 1513 and 1543, therefore, the Spanish completed a remarkable reconnaissance of the continental coastlines—up the Atlantic to Maine, around the entire Gulf of Mexico, and along the Pacific to the 42° parallel. Inland by 1543, De Soto and Coronado had explored much of the South and Southwest. As a result, the contours of the continent began to appear on European maps and Spain's King Carlos could indulge himself in the common European conceit that discovery gave him a strong claim to lands actually held by a variety of native peoples.

But Spaniards had little motive to return to North America, much less venture into the unknown northerly latitudes of what are now Oregon, Washington, and British Columbia. The northern reaches held little attraction for a people who had stumbled upon the wealth of the Aztec and Inca empires. Moreover, conventional wisdom suggested that precious metals abounded in hot rather than cold climates, and the tropics yielded other valuable commodities, including sugar and spices not susceptible to cultivation in northern latitudes. As Peter Martyr, the Italian humanist in the Spanish court, explained:

> But what need have we of what is found everywhere in Europe? It is towards the south, not towards the frozen north, that those who seek their fortune should bend their way; for everything at the equator is rich.[9]

Following the great explorations of the early-16th century, Spain concentrated on building colonies in lands farther south—closer to mineral wealth and tractable Indian laborers. Spain might have forgotten the Pacific coast of North America had it not been for the growth of a valuable trade between New Spain and the Philippines. Prevailing winds propelled Spanish vessels from Mexico to the Philippines, but returning home proved impossible until Andrés de Urdaneta discovered the solution in 1565. Thereafter, galleons returned to Mexico from Manila by sailing north into Japanese waters, then picking up westerlies in those latitudes that took them to the California coast—sometimes as high as Cape Mendocino—and then running south with the winds and current to Acapulco.

The long California coast now took on importance. The scurvy-ridden crews on returning galleons needed a place to take on fresh water, fruit, and vegetables after crossing the Pacific, and Spain needed to challenge Dutch and English pirates lurking in quiet coves along the coast, awaiting treasure-laden galleons. Thus, Spain began a search for a suitable place to establish a base in California—a search that culminated with the voyage of Sebastián Vizcaíno, an energetic merchant with long experience in the Pacific trade and in Baja California.

In 1602–1603, Vizcaíno accurately mapped the California coastline as far as Cape Mendocino and bestowed new names, replacing those left sixty years before by Cabrillo, whose charts apparently had been forgotten.[10] With few exceptions, Vizcaíno's names remain unchanged today. Vizcaíno recommended that Spain occupy the bay that he named for the conde de Monterrey, the viceroy who sponsored the expedition. In retrospect, it seems a curious decision because California had two bays manifestly superior to Monterey. One, San Diego Bay, Vizcaíno judged too far south for the landfall of ships returning from Manila; it also seemed to lack sufficient wood and game. San Francisco Bay, not being clearly visible from the sea, had simply eluded Vizcaíno—as it would other mariners.

If Spaniards had established a permanent settlement on Monterey Bay early in the 17th century, as Vizcaíno recommended, it would have brought them within convenient sailing distance of the Pacific Northwest. But in 1607, a new viceroy, the marqués de Montesclaros, shelved plans to build an outpost on the California coast. Rather than repel foreign interlopers and protect the Philippine trade, Montesclaros decided that a Spanish base would attract English and Dutch smugglers, who would come to trade (as they did in the Caribbean and on the Florida coast). California's security, Montesclaros believed, depended on its inaccessibility, and the passage of time confirmed his judgment. Finally, he did not believe that the benefits of building a base fifteen- to twenty-days' sail from Acapulco would justify its costs.

In the decades that followed, Spanish officials occasionally tried to resurrect the California project. A port far up the Pacific coast would not only support the Manila trade, but would serve as a supply base for New Mexico, where Spain had established a permanent colony in 1598. (The Spanish did not fully appreciate the great distance between Santa Fe and San Francisco Bay until the late-18th century.) The idea, however, failed to advance beyond the talking stage. Spain did not occupy the coast of what is today California until 1769—over a century and a half after Viceroy Montesclaros declared such a plan impractical.

There is no firm evidence that Spaniards deliberately explored the Northwest Coast during that century and a half, although some returning galleons accidentally approached the region or made landfall. One galleon, perhaps the *San Francisco Xavier* in 1707, crashed at Nehalem Beach, thirty-five miles south of the Columbia's mouth. Its cargo included over sixty tons of beeswax intended for candles for New Spain altars, homes, and mines. The castaways—the first European subjects known to have come ashore in the Pacific Northwest—lived long enough among Indians to leave descendants. Nehalem Indians and other tribes salvaged beeswax from the wreck well into the 19th century.[11]

Through most of the colonial era, then, the Spanish had no compelling reason to explore or settle in the Pacific Northwest. Pointing to Spain's rational calculations would seem sufficient to explain its absence from the region, but American historians, who often have approached the past with an anti-Spanish bias, have suggested a simpler explanation—Spanish lethargy. Historian Oscar Winther, for example, contrasted English settlement of the Atlantic coast with Spain's neglect of the Pacific Northwest. "From the founding of Jamestown to the close of the French and Indian War," Winther wrote, "the Spanish remained relatively inactive."[12] Winther chose to overlook Spain's considerable activity elsewhere in North America—in Florida, Texas, and New Mexico—as well as in Mexico, Central America, and South America.

Spain's "relative inactivity" ended, as Winther put it, when "two nerve-racking nightmares…contrived to disturb the Spanish *slumbers*."[13] Russian and English threats to Spanish claims to the Pacific coast of North America aroused the "suspicious Spaniards," Winther wrote. Had he been describing Englishmen or Americans, one suspects that Winther might have referred to them as "vigilant" or "alert," rather than "suspicious." Whatever adjective we apply, however, the defensive measures that Spain took against its European rivals brought Spaniards into Upper California and the Pacific Northwest in the last half of the 18th century.

The architect of Spanish expansion into California was José de Gálvez, who served as a nearly omnipotent royal inspector in New Spain from 1765 to 1770. Gálvez regarded both England and Russia as threats to Spanish claims. Gálvez feared that English vessels would soon enter the Pacific from the north if England's well-publicized search for the Northwest Passage succeeded, and he correctly predicted that the English pushing westward from Canada and the Mississippi would find their way to California. The threat from Russian fur traders seemed even more immediate. In 1759, a book by a Spanish Franciscan, José Torrubia, had appeared in Italy with the alarming title, *Muscovites in California.*

Fired by considerable ambition, the energetic Gálvez began, on his own initiative, to lay the foundations for Spanish expansion into the northwest of New Spain. In 1768, when reports of Russian activity on the California coast prompted Madrid to order Gálvez to secure Monterey Bay, he already was prepared to move swiftly.

With the founding of Spanish missions and presidios at San Diego and Monterey in 1769 and 1770, Spain moved closer to the Pacific Northwest. In

1773, a new viceroy, Antonio María Bucareli, became convinced of a renewed Russian threat to California and the need to occupy the extraordinary San Francisco Bay locality, which Spaniards had sighted in 1769 from a high point on the San Francisco Peninsula. Though cautious, Bucareli moved by land and sea to meet Russian expansion. First, he granted permission to a frontier presidial officer, Captain Juan Bautista de Anza, to blaze an overland trail from Sonora to Monterey. Second, he sent vessels beyond San Francisco to search the coast for foreigners and for sites for further Spanish defensive settlements.

Strapped for officers, men, and ships, Bucareli entrusted the naval exploration to a pilot, Juan Pérez, and to a single vessel that would double as a supply ship, the frigate *Santiago*. In January 1774, Pérez set out from San Blas on a voyage whose destination the viceroy hoped to keep secret, but that quickly became identified as "going to Russia." After dropping supplies off at San Diego and Monterey, Pérez set course far from the continent, then beat north into waters that no European had sailed in before. Near the present-day Canadian-Alaskan boundary at about 54° 40', Pérez made landfall. From there, he cruised south for a closer look at the coastline of British Columbia, Washington, and Oregon. He could not, however, comply with orders to inspect the coast carefully in a search for foreigners, or to stop frequently to ceremonially claim possession for Spain. Bad weather, crippling scurvy, and a fear of cold, uncharted coastal waters forced the *Santiago* and its crew to mostly stay far from shore.

These failures notwithstanding, the Pérez exploration did establish Spanish claims to the Northwest Coast, and identified a number of key geographical places, including Nootka Sound of western Vancouver Island, soon to be a place of international contention, and Mt. Olympus, which Perez christened "Cerro Nevado de Santa Rosalía."[14] A half-century later, American heirs to Spain's claims to the Pacific Northwest would use Pérez's voyage to assert 54° 40'—the present southern boundary of the Alaska panhandle—as the northern boundary of the Oregon Country.[15]

Soon after Pérez's return, however, Spanish mariners ranged well beyond 54° 40'. In 1775, in conjunction with Juan Bautista de Anza's successful plan to move colonists by land over 1,000 miles from Sonora to San Francisco Bay, Viceroy Bucareli ordered another maritime reconnaissance. This time he dispatched three vessels from San Blas, each commanded by young naval lieutenants, recently transferred from Spain specifically to reconnoiter the northern reaches of the California coast in search of Russians and sites for future Spanish bases. One vessel, the California supply ship *San Carlos*, commanded by Juan de Ayala, explored San Francisco Bay—the first non-Indian vessel to enter the Golden Gate and demonstrate its navigability.[16]

Two other ships, the *Sonora* under Juan Francisco de la Bodega y Quadra and the *Santiago* commanded by Bruno de Hezeta, continued northward. Against great odds, the heroic Bodega y Quadra pushed his ailing crew and the tiny, leaky *Sonora* up the Alaskan coast to 58° 30', near present-day Juneau, taking possession of the coast for Spain at four points, including a place on Prince of Wales Island that still bears the name of the viceroy, Bucareli Sound.

But the same difficulties that had plagued Juan Pérez—who now served as pilot on the *Santiago,* and who was one of the many sailors to die of scurvy on the expedition—also hindered Bodega and Hezeta from preparing careful charts that would document their accomplishments, and thereby establish an indelible Spanish claim to the coast. Hezeta, for example, made the first known European sighting of the mouth of the Columbia River, which appeared on subsequent maps as the "Entrada de Hezeta," but his failure to explore the river itself, coupled with the lack of publicity about the expedition, made the discovery easy for other nations to ignore. Seventeen years later, the American Robert Gray entered the river and named it the Columbia, after his ship, the *Columbia Rediviva.* The name stuck, even on Spanish maps, and helped strengthen American claims to the Pacific Northwest.

Thus, Spain had made a rapid thrust up the Pacific coast, planting settlements from San Diego to San Francisco and exploring into present-day Alaska. At the same time, the Spanish tried to block British expansion in the South Pacific. From Patagonia through the Straits of Magellan, to the islands of Juan Fernández, Easter Island, and even Tahiti, where two Spanish missionaries had failed dismally to convert natives, Spain sought to anticipate British attempts to establish South Pacific bases in the late 1760s and early 1770s. Its treasury overextended, and chronically short of ships, crews, arms, and equipment, Spain could not realistically defend the vast Eastern Pacific with force. Instead, Spain tried, in the words of its secretary of state, to avoid constructing "costly defended posts, but…[to] give signs that the land is ours."[17]

Although Spanish officials continued to invoke a 1692 royal decree that forbade foreigners from entering the Eastern Pacific without Spanish permission and required that violators be treated as enemies, the 1780s saw Spain's already limited ability to defend the Pacific decline even further as its priorities shifted.[18] In South America, for instance, the great revolts of Tupac Amaru in Peru and the *comuneros* in New Granada forced Spain to turn its attention inward; in North America, the rebellion of the British colonies gave Spain an opportunity to avenge itself against its recent humiliation in the Seven Years War, and to regain the Floridas.

Spain took the side of the rebellious American colonists, diverting resources away from California and the Pacific Northwest and into the fight against England. Spain drove Britain out of the lower Mississippi Valley, and off the northern shore of the Gulf of Mexico. Spain's little-known victories at Baton Rouge, Natchez, Mobile, and Pensacola not only facilitated American independence, but enabled Spain to extract the Floridas from Britain at the war's conclusion in 1783.

These victories in southeast North America came at a cost, however, to Spain's position in the Southwest. Spain lost control of the vital Yuma crossing of the Colorado River—an essential link on Anza's trail that connected California by land to Sonora and the rest of New Spain. Quechan Indians, whom the Spaniards knew as Yumas, had driven Spanish missionaries and soldiers away in 1781, the same year that Spanish forces defeated the British at Pensacola. Spain never again made a serious effort to regain the Yuma crossing. Initially, war with the Apaches and other tribes took priority over the Yumas. After the Spanish brokered a peace with the Apaches in the mid-1780s, projects to reopen the Sonora route failed to get off the drawing board because Spain had more pressing concerns on the edges of the expanding American settlers' frontier. For the remainder of the Spanish era, California depended upon the sea for supplies and immigration. This stunted growth, and halted Spanish expansion beyond San Francisco to the north.

Spain's position throughout the hemisphere suffered as leadership at the highest levels shifted to new and less able hands after the deaths of José de Gálvez and Carlos III in 1787 and 1788. Under the phlegmatic King Carlos IV (1788–1808), Spain staggered into several decades of catastrophic decline. In 1789, within a year after Carlos IV came to power, Parisians stormed the Bastille and seized his Bourbon cousin, Louis XVI. Carlos IV's ill-advised effort to reverse the direction of the regicidal French Revolution represented the beginning of Spain's decline—an eclipse that saw it go to war with England, as well as France, and eventually cost it nearly all of its American empire.

One of Spain's first setbacks in North America occurred in the Pacific Northwest. There England forced Spain to surrender its exclusive claims to the region as a result of an episode at Nootka Sound on Vancouver Island. The troubles at Nootka originated with the 1778 visit of the celebrated Captain James Cook, whose landing at Nootka on his third and final voyage of Pacific discovery, according to recently discovered evidence, was deliberate rather than coincidental. Cook knew even before leaving London in 1776 that Juan Pérez and the *Santiago* had met friendly Indians at the latitude of Nootka in 1774.[19] There, Cook found more than friendly Indians. Cook's report told of fortunes to be made by marketing silky sea otter pelts in Canton, China. Published in 1784, Cook's account brought merchant vessels from several nations scrambling to the otter-rich coastal waters off present-day Oregon, Washington, and British Columbia.

Alarmed by these new intrusions, New Spain's viceroy, Manuel Antonio Flores, on his own initiative sent Captain Esteban José Martínez in 1789 to warn foreigners away from this region, which Spain claimed by right of discovery. Viceroy Flores also ordered Martínez to establish a base at Nootka Sound—then believed to be on the North American mainland. The viceroy had evidence that Russians or the English might occupy this spacious harbor, and he also foresaw that Americans might try to establish themselves on the Pacific "above our possessions of Texas, New Mexico, and the Californias," and thus "obtain the richest trade of Great China and India."[20]

When Esteban Martínez arrived at Nootka Sound in early May 1789, he found British and American trading vessels already riding at anchor. More continued to arrive. One British fur trader, Captain James Colnett, professed to carry orders from George III to take possession of the region on the strength of Captain Cook's discoveries. Captain Martínez objected strenuously, noting that Juan Pérez had discovered Nootka in 1774, four years before Cook; Martínez knew that for a fact since he had served under Pérez on that voyage. Martínez and Colnett began to discuss their differences amicably, but in Martínez's cabin the morning after a late night of drinking "freely," as Colnett put it, the two headstrong men lost their tempers. Even without the aid of an interpreter, Martínez understood the meaning of what sounded to him like "Gardem España [God Damn Spain]."

Although he had received instructions to avoid words and actions that "might bring about a clash," Martínez arrested Colnett, and as part of a series of provocative events, seized two British trading ships and sent crewmen to Mexico in chains.[21] Word of these events soon spread to western Europe, causing a flurry of intense diplomatic activity.

The Nootka Incident quickly grew into a very serious international crisis, and spurred the "Spanish Armament" in Great Britain as that nation prepared its armed forces for possible hostilities. Hoping to gain commercial concessions from Spain (but anticipating that Spain ultimately would not fight), English officials whipped up latent anti-Spanish sentiment among the public and threatened war. Spain in turn alerted its overseas bases to the possibility of conflict and appealed to its French ally for help, but the French Revolution had begun and the French National Assembly had little enthusiasm for past alliances made by monarchs. Spain, then, declined to play its weak hand with Britain.

At the Escorial in October 1790, the Spanish court and diplomats capitulated to British demands. In the Nootka Convention, Spain agreed to share the Pacific Northwest and the North Pacific with Britain, return the British traders' property seized at Nootka, and make reparations.[22] Appeasement averted an almost certain and potentially disastrous war for Spain, but its relinquishment of exclusive sovereignty of a portion of the Pacific coast also marked the beginning of its slow withdrawal from North America.

The significance of this setback is clearer in retrospect than it was to contemporaries, for Spain did not immediately abandon its interest in the Pacific Northwest. From distant New Orleans in the early 1790s, the barón de Carondelet, the governor-general of Spanish Louisiana, envisioned an overland route up the Missouri River to "near Nootka Sound," where Spain would establish a settlement "to prevent the English or the Russians from establishing themselves or extending themselves on those coasts."[23] He offered a large cash prize to the first Spanish subject to reach the Pacific from the Missouri.

Carondelet's project represented part of a larger plan to block the advance of Canadian-based British fur traders all along the Upper Missouri—in order to prevent them from extending smuggling operations into New Mexico and Louisiana, or invading Spanish Upper Louisiana in time of war. Anticipating Thomas Jefferson's outfitting of the Lewis and Clark Expedition, a group of merchants in Spanish St. Louis (the nerve center of Upper Louisiana or the Illinois country) formed the Missouri Company and sent three exploring parties toward the Pacific between 1794 and 1796. The most successful of them reached the Mandan tribal villages in present-day North Dakota, but, of course, failed to connect St. Louis to the Pacific Northwest.

Meanwhile, Spanish ships had continued to explore the Pacific Northwest in 1791 and 1792. In conjunction with concurrent British Royal Navy investigations, teams of Spanish scholars and artists examined the region's native peoples, topography, flora, and fauna, as part of the brilliant five-year, round-the-world scientific expedition that Alejandro Malaspina had begun from Cádiz in July 1789. Among their achievements, these last explorers that Spain sent to the Pacific Northwest made a careful reconnaissance of the Strait of Juan de Fuca "to decide once and for all," as Malaspina put it, if a strait connected the Pacific and Atlantic. The idea of the mythic Strait of Anian had surfaced again.[24] Meanwhile, at Nootka Sound, the temporary Spanish shoreline cantonment, "Santa Cruz de Nootka," was the first white settlement west of the Rockies in what is today Canada.

Spain maintained political as well as scientific interests in the coast north of California. Although the Nootka Convention granted England rights to the Pacific Northwest, it had not given England exclusive rights or precluded Spaniards from also remaining or settling in the region. Nor had the Nootka Convention set a clear northern boundary for Spanish California. England claimed that the Convention permitted its subjects to range freely down the coast to San Francisco Bay, the northernmost Spanish settlement. Spain, however, hoped to place California's boundary farther north, at the Strait of Juan de Fuca.

Toward that end, in 1792 Spain established a short-lived settlement, Núñez Gaona, at Neah Bay, commanding the entrance to the Strait of Juan de Fuca on what is today the Washington side. The first white settlement in the continental United States west of the Rockies and north of San Francisco, "Núñez Gaona" consisted of "a Cross upon the beach, and…about 10 Houses and several good *Gardens*," in the words of one English speaking visitor. Spaniards also built a small barracks with four cannons atop it and some corrals before they abandoned the place in the autumn of 1792, when Spain's position in negotiations with Britain over the Nootka controversy fell apart.[25]

In the summer of 1792, English and Spanish negotiators had traveled to the busy harbor of "Santa Cruz de Nootka" on Vancouver Island to work out the details of the recently concluded Nootka Convention. Although his position was weak, Spain's negotiator, Juan Francisco de Bodega y Quadra, a hospitable and cunning diplomat as well as a courageous mariner, charmed his worthy opponent, George Vancouver, into a stalemate. Negotiations shifted back to European drawing rooms, where Spain finally surrendered its *exclusive* claim to the region, and both sides agreed to leave unresolved the question of California's northern boundary. On March 23, 1795, ceremonies at Nootka brought the quarrel to a formal end, with both sides abandoning the site—to the relief of the Mexican-born soldiers who had suffered from an unfamiliar cold and damp climate, a poor diet, and isolation.[26]

Spain had lacked the resources and the military muscle to appropriate more than scientific knowledge in this remote corner of the Pacific. Possession, as Spain had discovered elsewhere, no longer was determined by Papal bulls, claims to prior discovery, or to scrupulous attention to acts of possession that included the erection of wooden crosses and the burying of declarations in bottles sealed with tar.[27] Sovereignty had come to depend on occupancy, and occupancy depended on economic development. Capable officers close to the scene had proposed ways to use private companies to compete for a share of the profits that foreigners reaped from the sea-otter trade, but Spanish officials failed to heed this advice. Bureaucratic obstacles to entrepreneurial activity, an essentially reactive policy, and ongoing crises in the mother country left a vacuum in the Pacific Northwest that Spain never filled.

Although a declining Spain never planted another settlement in the Pacific Northwest, it continued to claim the right to do so. Finally, under pressure to cede Florida to the United States for some advantage, or lose it entirely, Spain renegotiated its North American boundaries. In 1819, Spain and the United States agreed on a new transcontinental boundary that saved Texas for Spain and created a large buffer zone between New Mexico and American territory, but that cost Spain its claim to the Pacific Northwest. In the 1819 agreement, Spain surrendered its claims to territory north of the 42nd parallel, today's California-Oregon border, to the United States (and Great Britain).

Spain lost the international struggle for the Pacific Northwest, leaving little trace of its presence. Beyond the tiny military and naval bases at Nootka and Neah Bay, it never extended its towns, ranches, fortifications, or missions north of the San Francisco Bay area.[28] In the six-year existence of Santa Cruz de Nootka itself, Spanish Franciscans made no serious effort to replace native religion with Christianity—a rare case where missionization was not part of the process of Spanish expansion.[29] Nor did Spain make a serious effort at colonization. It would not strain the analogy to argue that Santa Cruz de Nootka was a Potemkin village—a theater set, with an all-male cast numbering between 200 and 250, raised by a vastly overextended empire to fool European powers into believing that Spain had achieved sovereignty through occupancy.[30] As in the South Pacific, Spain could only afford the appearance of occupancy.

When Spain withdrew from its most northerly outpost in the empire in 1795, much of the physical evidence of its presence vanished. Following orders, soldiers tore down the wooden chapel, houses, and other structures at Nootka prior to their departure. Nootka Indians rebuilt Yuquot, one of their summer villages, on the site.[31]

In written records, too, the activities of Spaniards along the Northwest Coast became hazy, hidden by a fog of Spanish secrecy. As historian Hubert Howe Bancroft noted over a century ago, Spain's failure to publish the results of the great exploring expeditions of 1774–1775—by Pérez, Hezeta, and Bodega y Quadra—meant that "the Spanish discoverers lost much of the honor due them."[32] The loss of honor extended even to Spain itself, where an authoritative encyclopedia published in Madrid in the 1960s credited James Cook rather than Juan Pérez with the discovery of Nootka Sound.[33]

Even the voluminous work of Alejandro Malaspina's scientific expedition disappeared into Spanish archives and remained largely unpublished until the 20th century.[34] That misfortune resulted from chance rather than from Spain's penchant for secrecy. Celebrated on his return to Spain, Malaspina was arrested and exiled within a year, accused of intrigue and in such disgrace that some writers feared to mention his name. One of Malaspina's friends and the promoter of his expedition, Antonio Valdés for whom Valdez, Alaska, is named, observed that Malaspina was "a good mariner, but a very bad politician."[35]

Unable to gain easy access to Spanish sources, early Pacific Northwest historians, with few exceptions, relied on Hispanophobic English accounts of Spanish activities in the region and satisfied themselves with stereotypical or superficial analyses.[36] As the author of one survey of the history of the state of Washington concluded, Spain slighted the Northwest Coast because "Spaniards had accustomed themselves to thinking only of gold and silver as important natural resources."[37] (That generalization might have applied to the 16th century, but definitely not to the 18th.) With similar acumen, the same author analyzed Spain's failure to stay at Neah Bay: "Neither the fur trade nor the northern climate appealed to the Spaniards," she wrote, "so that maintaining a post there was too much of an ordeal for them."[38]

Indeed, Spain did not engage seriously in the Pacific fur trade, and, among other things, soldiers from Mexico disliked the cold, damp climate at Nootka, but if the Spanish Crown had had sufficient resources and intent to enforce its claim to the region by maintaining a colony there, Spanish soldiers would have endured the "ordeal."

Most early historians acknowledged early Spanish primacy in the area and chronicled Spain's role in the Nootka Sound controversy, but concentrated on the British and American dramatis personae.[39] For Anglocentric writers, Spaniards generally did not figure among the "Pioneers of the Pacific Coast"—a title they reserved for the likes of Francis Drake, James Cook, George Vancouver, Simon Fraser, and John McLouglin.[40]

On the Northwest Coast, visiting Spaniards did not even make good villains. Spaniards at Nootka and Núñez Gaona refrained from conquering Indians, bringing them into mission compounds, or subjecting them to systems of forced labor. Moreover, Spaniards in the region during the Enlightened 18th century operated under restrictions imposed by their government, in contrast to some unscrupulous American and British fur traders, who, historian Christon Archer has pointed out, could operate "well beyond the ordinary constraints and laws that governed in their own societies."[41] One Spanish observer deplored the occasionally extreme treatment of Indians by fur traders:

> Impiously, they rob these unfortunates and they force them with superiority of arms to give their furs…or to defend their possessions at the cost of their lives and the ruin of their temples and houses.[42]

In contrast, Spanish officers had orders to treat the natives respectfully. They went to such lengths to fulfill those orders that Christon Archer has calculated "Indians suffered less from the presence of Spain than they did from any of the other nations there to make profits from the fur trade."[43]

Archer made that judgment in an important article published in 1973, a year that marked a sea change in American and British historical sensibility toward the Spanish in the Pacific Northwest, because that same year also saw the publication of Warren L. Cook's magisterial work, *Flood Tide of Empire: Spain and the Pacific Northwest, 1543–1819*. The years since have brought a surfeit of studies of Spain's scientific legacy in the region, cresting in the years leading up to and during the bicentennial of Malaspina's round-the-world voyage (1989–1994). Some of those new studies narrate the story of Spanish scientific exploration,[44] others contain transcriptions or translations of primary sources,[45] and still others provide guidance to sources[46] or describe exhibitions that have made many of the expedition's artifacts and artistic representations available for the first time.[47]

As a result of this astonishing array of new work brought to light from Spanish archives, Spaniards in the Pacific Northwest seem likely to be remembered as collectors of knowledge rather than as conquerors of Indians. Indeed, Spanish scientists, rather than priests or soldiers, have become the most celebrated symbol of Spain's presence in the Pacific Northwest. These scientists, Spanish historian Mercedes Palau has noted somewhat extravagantly,

> risked their lives individually and collectively, setting an example of vigor and courage in the service of their country…with no attempt made to seek economic benefits.[48]

As we now know, Iberian scientists under Carlos III produced incomparable written and graphic representations of natives and regional life, just before Old World diseases began to take a toll on Indian lives, and before the importation of European biota transformed the natural flora and fauna in this corner of the continent. Indeed, Spaniards documented the region in much greater detail than they did any other part of North America, including such bastions of Spanish settlement as California, New Mexico, or Florida. The explanation for this paradox lies in the fact that the Pacific Northwest remained especially primitive and exotic to Europeans in the late-18th century, luring the Spanish, British, and French governments to send scientists and artists by sea.

Given the current scholarly literature on this time and place, one can no longer sustain the argument that the early activities of the English and Americans overshadowed those of Spaniards. The Spanish moment in the Pacific Northwest, however, remains little known outside of a small circle of specialists. One need only consult recent general histories of the region to see that Spanish explorers continue to receive cursory treatment, compared to their English and American counterparts.[49] Even stories of extraordinary human interest, such as the Spaniards' relationship with the complex Nootka chief, Maquinna, or the lurid aspects of native culture, such as Spanish inquiries into prostitution and cannibalism, remain more obscure than if they had been reported by British and American observers.[50]

Such oversights and emphases are consistent with our larger reconstruction of the American past. The United States always has been a multi-ethnic society, but in American popular culture, and in most general histories, America's past has been generally understood as the story of English America, rather than as the stories of the diverse cultures that comprise our national heritage. The Spanish colonial origins of the United States, then, remain to be better woven into the fabric of American history—in classrooms, textbooks, and our national consciousness. This is true not only for the Northwest, but even for the Southwest, where Spaniards left their most enduring mark on what is now the United States.

It also appears, however, that a reshaping of our nation's story is well underway, even without the visit of Spain's king and queen to serve as a catalyst. Growing interest in environmental and Indian history has renewed investigations of Spanish sources, since those accounts provide a graphic baseline for measuring historic change in the Pacific Northwest. Regardless of whether Spain won or lost, a fuller and fairer understanding of our nation's fascinating multiethnic and multinational past requires that we know how, when, and where Spain played the game.

Notes

1. This essay derives in part from my book, *The Spanish Frontier in North America* (1992), and is presented here with permission from Yale University Press. Sources not noted in this essay can be found in that book. I use the term North America in reference to present-day Canada and the United States, and apply Spaniard as a political and cultural term, not a racial category, with full awareness that many of the Spaniards who explored or occupied the Pacific Northwest were Mexican-born mestizos. For careful readings of this manuscript and useful suggestions, I am grateful to Christon Archer, Janet Fireman, Heather and Gordon Forward, and Carlos Schwantes.

2. Told by B. Guild Gillespie in the preface to *On Stormy Seas: The Triumphs and Torments of Captain George Vancouver* (Victoria: Horsdal and Schubart, 1992). I am grateful to Vancouver expatriates Gordon and Heather Forward of Dallas for calling this episode to my attention.

3. Booknote by Bernard L. Fontana in the *Southwest Mission Research Center Newsletter,* June 1993, 31.

4. Nicholas Lemann, "A Failed Dominion," *Atlantic Monthly* 270 (November 1992):149–50.

5. Michael C. Scardaville, "Approaches to the Study of the Southeastern Borderlands," in *Alabama and the Borderlands from Prehistory to Statehood,* R. Reid Badger and Lawrence A. Clayton, eds., (Tuscaloosa: University of Alabama Press, 1985), 185–88.

6. Cabrillo has been incorrectly identified as a Portuguese mariner sailing for Spain—a notion so well established that it probably will persist in the literature.

7. [Andrés de Urdaneta's summary of the expedition's log], "Relation of the Voyage of Juan Rodriguez Cabrillo," in Herbert E. Bolton, ed., *Spanish Exploration in the Southwest, 1542–1706* (New York: Charles Scribner's Sons, 1908), 37.

8. For an analysis of the Juan de Fuca story and legend, see Warren L. Cook, *Flood Tide of Empire: Spain and the Pacific Northwest, 1543–1819* (New Haven: Yale University Press, 1973), 22–29.

9. Peter Martyr, *De Orbe Novo: The Eight Decades of Peter Martyr D'Anghera,* F.A. MacNutt, ed. and trans., 2 vols. (New York: G.P. Putnam's, 1912), 2:419.

10. One of Sebastián Vizcaíno's vessels, the *Tres Reyes,* apparently passed Cape Blanco, in present-day southern Oregon—beyond the point that Cabrillo-Ferrer attained—but no good charts resulted and, indeed, the ship may have been blown in that direction accidentally. See W. Michael Mathes, *Sebastián Vizcaíno and Spanish Exploration of the Pacific Ocean, 1580–1630* (San Francisco: California Historical Society, 1968), 98, 104, 107.

11. Cook, *Flood Tide of Empire,* 31–40. For more speculative but interesting scenarios, see J. Neilson Barry, "Spaniards in Early Oregon," *Washington Historical Quarterly* 23 (January 1932):25–34.

12. Oscar O. Winther, *The Great Northwest: A History* (1st ed., 1947; rev. ed., New York: Alfred A. Knopf, 1950), 22.

13. Ibid. Emphasis mine. Historian Joseph Schafer sounded a similar note of Spanish somnolence: British and Russians "roused the Spaniards of Mexico to undertake new schemes of conquest, settlement, and exploration." Joseph Schafer, *A History of the Pacific Northwest* (1st ed., 1905; rev. ed., New York: Macmillan, 1918), 11.

14. The two quotes in this and the previous paragraph, "Ir a la Russia" and "Cerro Nevado," are in Salvador Bernabeu Albert, "Juan Pérez, Navegante y Descubridor de las Californias (1768–1775)," in José Luis Peset, ed., *Culturas de la costa noroeste de América* (Madrid: Turner, 1989), 286–87.

15. Herbert K. Beals, ed. and trans., *Juan Pérez on the Northwest Coast: Six Documents of His Expedition in 1774* (Portland: Oregon Historical Society Press, 1989), 41.
16. One of the ship's boats was actually the first vessel to enter the bay.
17. The marqués de Grimaldi to Viceroy Bucareli, 1773, quoted in Christon I. Archer, "Spain and the Defense of the Pacific Ocean Empire, 1750–1810," *Canadian Journal of Latin American and Caribbean Studies* 11, no. 21 (1986):25. See also, Archer, ibid., 20–23, 34–35.
18. See, for example, the royal cédula of November 25, 1692, invoked by Viceroy Caballero de Croix on July 31, 1788, cited in Christon I. Archer, "Review Article [of Frederic W. Howay, *Voyages of the 'Columbia' to the Northwest Coast, 1787–1790 and 1790–1793*]," *BC Studies* 93 (Spring 1992):74; and also, Christon I. Archer, "Russians, Indians, and Passages: Spanish Voyages to Alaska in the Eighteenth Century," *Exploration in Alaska,* Antoinette Shalkop, ed., (Anchorage: Cook Inlet Society, 1980), 134.
19. Dagny B. Hansen, "Captain James Cook's First Stop on the Northwest Coast—By Chance or by Chart?" *Pacific Historical Review* 62 (November 1993):475–84.
20. Flores to Secretary Antonio Valdés, Mexico, December 23, 1788, quoted in Warren L. Cook, *Flood Tide of Empire,* 130. The Nootka Crisis has been the object of considerable study. Christon I. Archer, "The Transient Presence: A Re-Appraisal of Spanish Attitudes toward the Northwest Coast in the Eighteenth Century," *BC Studies* 18 (Summer 1973):3–32, noted the anti-Spanish bias in much of the literature, and offered a fine corrective. Also in 1973, Warren L. Cook's more balanced work appeared; it remains the indispensable starting point. Derek Pethick, *The Nootka Sound Connection: Europe and the Northwest Coast, 1790–1795* (Vancouver, B.C.: Douglas and McIntyre, 1980), reviews the story.
21. For the heavy drinking, see Cook, *Flood Tide of Empire,* 169, 175; for "Gardem España," see p. 172; for Martínez's instructions, see p. 132. For Martínez's sometimes "irrational" behavior, see Christon I. Archer, "The Political and Military Context of the Spanish Advance into the Pacific Northwest," in Robin Inglis, ed., *Spain and the North Pacific Coast: Essays in Recognition of the Bicentennial of the Malaspina Expedition, 1791–1792* (Vancouver, B.C.: Vancouver Maritime Museum, 1992), 14. Archer argues, however, that Martínez exercised "logical defensive thinking" on this occasion.
22. For a readable and easily approachable account focusing on the series of events and the far-reaching importance of the Nootka affair with its international diplomatic ramifications, see J. Richard Nokes, *Almost a Hero: The Voyages of John Meares, R.N., to China, Hawaii and the Northwest Coast* (Pullman: Washington State University Press, 1998).
23. Carondelet to the duque de Alcudia, New Orleans, January 8, 1796, in A.P. Nasatir, ed., *Before Lewis and Clark: Documents Illustrating the History of the Missouri, 1785–1804,* 2 vols. (St. Louis: St. Louis Historical Documents Foundation, 1952), 2:388.
24. The quote is from Malaspina's instructions to the commanders of two vessels sent to the Pacific Northwest in 1792, in John Kendrick, ed. and trans., *The Voyage of the SUTIL and MEXICANA, 1792: The Last Spanish Exploration of the Northwest Coast of America* (Spokane: Arthur H. Clark, 1991), 41.
25. Cook, *Flood Tide of Empire,* 350–51, 382–86. The quote is from "John Boit's Log of the Second Voyage of the 'Columbia,'" in *Voyages of the "Columbia" to the Northwest Coast, 1787–1790 and 1790–1793,* Frederick W. Howay, ed., (Massachusetts Historical Society, 1941), 416. The port was named in 1790 for Admiral Manuel Núñez Gaona of the Spanish Navy.
26. Christon I. Archer, "Retreat from the North: Spain's Withdrawal from Nootka Sound, 1793–1795," *BC Studies* 37 (Spring 1978):20, 28–30, 32.

27. See, for example, the instructions to Juan Pérez of 1773, summarized in Archer, "The Political and Military Context of the Spanish Advance," 12–13.

28. The one "Spanish" mission to the north of San Francisco Bay, at Sonoma, was founded in 1823 when independent Mexico governed California.

29. By 1791, Franciscans had converted only seventeen Indians at Nootka, but these were outcasts whom Spaniards had purchased. Archer, "Spain and the Defense of the Pacific," 36; Archer, "Retreat from the North," 20–22.

30. Archer, "The Transient Presence," 11, and Luis Navarro García, "Política indígena de España en el noroeste," in Peset, ed., *Culturas de la costa noeste,* 209–22, make this argument. Navarro García also offered several explanations for the Franciscans' failure to attempt conversions.

31. Archer, "Spain and the Defense of the Pacific," 32–33, 34, corrects the assertion by Cook (*Flood Tide of Empire,* 423) and others that natives in search of iron nails tore down the village.

32. Hubert Howe Bancroft, *History of the Northwest Coast,* 2 vols. (San Francisco: History Company, 1886) 1:166. For a sense of how far Bancroft had come in reaching this realization, see Robert Greenhow's scholarly *History of Oregon and California* (Boston: Charles C. Little and James Brown, 1844), a serious work of scholarship, but one hindered by scanty sources.

33. Archer, "The Transient Presence," 8, n. 19; and Christon I. Archer, "The Spanish Reaction to Cook's Third Voyage," in *Captain James Cook and His Times,* Robin Fisher and Hugh Johnston, eds., (Vancouver, B.C.: Douglas and McIntyre, 1979), 99.

34. The great exception was the *Relación del viaje hecho por las goletas Sutil y Mexicana en el año 1792,* 2 vols. (Madrid: 1802).

35. Quoted in Emilio Soler Pascual, *Antagonismo político en la España de Godoy: la conspiración Malaspina, 1795–1796* (Alicante: Instituto de Cultura "Juan Gil-Albert"/Diputación de Alicante, 1990), 72. For explanations for Malaspina's disgrace, none fully accepted, see also Donald C. Cutter, *Malaspina and Galiano: Spanish Voyages to the Northwest Coast* (Seattle: University of Washington Press, 1991), 113, 137–38; and Eric Beerman, *El diario del proceso y encarcelamiento de Alejandro Malaspina (1794–1803)* (Madrid: Editorial Naval, 1992).

36. Archer, "The Transient Presence," 3, notes some exceptions.

37. Mary W. Avery, *Washington: A History of the Evergreen State* (Seattle: University of Washington Press, 1965), 72.

38. Ibid., 79.

39. See, for example, Joseph Schafer, *A History of the Pacific Northwest* (1st ed., 1905; rev. ed., New York: Macmillan, 1918), 20; George W. Fuller, *A History of the Pacific Northwest with Special Emphasis on the Inland Empire* (1st ed., 1931; 2nd ed., rev., New York: Knopf, 1938), 45–48; Sidney Warren, *Farthest Frontier: The Pacific Northwest* (New York: Macmillan, 1949), 2; Winther, *The Great Northwest,* 21–25; Dorothy O. Johansen and Charles M. Gates, *Empire of the Columbia* (New York: Harper and Row, 1967), 1–62; Lloyd Spencer, *A History of the State of Washington,* 4 vols. (New York: American Historical Society, 1937); Ephraim W. Tucker, *History of Oregon* (1st ed., 1844; Fairfield, Washington: Ye Galleon Press, 1970), 13–15; Charles H. Carey, *General History of Oregon through Early Statehood* (1st ed., 1922; 3rd ed., Portland: Binfords and Mort, 1971), 17–33, 62–68, 89–90.

40. Agnes C. Laut, *Pioneers of the Pacific Coast: A Chronicle of Sea Rovers and Fur Hunters* (Toronto: Glasgow, Brook, 1915).

41. Archer, "Review Article," 81.

42. "Apuntes…de los salvajes habitantes del Estrecho de Fuca," Secundino Salamanca, 1792, ms., quoted in Christon I. Archer, "The Voyage of Captain George Vancouver: A Review Article," *BC Studies* 73 (Spring 1987):60.

43. Archer, "The Transient Presence," 23. See also, Christon I. Archer's later superb articles: "The Making of Spanish Indian Policy on the Northwest Coast," *New Mexico Historical Review* 52 (January 1977):45–70; "Seduction before Sovereignty: Spanish Efforts to Manipulate the Natives of the Northwest Coast," in Robin Fisher and Hugh Johnston, eds., *From Maps to Metaphors: The Pacific World of George Vancouver* (Vancouver: University of British Columbia Press, 1993), 127–59; Archer, "Spain and the Defense of the Pacific," 31–36.

44. Cook's splendid narrative in *Flood Tide of Empire* places the work of these scientists in the largest context and offers guidance to sources as of 1973—including the important pioneering work of Henry Raup Wagner. Cutter, *Malaspina and Galiano,* is the best single volume treatment. Mercedes Palau, "The Spanish Presence on the Northwest Coast: Sea-going Expeditions, 1774–1793," in Francisco Morales Padrón, et al., *To the Totem Shore: The Spanish Presence on the Northwest Coast* [World Exposition, Vancouver, 1986, Pavilion of Spain] (Madrid: Ediciones El Viso, 1986), 38–89, is the best short introduction in English (and the bibliography in *To the Totem Shore* is comprehensive and up to date). Derick Pethick, *First Approaches to the Northwest Coast* (Seattle: University of Washington Press, 1979), traces European voyages to 1792 in short compass and contains a good bibliography. For a more recent popular account, see John Kendrick, *The Men with Wooden Feet: The Spanish Exploration of the Pacific Northwest* (Toronto: NC Press, 1986). Among recent detailed accounts of the scientific expeditions in the larger context, see especially Juan Carlos Arias Divito, *Las Expediciones Científicas Españolas durante el siglo XVIII* (Madrid: Ediciones Cultura Hispanica, 1968); Iris H.W. Engstrand, *Spanish Scientists in the New World: The Eighteenth Century Expeditions* (Seattle: University of Washington Press, 1981); Fermín del Pino Diaz, ed., *Ciencia y contexto histórico nacional en las expediciones ilustradas a América* (Madrid: Consejo Superior de Investigaciones Científicas, 1988); Salvador Bernabeu Albert, "Viajes marítimos y exploraciones científicas al Pacífico Septentrional, 1767–1788," 6 vols., Ph.D. diss., Universidad Complutense de Madrid, 1989. More focused on the Pacific Northwest are the essays in Peset, ed., *Culturas de la costa noroeste*; and Inglis, ed., *Spain and the North Pacific Coast.*

45. The first-hand accounts in English published in recent years include José Mariano Moziño, *Noticias de Nutka: An Account of Nootka Sound in 1792,* Iris Wilson [Engstrand], ed. and trans., (Seattle: University of Washington Press, 1970). Recent titles in Spanish include Alejandro Malaspina, *Viaje científico y político a la América Meridional Diario de viaje de Alejandro Malaspina,* Mercedes Palau, ed., (Madrid: Ediciones El Museo Universal, 1984); and most impressively Alejandro Malaspina, et al., *La expedición Malaspina, 1789–1794,* 7 vols. (Madrid: Ministerio de Defensa, Museo Naval, and Lunwerg Editores, 1987–94).

Primary sources regarding Spanish expeditions prior to the surge of scientific interest also have appeared recently: Herbert K. Beals, ed. and trans., *For Honor and Country: The Diary of Bruno de Hezeta* (Portland: West Imprints, Oregon Historical Society Press, 1985); Herbert K. Beals, ed. and trans., *Juan Pérez on the Northwest Coast*; John Kendrick, ed. and trans., *The Voyage of the SUTIL and MEXICANA, 1792*; and Salvador Bernabeu Albert, ed., *Juan Francisco de la Bodega y Quadra: El descubrimiento del fin del mundo (1775–1792)* (Madrid: El Libro de Bolsillo Alianza Editorial, 1990).

These Spanish scientists visited the California coast, too, and the first-hand accounts published in English include Donald C. Cutter, *Malaspina in California* (San Francisco:

John Howell Books, 1960), and *California in 1792: A Spanish Naval Visit* (Norman: University of Oklahoma Press, 1990).

46. Mercedes Palau, *Catálogo de los dibujos, aguadas y acuarelas de la expedición Malaspina, 1789–1794* (Madrid: Museo de América, 1980); Carmen Sotos Serrano, *Los pintores de la expedición de Alejandro Malaspina*, 2 vols. (Madrid: Real Academia de la Historia, 1982); Dolores Higueras, *Catálogo crítico de los documentos de la expedición Malaspina*, 3 vols. (Madrid: Museo Naval, 1985); Blanca Sáiz, *Bibliografía sobre Alejandro Malaspina…* (Madrid: Ediciones el Museo Universal, 1992).

47. Exhibition catalogues include *La expedición Malaspina, 1789–1794: Viaje a America y Oceania de las corbetas "Descubierta" y "Atrevida"* (Madrid: Ministerio de Cultura and Ministerio de Defensa, 1984); [Mercedes Palau, ed.,] *El ojo del tótem. Arte y cultura de los indios del noroeste de América* (Madrid: Biblioteca V Centenario, 1988); John Kendrick and Robin Inglis, *Malaspina and Galiano on the Northwest Coast, 1791–1792* (Vancouver, B.C.: Vancouver Maritime Museum, 1991). Several books cited above, such as Cutter's *Malaspina and Galiano,* were published in conjunction with exhibits.

48. Mercedes Palau, "The Spanish Presence on the Northwest Coast: Sea-going Expeditions, 1774–1793," in Morales Padrón, et al., *To the Totem Shore, 39.*

49. An exception is Gordon B. Dodds, *The American Northwest: A History of Oregon and Washington* (Arlington Heights, Illinois: Forum Press, 1986), 19–21, 24, and his less balanced *Oregon: A Bicentennial History* (New York: W.W. Norton, 1977), 12–25. More typical are: Norman H. Clark, *Washington: A Bicentennial History* (New York: W.W. Norton, 1976), who confines his brief discussion of the age of maritime discovery to George Vancouver; Robert E. Ficken and Charles P. LeWarne, *Washington: A Centennial History* (Seattle: University of Washington Press, 1988), 8–9; Carlos A. Schwantes, *The Pacific Northwest: An Interpretive History* (Lincoln: University of Nebraska Press, 1989), 38–46; Edward Nuffield, *The Pacific Northwest: Its Discovery and Early Exploration by Sea, Land, and River* (Surrey, B.C.: Hancock House, 1990), 62–67, 98.

50. Cutter, *Malaspina and Galiano,* 61–63, 100–3.

II

Two Faces West:
The Development Myth in Canada
and the United States

Donald Worster

A LOCOMOTIVE WHISTLES SHRILLY as it approaches a small town on the
North American prairie. Along the tracks ahead stands a grain elevator
on one side, a wooden station and a brick hotel on the other, and behind
them a checkerboard of streets marking off a community's life. On the out-
skirts of the town, a woman peers from her farmhouse window, watching
the train approach against a background of snow-crusted mountains. A man
plowing a field, preparing to plant wheat, stops to watch and listen too. All
these images have been popular in the Canadian and American West for more
than a century. They are signs of what the two nations have in common—a
landscape, a technology, a set of hopes, and a story of development.

The two nations share other signs and memories as powerful as that prairie
scene—the slap of a beaver tail on a lake; bison streaming over a wide plain,
and of their carcasses lying in the grass; cattle bawling and shoving, taking the
bison's place; oil wells pumping wealth from the ground, smelly and viscous;
and gold dust glinting in a miner's pan, mixed with gravel and snow melt.
Both nations displaced proud Indian peoples, who once occupied the land
and now are living on the margins, expected to turn to farming or manufacturing to survive. Both nations witnessed a diverse immigration of Chinese
railroad workers, Russian peasant farmers, French or Spanish missionaries in
black robes, and millions of English-speaking poor people.

Despite all these commonalities, however, interesting differences have
separated the Canadian from the American West. There were differences, for
example, in the Indian policies adopted on either side of the border and in the
degree of violence occurring between native inhabitants and white Europeans.
Historians have compared the "Wild West" of America to the "Mild West"
of Canada.[1] Rather than treading down that familiar path, I want to suggest

another comparison between our two countries, and between the two Wests within them, by focusing on a seemingly more innocuous subject—the idea of development. Despite its prosaic if not trite sound, that idea offers a fresh, provocative basis for exploring our differences.

Canadian historians, like their American counterparts, frequently have told the story of development, writing extensively on the expansion of railroads, industry, agriculture, and towns and cities, as well as culture, religion, and education. That fact may not seem particularly noteworthy, but I want to argue that it is highly significant. Ubiquity, familiarity, and habit have all made us indifferent toward what we have been saying or about how we have imagined the past. There has been too little critical inquiry on either side of the Canadian-U.S. border into what the word "development" has meant, or its darker implications including the costs to both people and nature, or the question of how well the development idea accounts for our distinctive national and regional characteristics.

Both Canadians and Americans have given one fundamental meaning to development from which all other meanings derive—development refers to exploiting the land to get the wealth out of it. "Undeveloped" land is terrain that lacks roads, buildings, or mines; it is land that produces little or no profit. There is little difference between the views of both nations in this regard. When the two Wests were at an early stage of exploitation, they saw themselves as economically underdeveloped, or put more positively, as economically developing—the advancing edge of two new nations. Today, on the other hand, both Wests see themselves as having mature, well-financed economies, though both also describe themselves as still developing in the sense that all regions and nations see themselves as tirelessly driving to turn nature into wealth, with no end in sight.

Even on this basic level of economics, however, the word development has had a complicated set of meanings. Development first came into common use in the 19th century, an era that was awestruck by advances in biological science that had begun to show how organisms mature and evolve, not only in size but changing in form, passing from youth to maturity, or advancing from the one-celled amoeba to multi-celled plants and animals. By analogy, human social development was supposed to follow a similar progression, as natural as the passage from the embryo to the adult, starting with the savage life and ending up with the English gentleman.

The idea of development as the progressive law of nature inspired not only the Victorians, but also such social philosophers as Karl Marx and Friedrich Engels, for whom history was an inexorable advance from primitive society to industrial capitalism and on to a socialist future, all stages in the techno-logical domination of nature. According to Gustavo Esteva, "development became the central category of Marx's work: revealed as a historical process that unfolds with the same necessary character of natural laws."[2]

In the 19th century, development also became a transitive verb, with humans as the subject, nature as the object. That is, it became man's proper role on earth to "develop nature," meaning to make nature over into useful, marketable commodities. Unaltered nature, civilized people believed, was incomplete and embryonic, a possibility waiting to be achieved. The special role of humankind was to release nature from its slumber, awaken its poten-tialities, and enable it to reach its grand destiny, which was nothing less than service to our own species' comfort and well-being.

This second use of the word as a transitive verb first became popular in the outposts of the British Empire, particularly Australia and Canada, and later in the United States. The Australian scholar H. W. Arndt, who has writ-ten an interesting history of the word, quotes from an 1846 article in the *Canadian Economist*: "Canada is now thrown upon her own resources, and if she wishes to prosper, these resources must be developed."[3] Challenged to achieve a measure of independence, Canadians understood that they must become an active agency in nature, no longer content to buy many of their necessities from England.

Development thus became a compelling international myth about the growth of nation-states. By myth I mean simply that it told a popular story about origins and destiny—one progressing from primitive life to civilization, from the simple to the complex, from an inferior colonial dependency to nation-state maturity. It was a heroic story that both capitalists and commu-nists could share because it expressed their common ideals. The myth was part of the justification of European imperialism—helping other peoples achieve their own state-based identities and secure places in the global economy. It told what all people's attitudes and behavior toward the rest of nature ought to be, especially among those backward areas far from the centers of civili-zation. By the time of World War II, the myth of development had spread everywhere, replacing older traditions of stasis and equilibrium. Wherever it went, it offered a similar formula for improving the life of a nation and its people—one measured in higher per capita income and, so the promise goes, greater happiness and moral enlightenment.[4]

Because the United States and Canada emerged as nations during the very era when development was becoming the dominant political myth, their national histories were both conceived in terms of this myth. However, not one but two stories emerged to describe North American national development. Historians have analyzed them in isolation from one another, but I want to consider them together as different versions of the same myth. Both predict the final success of industrial capitalism, but then they veer off into different emphases and implications. And, those differences reveal a great deal about each nation, especially how each has envisioned its place in history and has conceived of its relation with nature in the New World.

The first of those two stories may be summed up in these famous words: "The existence of an area of free land, its continuous recession, and the advance of American settlement westward, explain American development."[5] They come, of course, from Frederick Jackson Turner, whose Frontier Thesis, first presented in 1893, spawned an influential American school of development thinking. Turner was mainly interested in the origins of liberal democracy, which was an American invention in his view, and he saw it deriving from the extraordinary potential of the American land—its untapped abundance. True to his age, Turner portrayed nature as undeveloped and raw, inviting a series of resource exploiters, beginning with traders and trappers, followed by miners, ranchers, and farmers—a succession of distinct groups who gave way eventually to a more impersonal set of exploiting *institutions* in the form of cities, factories, corporations, and the nation-state. Turner accepted this growing exploitation of nature, even celebrated it, although ironically at the same time he celebrated the American love affair with a glorious pristine wilderness.

The most distinctive theme in Turner's story is the notion that development in America is always starting over, like an organism that returns repeatedly to its embryonic state. "All peoples show development," Turner acknowledged, but only in America did development become not a single linear process, but a whole series of new beginnings, a process of birth and rebirth. "American social development," he pointed out, "has been continually beginning over again on the frontier."[6]

Each new frontier offered an exhilarating moment of what we might call "un-development," when complex European civilization reverted to a more archaic life. From that moment came a sense of freedom from distant centers of power, a freedom that spawned democracy, egalitarianism, and individualism. Regrettably, Turner wrote, the rebirthing opportunities eventually must end, and development must become a fixed linear progression here as in Europe, leading to a single common destiny. Turner found that outcome disturbing because increasingly the American scene would become unfriendly to the freedom and democracy that had come out of the primitive wilderness. He could only hope that what had been so often born and reborn would not quickly fade away.[7]

North of the Great Lakes, we find quite another story of development appearing. Often referred to as "metropolitanism," it was the creation of such famous Canadian historians as Harold Innis, Arthur Lower, and Donald Creighton, writing in the 1920s and 1930s, and more recently of Maurice Careless. All were as fascinated as Turner with the great interior of North America—its forests, grasslands, waterways, mountains, and wildlife—and with the dramatic changes in the natural environment caused by European settlement. However, the Canadians could find none of Turner's multiple new beginnings in the wilderness; instead, they saw development as a straight-forward march, controlled and directed by metropolitan forces far removed from the wilds. The march had begun in Europe, and it was Europe's urban centers that continued to set the pace, along with the rising Canadian centers of Toronto and Montreal. Cities defined what development meant; they made sure that development was secure and orderly; and they propelled the frontier through its various stages of progress, from gathering beaver pelts to planting wheat.[8]

Despite this strikingly different emphasis on a continuity with Europe, Canada's historians seem to have been at times as nationalistic and exceptionalist as those in the United States. For them, as for Turner, the natural environment played a major role in creating a national identity, giving Canada a peculiar place among the nations of the world. Wilderness conditions forced Canadians to become harvesters of raw natural resources called staples. "The trade in staples," wrote Harold Innis, "has been responsible for various peculiar [i.e., distinctive] tendencies in Canadian development." Beaver was one of the most important of those staple products, he argued, and beaver had made a unique nation to the north, while fish, lumber, and wheat would contribute to its further growth.[9]

If Canada looked to England for its model of economic progress, it also depended on those staples taken from and determined by nature. To be sure, in Innis's view as in Turner's, European technology must eventually overcome environmental factors, bringing industrial development.[10] The effect was to free the country, region by region, from a dependence on the local products of nature while increasing the hold of technology and distant markets. Nonetheless, Canada's special historical relation with nature in the New World would never altogether lose its significance. The primitive extraction of fur and pine would leave its trace on the Canadian identity.

Another leader of the metropolitan school, Donald Creighton, echoed this ambiguity about Canada's relationship to the Old World. Following the standard terms of European development, he argued that Canada had emerged as a vibrant "commercial empire" by exploiting the vast Saint Lawrence River system.[11] The phrase "commercial empire" indicated that the country was not traditional in its relation with nature; it was modern and capitalistic, with businessmen at its center. Yet those businessmen, Creighton suggested, even while following the established European model, had their lives shaped in subtle ways by the power of nature; the very form of the Saint Lawrence waterway, for instance, gave shape to their enterprise.

Like Turner's Frontier Thesis, this metropolitan story has had its own rich mythic potential. Canadians have liked to describe themselves as gathering staples from a vast northern country while becoming spiritually part of what they exploit. A nation pursuing capitalistic gain with great fervor, all the while remaining faithful to an ancient cultural heritage. A nation bringing law and order to the continent while obeying the laws of nature. A nation of traditionalists, unlike the Americans, yet like the Americans creating a distinctive civilization from the Europeans. While Turner hoped his countrymen always would remember their wilderness past as they gained in prosperity, the Canadians hoped that they would remain true to their European heritage while doing the same. Although both myths ended up in exactly the same place—in powerful industrial-capitalist economies ransacking the land for raw materials—they arrived there with different memories of where they had been, of what nature had allowed them to do, and of what their relation to the Old World had been.

For reasons that Canada's historians understand better than anyone else, Turner's frontierism never quite caught on north of the border, although it has had a few advocates.[12] On the other hand, the metropolitan school of Canadian history recently has begun to creep south and influence a few American scholars. A leading example is William Cronon's book, *Nature's Metropolis: Chicago and the Great West*, published in 1991, which is clearly indebted to the staples history of Innis, the commercial empire history of Creighton, the forest history of Lower, and the urban history of Maurice Careless.[13] Like the Canadians, Cronon shifts the development focus from the frontier to the city, repudiating Turner's legacy.[14] He puts ambitious capitalists at the center of the story—men who set out to remake the face of the land, becoming developers on a continental scale, building railroads from Chicago into the prairies, while using the Great Lakes as a supplementary mode of transportation. They transform the broad countryside into a mechanized, commercial system of agriculture and forestry, and they bring the land's products into the cities for mass consumption.

Cronon's book is an important work, not only in "New Western" history, but also in the field of environmental history, which deals with human relationships with nature. Among other things, he is concerned with the impact that urban people have had on nature, and with the ecological consequences of their consumption. In keeping with the conventions of development thinking, however, Cronon portrays nature mostly as passive before the onslaught of boosters, businessmen, and consumers. Nature provides a flow of commodities, but in that role it is responsive to whatever demands people make, never becoming an active or disruptive obstacle in mankind's way or forcing adaption. Nature does not wreak any vengeance, despite the many ravages committed by capitalist development. The urban consumers, for all their ignorance and indifference toward the land that supports them, apparently suffer no disruption when they deplete the land. In the face of capitalism's overwhelming power, nature rapidly disappears from the scene, becoming transformed into what Cronon calls "second nature," an artificial world designed according to "the logic of capital."[15] Like the 19th century's natural law of development, Cronon's logic of capital moves across the landscape like an iron horse of destiny—it being irrational and futile to oppose its progress.

Yet despite his fascination with the transforming logic of capital, Cronon also describes, with all the ambivalence of the Canadian metropolitan historians, a permanent legacy of nature in American cultural life in the area of Cronon's focus, the Midwest. The "logic of nature," it turns out, is as important as the logic of capital in the making of that region. Corn and other lush crops coming into the metropolis from Iowa are the products of rich, moist prairie soils, while range livestock coming in from the short grasslands to the west and southwest are the products of areas that are too dry to become a corn belt. The lumber furnishing housing for Chicago's immigrant multitudes is the product of white pine forests in Michigan and Wisconsin. Depleting or destroying any of these environmental support systems would have a profound impact on the fate of the Midwest.

Nature is, therefore, not truly passive before the onslaught of economic development—rather, capital says to nature, here is what we intend to do in this place, and nature replies, here is what you *may* do. So a reader of Cronon's book may find in its narrative more than one conclusion. As with Canada's great metropolitan historians, an ambivalence between admiring the invading, unstoppable power of the metropolis, and admiring the absorbing, shaping power of nature, lies at the heart of Cronon's work.

Both of these influential schools of North American history—frontierism and metropolitanism—focus on the process of economic and social development. Both define development as man's inexorable conquest over nature, of ever greater levels of wealth accumulation, and of an increasing degree of technological control. Both see the process leading to the triumph of industrial capitalism on a global scale, and both hint of a withering away of national and regional distinctions.

Then, unexpectedly, in contrast to the classical development myth, both schools testify that Canadians and Americans have wanted different things—different relationships with the wilderness, with Old World culture, and with capital. They also suggest that nature does not always give people what they want, that nature has a continuing power over human lives—a power the development myth never allowed for. Consequently, environmental differences (soil, climate, vegetation, the flow of waters) as well as cultural differences separate our two nations from each other, as they separate us from the European centers of civilization Also, differences likewise show up *within* our two nations, creating distinctive regions, such as the prairie West.

Let us now turn to the westernmost part of North America to see how the same international mythology of development has come into this vast area. But here, too, as elsewhere, there have been surprising, unpredictable outcomes.

Again, the story takes an unanticipated turn or two, despite the spread of homogenizing railroads, grain elevators, and oil wells. By the western regions I mean Canada that lies beyond the Shield, beginning with Manitoba and extending to British Columbia; and I mean the part of the United States that lies west of the Mississippi Valley, beginning with the Great Plains and stretching on to the Pacific Coast.[16] Neither has developed into a form that any European thinker, or for that matter any early historian from Ontario or Wisconsin, ever quite anticipated.

If we take the coming of transcontinental railroads as signaling the beginning of full-fledged capitalist development in these two regions, then we have on the American side of the border the critical date of 1869, the year of the driving of the "golden spike," and on the Canadian side, 1885, the year of the "plain iron spike"—a mere sixteen-year gap. Before those dates there had been a great deal of exploring, trapping, mining, even some farming, but the railroads were to be the magical key that would release the land from its bondage.[17]

In 1862, the U.S. Congress passed the Homestead Act, and ten years later the Canadians adopted the Dominion Lands Act, both of which aimed to give plots to homestead families. In each country, the official plan of development required the enticement of immigrants from Europe to resettle on New World soil, raising crops to sell in eastern cities, and buying finished goods from those cities. Thus, wheat was as critical as railroads. As a further part of the plan, each nation set up protective tariffs for their eastern manufacturers to secure an advantage in selling finished goods to western farmers.

Canadians call this triad of policies—a transcontinental railroad, an immigration and homesteading program, and a protective tariff for manufacturers—the "National Policy," and they credit Prime Minister John A. Macdonald with implementing it, though graciously acknowledging that he borrowed most of it from the United States.[18] It was not truly an American invention any more than it was Canadian; in its broad outlines the plan followed the international logic of capitalist development.[19]

If we look closely at the two development plans, we can detect small but intriguing differences. Canada, for example, was more accommodating to collective settlement, so that closely knit ethnic groups, such as the Doukhobors, could settle there easily.[20] Canada also was friendlier to rancher-capitalists than the U.S. government initially was. As David Breen has argued, Alberta set up a generous policy of leasing land on a large-scale to cattlemen, though within a few decades, as more farmers arrived in the province and as ranchers in the United States gained more recognition, the differences became harder to detect.[21] The railroad picture is more complicated in the United States, where many private corporations competed against each other and where a "government-owned" railroad was never attempted.[22] With such exceptions, the two nations did set off on similar paths to make the western continent a land of broad opportunity.

But here is how nature thwarted these grand designs. In the western United States, the land usually proved insufficiently watered to suit the original plans of railroad executives or government officials. Their logic of national development met rugged deserts and dry prairies, and plans began to run off-track. Even Turner, with his vision of a continually rejuvenating society in the wilderness, ran off the tracks. Early on, he had written that it would be useful to know how environment played a part in "determining our lines of development," words that would later come back to haunt him.[23]

Three years after the essay on the significance of the frontier, Turner discovered the writings of explorer John Wesley Powell, who described a West that was more arid than anything Turner had ever expected.[24] Though the popular perception of a great American desert had long been in vogue, Powell in 1878 was the first American to report a comprehensive analysis of the arid conditions in the West, and he also was one of the first to envision America as a land of diverse regions shaped by natural conditions. Turner, after reading a Powell essay written in 1896, began looking into ways to adjust his "wilderness" concepts to a complicated mosaic of natural environments, with diverse implications for development. Turner, however, never could quite figure out how to talk about that unfamiliar country beyond the 100th meridian.

Other Americans eventually did learn how, but doing so required a major revision in their thinking about development. The most serious weakness lay in the Homestead Act and its ambitious promise of an agricultural empire, based on a climate allowing for numerous fully watered farms—a dream coming out of such climatically homogeneous places as Illinois, Ohio, and Virginia, and drawing on older European models. Capital and agricultural interests together, however, could not find a way to make that dream real in such dry places as Idaho and Arizona. Both interests were forced to turn to the federal government as the chief organizer and bankroller of agricultural development if they were to go forward. Beginning in 1902, the U.S. government undertook to reclaim arid lands through large irrigation projects. To a degree unprecedented in the East, the West henceforth became the protégé of the federal government and the beneficiary of what now amounts to several hundred billion dollars' worth of infrastructure investment.

That unanticipated outcome was ironic in the extreme. Compared to Canada's citizens, Americans were not accustomed to looking favorably on a strong, centralized governmental role. Admitting their dependence on the federal government meant contradicting their self-image of frontier individualism and free enterprise, but the West's environmental conditions forced them to do just that—to adopt radical new policies, and to look eastward to Washington, D.C. Consequently, the real American West, the West of fact rather than romance, became the domain of the Bureau of Reclamation and the Bureau of Land Management more than of Wyatt Earp or Billy the Kid. One might call this outcome a triumph for metropolitanism, since it was the federal capital that henceforth began to lead and control western development.

No more than the western frontiersman or the Chicago capitalist, however, the federal bureaucracy was unprepared to fully cope with the western environment. It is still not fully prepared to do so today. After a century of federally funded water projects, the American West remains highly vulnerable to aridity—on the Great Plains, where another dust bowl disaster is never far off; in the Southwest, which is still desert the last time anyone looked; and, indeed, around practically every western city, except those located in the humid coastal strip of Oregon and Washington. The dream of developing the West into an empire inhabited by millions of agricultural producers has not come true on the vast scale that dreamers hoped. Even where agriculture has succeeded, as in California's Central Valley, it remains vulnerable to the limits of nature and to its own excesses—dams are silting up and soil salinity is increasing, the heavy pesticide use associated with irrigation is meeting public resistance, and there are fiercely competing claims on the limited supplies of water. As other countries have discovered, water development is a far more uncertain and expensive undertaking than once was believed.[25]

Canada, too, has built a number of irrigation dams, such as the Peace River and Bow-Saskatchewan projects, but there is no equivalent of the Bureau of Reclamation north of the border, nor anything like the hydraulic civilization that has appeared along the Colorado, Missouri, or Columbia rivers. Granted, there has not been much of an aridity problem there either. Aside from the little patch known as Palliser's Triangle, which is not truly arid, Canada's West has not required so profound an adjustment to the problem of dryness.

Nonetheless, nature has played a powerful role in the pace and success of development in western Canada, just as in the western United States. In Canada, the great obstacle to a broadening agricultural empire is the high latitude and a short growing season rather than a lack of moisture.[26] With the annexation of Rupert's Land in 1870, an immense country seemed ready for rural development. Toronto elites imagined a future West that would be the home of 100 million people, that would surpass the United States in size, stability, enlightenment, and prosperity, and that would become the world center of an invigorated British Empire.

As Doug Owram has shown, that unbounded optimism began to disintegrate by the mid-1880s, as it came under attack by disillusioned westerners themselves. In Owram's words, "the great partnership which was supposed to develop between the metropolitan center and the hinterland was rejected by the hinterland even before it had been fully formed."[27] Ever since that first moment of reassessment, western Canadians have doubted that the eastern provinces really understand their situation—the hard, physical reality of creating a life on the prairies and in the mountains—or sympathize as much as they should. Subsequently, the Canadian West went on to seek a separate identity, more local control over its resources, and a closer fit to the land. To be sure, much settlement occurred after those dark days of the 1880s and 1890s; so-called "improved land" in Manitoba, Saskatchewan, and Alberta increased from less than 300,000 acres in 1881 to nearly 60,000,000 acres in 1931.[28] However, as impressive an achievement as this expansion was, it never represented a great imperial power base.

Still another way in which development had to be radically rethought was in regard to land ownership in the West. The original idea in the United States was that development involved turning all of the terrain into fee-simple, private ownership plots, bounded by sturdy fences and stretching from the East Coast all the way to the Pacific. That plan broke down; it did not even get to the Rocky Mountains intact.

Thirty years after President Abraham Lincoln signed the Homestead Act—itself a monument to the private property ideal—another Congress gave another President the authority to withdraw government lands from homestead entry, in order to safeguard vulnerable watersheds and protect a timber supply.[29] That act, which Marion Clawson and Burnell Held have called "one of the most important land administration measures ever undertaken in the United States," eventually led to the National Forest system, which includes nearly 200 million acres.[30] Then in the 1930s, virtually all homesteading, and thus all further settlement of the public domain, came to an end, leaving much of the West in the hands of the federal government. Today, the U.S. government owns approximately one-third of the entire nation, making it the country's biggest landowner by far, and the dominant power over national as well as western development. In some western states, as much as fifty or even eighty percent of the land is public domain.[31]

Again, the impetus behind this change, of course, came partly from nature. The same environmental conditions that made federal water projects necessary, if agriculture was to succeed, required the preserving of watersheds from deforestation by private timber companies. Lands that could not be irrigated could not be homesteaded; therefore, they could not become fee-simple rural estates. Most of the public domain lies where nature has made the land too dry or too cold for agricultural settlement. What is more important is that these extraordinary changes in American land policy came about because of dramatic changes in peoples' attitudes toward private land ownership, and indeed toward the whole capitalist logic of development. By the 1890s, many citizens had begun to worry about where that logic was leading—to a landscape depleted and degraded, they feared, by frontier exploiters and metropolitan businessmen.

We call this reaction the Conservation Movement and note that it grew out of outrage over the decimation of American forests and a decline of wildlife. Organizations such as the Audubon Society and the Sierra Club appeared in the years of the first land withdrawals, and supported a permanent federal responsibility for controlling the effects of unbridled development. No one contemplating the West in 1869, when the first trains began running triumphantly across the continent, foresaw any of this change in public mood, any more than they understood the limits of the western land itself. They could not have imagined the intense reaction against privatization and exploitation of land that would begin to flare up within a few decades; nor foresee a future West perpetually under the management of federal resource agencies. The idea of federal subsidies to railroad construction was a familiar idea, but not a vast federal ownership and management of the land in perpetuity.

The Canadian government took a strikingly different course in land ownership, one that I believe has never received sufficient attention by historians in either country. Ottawa did not remain the major landowner in the Canadian West; in the North, it did, but not in the West. In 1930, the federal government turned over all its lands, except a few parks, to the western provinces. For the previous sixty years, those lands had been federal property, the so-called "Crown lands," acquired from the Hudson's Bay Company in 1870. British Columbia was an exception to that pattern; its Crown lands became the provincial government's responsibility immediately upon joining the Confederation.[32]

As other provinces formed, they too wanted the same local control over resources that British Columbia exercised, but for a lengthy time their pleas were ignored. The National Policy, directed from far-away Ottawa, allowed the prairie provinces little voice regarding railroad grants, agricultural development, and timber and mineral extraction. In 1930, that situation abruptly shifted. Ottawa proclaimed that it had fulfilled its major development goals in the West and handed over its huge estate to Winnipeg, Regina, and Edmonton.[33]

Exactly the same case could have been made in the American West, and around 1930 it indeed was being made, impatiently and stridently, by western governors. They could claim the same kind of precedent as their counterparts in Canada, since lands in eastern states, as well Texas, rather quickly and universally had gone from federal to private ownership. But despite strenuous arguments, no handover occurred. The American public would not let it happen, then or any time thereafter. They wanted the federal government to remain in charge of those acres simply because, in this regard, it was trusted more than the state governments, with their open-door attitudes toward mining and timber companies. New attitudes had emerged that encouraged American public leaders to assume a permanent resource stewardship in the West, thus breaking a very old precedent and disappointing many westerners.

Why did such a federal responsibility emerge in the United States, but not in Canada? Were the provinces such good resource stewards that the question of who to trust was never an issue? I doubt that such was the case.[34] One only has to look at the controversial record of British Columbia, where conservationists have severely criticized the cozy relation between the Ministry of Forestry and private timber companies, to see that there was reason enough to worry.

The issue of conservation, however, does not seem to have even come up in Canada in 1930. The most plausible reason for that silence is that conservation was a less potent political movement in Canada than the United States, for reasons of culture and politics that invite further research. Quite tellingly, there were at the time almost no popular conservation organizations north of the 49th parallel—nothing like America's Sierra Club and the rest—to stir up debate over issues of land and conservation. In contrast, such a debate had been going on in the United States since the 1890s, and it helps explains why a strong federal responsibility over land ownership emerged and why it continues down to this very day. Even as angry Sagebrush Rebels demand cession of the public domain to the states and its privatization, environmental groups such as the Wilderness Society and Earth First! still fight for federal ownership.

Obviously, the federal land managers in the United States also have not quite lived up to all of the early rosy expectations. These days, they are the target of as much criticism as the timber or mining companies; and, for a number of Americans, the government no longer seems to be the safe guardian of public lands that it once was. Moreover, conservation expectations themselves have changed from the late-19th century to the present, and changed unpredictably. A few decades back, the Forest Service could not have foreseen the degree to which its historic mission would be criticized by the post World War II environmental movement. Instead of aiming merely for sustainable timber harvests, the Forest Service now must learn to apply ecological science to land-use decisions. It must protect old-growth forests, endangered species, and millions of acres of wilderness, which was not part of the original responsibility.

Nor, for that matter, do any of these conservation demands of today fit easily into the traditional logic of capitalism. Where then did they originate? From a rising affluence, which is to say from the very success of capitalism? Or do they stem from deeper cultural shifts—from fears and anxieties about the course of development and progress—that have produced a powerful challenge to capitalism? We really do not fully know the answer.

Notes

1. A provocative discussion of these themes appears in William G. Robbins, *Colony and Empire: The Capitalist Transformation of the American West* (Lawrence: University Press of Kansas, 1994), chap. 3. Robbins tends to see Canada as less aggressive toward its native peoples than the United States, a view some observers might dispute.

2. Gustavo Esteva, "Development," in *The Development Dictionary: A Guide to Knowledge and Power*, Wolfgang Sachs, ed., (London: Zed Books, 1992), 9.

3. H.W. Arndt, "Economic Development: A Semantic History," *Economic Development and Social Change* 29 (April 1981): 461.

4. By the late-19th century, the United States saw itself, and was so seen by many others, as the quintessential developed nation, essentially capitalistic, but blending elements of socialism and populism. A stimulating account of this era of emergence is Martin J. Sklar, *The United States as a Developing Country: Studies in U.S. History in the Progressive Era and the 1920s* (New York: Cambridge University Press, 1992).

5. Frederick Jackson Turner, "The Significance of the Frontier in American History" [1893], in *Frontier and Section: Selected Essays of Frederick Jackson Turner*, Ray Allen Billington, ed., (Englewood Cliffs, New Jersey: Prentice-Hall, 1961), 37.

6. Ibid., 38.

7. "Today," Turner wrote, "we are looking with shock upon a changed world." The best he could offer were half-hearted words: "Let us hold to our attitude of faith and courage. Let us dream as our fathers dreamt and let us make our dreams come true"; from "The West and American Ideals" [1914], in *Frontier and Section*, 106.

8. Among the sources drawn on here are J.M.S. Careless, "Frontierism, Metropolitanism, and Canadian History," *Canadian Historical Review* 35 (March 1954):1–21; Ramsay Cook, "Frontier and Metropolis: The Canadian Experience," in *The Maple Leaf Forever: Essays on Nationalism and Politics in Canada* (Toronto: Macmillan, 1971), 166–75; Carl Berger, *The Writing of Canadian History: Aspects of English-Canadian Historical Writing since 1900*, 2nd ed. (Toronto: University of Toronto Press, 1986), esp. 174–78; W.L. Morton, "Clio in Canada: The Interpretation of Canadian History," *University of Toronto Quarterly* 15 (April 1946):227–34; Carl Berger, "William Morton: The Delicate Balance of Region and Nation," in *The West and the Nation: Essays in Honor of W.L. Morton*, Carl Berger and Ramsay Cook, eds., (Toronto: McClelland and Stewart, 1976), 9–32. The continuing appeal of the metropolitan school of thought is demonstrated by the various essays in *Heartland and Hinterland: A Geography of Canada*, 2nd ed., L.D. McCann, ed., (Scarborough, Ontario: Prentice-Hall Canada, 1987).

9. On the forest staple, see A.R.M. Lower, *The North American Assault on the Canadian Forest: A History of the Lumber Trade between Canada and the United States* (Toronto: Ryerson Press, 1938), and *Great Britain's Woodyard: British America and the Timber Trade, 1763–1867* (Montreal: McGill-Queens University, 1973).

10. Harold A. Innis, *The Fur Trade in Canada* (orig. pub. 1930; New Haven, Connecticut: Yale University Press, 1962), 401–2. See also Abraham Rotstein, "Innis: The Alchemy of Fur and Wheat," *Journal of Canadian Studies* 12 (Winter 1977):6–31; William Christian, "The Inquisition of Nationalism," ibid., 52–72. The similarity of Innis's work to modern dependency theory is the theme of Mel Watkins' "The Staple Theory Revisited," ibid., 83–95.

11. See D.G. Creighton, *The Commercial Empire of the St. Lawrence, 1760–1850* (Toronto: Ryerson Press, 1939). Creighton's "environmentalism" consisted of a great river system inspiring economic development, giving as it were nature's approval to commerce. In the

midst of a panegyric to the Saint Lawrence he wrote: "From the river there rose, like an exhalation, the dream of western commercial empire."

12. The reaction to Turner's thesis is summarized in Michael S. Cross, ed., *The Frontier Thesis and the Canadas: The Debate on the Impact of the Canadian Environment* (Toronto: Copp Clark, 1970). Most authorities seem to concur that the staple school (or Laurentian, or metropolitan—the names seem to be interchangeable) was influenced by Turner, but not in terms of explaining the origins of democracy. See also George F.G. Stanley, "Western Canada and the Frontier Thesis," *Canadian Historical Association Report* (Toronto: University of Toronto Press, 1940), 105–14; Paul F. Sharp, "Three Frontiers: Some Comparative Studies of Canadian, American, and Australian Settlement," *Pacific Historical Review* 24 (November 1955): 369–77; Robin Fisher, "Duff and George Go West: A Tale of Two Frontiers," *Canadian Historical Review* 68 (December 1987):501–28; Robin W. Winks, *The Relevance of Canadian History: U.S. and Imperial Perspectives* (Toronto: Macmillan, 1979), 14, 21.

13. Much of Cronon's book seems to be an application of ideas first laid out by J.M.S. Careless in "Metropolis and Region: The Interplay between City and Region in Canadian History before 1914," *Urban History Review* (1978):99–118. "Behind the rise of frontier, hinterland or region in Canada," writes Careless, "lay the power of the metropolis, which ultimately disposed of their resource harvest, strongly fostered their expansion, and widely controlled their very existence."

14. William J. Cronon, *Nature's Metropolis: Chicago and the Great West* (New York: W.W. Norton, 1991), 46–54.

15. Ibid., 85.

16. These two Wests include, of course, many diversities within them, as Jean Barman has argued, in "The West beyond the West: The Demography of Settlement in British Columbia," *Journal of Canadian Studies* 25 (Fall 1990):5–18.

17. The best guide to this subject for Canada is John A. Eagle, *The Canadian Pacific Railway and the Development of Western Canada, 1896–1914* (Kingston, Ontario: McGill-Queen's University Press, 1989). A splendid visual guide is Bill McKee and Georgeen Klassen, *Trail of Iron: The CPR and the Birth of the West, 1880–1930* (Vancouver, B.C.: Douglas and McIntyre, 1983).

18. Kenneth H. Norrie, "The National Policy and the Rate of Prairie Settlement," *Journal of Canadian Studies* 14 (Fall 1979):63–76.

19. This is not to deny that there were many ways in which Canada looked south for a model, if only a reaction to American policies; see, Richard Preston, ed., *The Influence of the United States on Canadian Development: Eleven Case Studies* (Durham, N.C.: Duke University Press, 1972).

20. C.J. Tracie, "Ethnicity and the Prairie Environment: Patterns of Old Colony Mennonite and Doukhobor Settlement," in *Man and Nature on the Prairies*, Richard Allen, ed., Canadian Plains Studies 6 (Regina: Canadian Plains Research Center, 1976), 46–65.

21. David H. Breen, *The Canadian Prairie West and the Ranching Frontier, 1874–1924* (Toronto: University of Toronto Press, 1983), 125–27, and the same author's "The Turner Thesis and the Canadian West: A Closer Look at the Ranching Frontier," in *Essays on Western History*, Lewis H. Thomas, ed., (Edmonton: University of Alberta Press, 1976), 147–58.

22. That a conservative such as Robert Borden would support nationalization of railroads would be unthinkable in the United States. See John A. Eagle, "Sir Robert Borden, Union Government and Railway Nationalization," *Journal of Canadian Studies* 10 (November 1975):59–66.

23. Turner, "Problems in American History" [1892], in *Frontier and Section*, 30.

24. Ray Allen Billington, *Frederick Jackson Turner: Historian, Scholar, Teacher* (New York: Oxford University Press, 213–14. Turner read Powell's 1896 essay, "Physiographic Regions of the United States," and thereafter began working on a "sectional" interpretation of American history, though it never quite achieved the impact of his Frontier Thesis.

25. The literature on western water development has grown rapidly. For a overview of the environmental problems it has created, see Marc Reisner, *Cadillac Desert: The American West and Its Disappearing Water* (New York: Viking, 1986); and for historical perspectives, see Norris Hundley Jr., *The Great Thirst: Californians and Water, 1770s–1990s* (Berkeley and Los Angeles: University of California Press, 1992); Donald Pisani, *To Reclaim a Divided West: Water, Law, and Public Policy, 1848–1902* (Albuquerque: University of New Mexico Press, 1992); Donald Worster, *Rivers of Empire: Water, Aridity, and the Growth of the American West* (New York: Oxford University Press, 1995), and "Water as a Tool of Empire," in *An Unsettled Country: Changing Landscapes of the American West* (Albuquerque: University of New Mexico Press, 1994), 31–54.

26. For a fine study of Alberta settlement, with a shrewd discussion of the interactive role of the metropolis, the frontier, and the environment, see Paul Voisey's *Vulcan: The Making of a Prairie Community* (Toronto: University of Toronto Press, 1988). See also Max G. Geier, "A Comparative History of Rural Community on the Northwest Plains: Lincoln County, Washington, and the Wheatland Region, Alberta, 1880–1930," Ph.D. thesis, Washington State University, 1990.

27. Doug Owram, *Promise of Eden: The Canadian Expansionist Movement and the Idea of the West, 1856–1900* (Toronto: University of Toronto Press, 1980), 220. Also, regarding the rise of a western identity, see R. Douglas Francis, "From Wasteland to Utopia: Changing Images of the Canadian West in the Nineteenth Century," *Great Plains Quarterly* 7 (Summer 1987):178–94, and "In Search of a Prairie Myth: A Survey of the Intellectual and Cultural Historiography of Prairie Canada," *Journal of Canadian Studies* 24 (Fall 1989):44–69.

28. R.W. Murchie, assisted by William Allen and J.F. Booth, *Agricultural Progress on the Prairie Frontier*, vol. 5, *Canadian Frontiers of Settlement* series (Toronto: Macmillan, 1936), 8.

29. On March 3, 1891, Congress passed the Forest Reserve Act, authorizing the President to reserve forested lands from the public domain. An earlier set-aside of land took place in 1872, with the creation of Yellowstone National Park, as "a public park or pleasuring ground for the benefit and enjoyment of the people."

30. Marion Clawson and Burnell Held, *The Federal Lands: Their Use and Management* (Lincoln: University of Nebraska Press, 1957), 28. The Americans had, in effect, to reinvent an institution of public ownership that never was discarded in Canada. See H.V. Nelles, *The Politics of Development: Forests, Mines, and Hydro-Electric Power in Ontario, 1849–1941* (Hamden, Connecticut: Archon, 1974), 2–9.

31. U.S. Department of the Interior, Bureau of Land Management, *Public Land Statistics 1990*, vol. 175 (Washington: Government Printing Office, 1991).

32. See Robert E. Cail, *Land, Man, and the Law: The Disposal of Crown Lands in British Columbia, 1871–1913* (Vancouver: University of British Columbia Press, 1974), which focuses on the wise leadership of Governor James Douglas in forming a provincial land policy.

33. For an early, though still valuable, discussion of this issue, see Chester Martin, "Dominion Lands Policy," which comprises the second half of volume II of the *Canadian Frontiers of Settlement* series, edited by W.A. Mackintosh and W.L.G. Joerg (Toronto: Macmillan, 1938). See especially chap. 12, which deals with the transfer of 1930. Martin was a strong

province-rights advocate, particularly for Manitoba. For a general review of federal policy, see Kirk N. Lambrecht, *The Administration of Dominion Lands, 1810–1930* (Regina: Canadian Plains Research Center, 1991).

34. According to John Herd Thompson and Allen Seager, "the attitude of the federal government, Liberal or Conservative, to resource development did not differ significantly from that of the provinces"; in *Canada, 1922–1939: Decades of Discord* (Toronto: McClelland and Stewart, 1985), 84.

III

Almost Columbia,
Triumphantly Washington

John McClelland Jr.

*T*HE HUDSON'S BAY COMPANY'S *red banner, which flew authoritatively on both sides of the Cascade Range from 1821 until the Oregon Treaty of 1846, had been replaced by the Stars and Stripes only three years when Oregon Territory was formed. Four years later in 1853, the relatively few Americans busy claiming and settling land north of the Columbia River successfully campaigned to divide Oregon and create still another new territory. Their petitions to the national capital asked that it be called Columbia, but Congress decided to name it Washington.*

The original Washington extended from the Pacific Ocean to the crest of the Rocky Mountains. Probably never in American history have so few achieved self-governance over so much terrain. The motivations for a hurried division of Oregon Territory, the condition of the sparse clusters of settlement between the Columbia and Puget Sound, and the determined leadership of the enthusiasts—who rallied nearly every white settler to support their pioneering political crusade—form the basis for the first, and one of the most interesting, chapters in Washington history.

In 1889, Washington was well on its way to full social and economic development when it finally achieved statehood. By that date, the population stood at nearly 350,000, and a long-sought railroad link with the East—reviving dreams of economic progress delayed by 36 years of isolation—was at last completed.

By contrast, in 1853 when Washington Territory was formed, the population was 3,965 and a route for a rail line across the northern United States had not even been surveyed. Despite these raw conditions, the newly arrived emigrants settling along the banks of the lower Columbia and Cowlitz rivers, and northward to Puget Sound, had convinced themselves that their destiny lay in breaking away from Oregon Territory and establishing a territory of their own.

Why were these frontiersmen in such a hurry beginning in 1851? Why were they so eager to assume the responsibilities of government while still preoccupied with the dawn-to-dusk labor of building log cabins and clearing land for farming? At that time, the Pacific Northwest had been a part of the United States for just five years and the Oregon Territory for only three. Everything was new. Yet these settlers north of the Columbia were dissatisfied and restless.

They wanted the usual necessities—roads, mail service, towns—as well as self-government. In addition, they sought assistance in dealing with their most troublesome obstacle—not the Indians, who were not yet openly hostile—but the British, particularly the Hudson's Bay Company (HBC) and its subsidiary, the Puget Sound Agricultural Company, centered at Cowlitz Prairie and at Fort Nisqually on Puget Sound, which claimed much of the best land. The seat of territorial government lay far away in the Willamette Valley and all but two members of the legislature lived their. What chance did the north have for good representation, especially in the distribution of what few federal appropriations Oregon Territory received?

These reasons and more persuaded the settlers to seek independence from the south. Had they concluded otherwise, had they been less persistent and resourceful, and had the first newspaper in the region not cheered them on, Washington might never have come into being. Oregon was only eight years away from statehood in 1851. If the northern part had not seceded when it did, much of it might now be in Oregon—a state perhaps comparable in size to California. No western state has ever been divided after admission to the Union.

Before the signing of the Oregon Treaty in 1846, ending almost 30 years of joint occupation by the United States and Great Britain, most Americans migrating to the Oregon Country settled south of the Columbia in the Willamette Valley. In the "Great Migration" of 1843, for instance, almost 900 traveled over the Oregon Trail to the Pacific Northwest, yet none had tried their luck north of the river. The HBC, with its fur-trading headquarters at Fort Vancouver, initially provided law enforcement and some social services in old Oregon.

Soon, following frontier tradition, Americans in the Willamette Valley employed the time-honored social compact principle by forming the Oregon Provisional Government in 1843. This fledgling government had no authority to rule, except by frontier necessity and tradition. In actuality, the early

Oregon-bound emigrants came not to a "no-man's land," but to a "no-country land" beyond the boundaries of the United States.

The imperious HBC steered the earliest American arrivals southward into the Willamette Valley and discouraged them from going north. The HBC hoped that the absence of Americans north of the Columbia would strengthen the British objective of making the river the international boundary line. But this well-calculated plan failed. Americans were inevitably drawn northward along the swift rivers and through the dense forests, where only a few rough trails provided passage.

Emigrant interest in northern Oregon began in 1844 when the Michael T. Simmons party arrived at Fort Vancouver. One member of this group was George Washington Bush, part black and thus not allowed to settle in the Willamette Valley, because the provisional government prohibited blacks. Bush had made good friends among his traveling companions on the long journey westward and they would not desert him now. They all spent the winter at Fort Vancouver, splitting shingles for the HBC.

Then Simmons, after exploring to the north, led the party to that spot on the Deschutes River where it tumbles into the southern end of Puget Sound with enough flow to turn the wheels of grist mills and sawmills. There, at a place called Newmarket and later Tumwater, they established the first permanent American settlement in what is now Washington. It was the fall of 1845.

Other Americans followed the Simmons party, staking claims in the few non-forested areas not already occupied by the Puget Sound Agricultural Company between Cowlitz Prairie and the Nisqually Valley. By this time the "Oregon Question"—whether Britain or the United States should prevail there—had become a raging national issue. The new settlers, recognizing the importance of getting more Americans into the area, encouraged friends and relatives to join them. So many came that four years later a census counted about 1,000 white people north of the Columbia River.

As scholars have noted, however, the influence of increasing numbers of Americans in the Oregon Country, who in effect colonized a region dominated by the British, remains a matter of conjecture. Perhaps more importantly regarding the Oregon Treaty of 1846, a combination of diplomatic events and political conditions in both nations turned the tide for the United States, resulting in the international boundary being established to the north along the 49th parallel.[1]

Soon after Oregon became a territory in 1848, the northern settlers realized they were poorly situated in relation to the territorial capital and the seat of political power in the Willamette Valley, up to 300 miles and several days of travel time away from Puget Sound. Even more bothersome was the likelihood that the federal assistance Oregon might receive would be used in the south, leaving little for the north. These and other circumstances spawned an idea. Oregon Territory was large—why not divide it and give the northern part a government of its own?

Just where the idea originated is not known; it may simply have evolved out of the grievances and complaints among northern settlers. But it was an ambitious young lawyer, perhaps hoping to be identified as the proposal's originator, who first put it in print. John B. Chapman of Oregon City, recently arrived in the territory, wrote a letter to the editor of the *Oregon Statesman* urging that all of Oregon lying north of the Columbia be made a separate territory called "Columbia."

Shortly afterward, Chapman went north to see the area for himself. From Steilacoom, he wrote to A.A. Durman at Oswego, near Portland, saying he had found "the fairest and best portion of Oregon north of the Columbia." Inevitably, he said, "the north must be Columbia Territory and the south the state of Oregon. How poetical!"[2]

When Chapman was admitted to the bar by Judge William Strong at John R. Jackson's log cabin, which served as a courthouse (located north of present-day Toledo), he became the first practicing attorney in what is now Washington. His proposal for a new territory found ready acceptance among northern settlers, especially after he delivered an oration at the 1851 Independence Day celebration in Olympia, where he expounded on the division, insisting the time had come for action. Listeners applauded the speech enthusiastically. Some were at first skeptical about the chances of Congress creating a new territory out of one that had existed only three years, but they believed it worth considering.

Soon, settlers at the south end of Puget Sound and in the prairies along the trail to the Columbia River eagerly embraced the proposal for a government, whose elected officers could meet close to home and thus respond to local needs. Some of them had been leaders in the Midwest and elsewhere, and were ready to exercise their political talents again as founders of a new government on the farthest frontier of the land.

Calling meetings to discuss public affairs was not a new experience for the settlers. They had earlier contemplated a problem involving the Puget Sound Agricultural Company's large cattle herds in the Nisqually locality. They had held a meeting—a protest session—and passed a series of resolutions demanding that the British herds be moved north of the Nisqually River and declaring that none but Americans, or those intending to become

Americans, were eligible to claim the land. The British decided not to antagonize the determined settlers; they moved the herds. This initial triumph of collective will encouraged more action—the determined steps leading toward self-government.

In another meeting, northerners launched the movement to convince Congress it should designate this corner of the continent as a separate territory. They met at Cowlitz Landing (today's Toledo), a riverbank hamlet central to the area of settlement, but consisting of little more than a store and small hotel where travelers going north or south changed from canoes to horses, or the other way around. The gathering, given the dignified name of being a convention, with those attending identified as delegates, opened on August 29, 1851. Nineteen people attended. Representatives elected Seth Catlin, an older settler from the lower Cowlitz River, as chairman. They also appointed five standing committees—territorial government, districts and counties, rights and privileges of citizens, internal improvements, and ways and means.

The committees met on the first day and were ready to report the next morning. Headed by Chapman, the territorial committee unanimously recommended a new territorial government be organized, and called for the appointment of a panel of three to draw up an appropriate memorial to Congress. The convention immediately accepted the report, appointing Chapman, F.S. Balch, and Michael T. Simmons to draft the memorial.

Next, the internal improvements committee called for a road between Puget Sound and old Fort Walla Walla (near present-day Wallula), to be built with a $100,000 federal appropriation. Since there was no commerce between this eastern region and the Puget Sound country, and few occasions for travelers to go east, they obviously intended for the road to bring immigrants into northern Oregon rather than going down the Columbia River to the Willamette Valley. It was not too early, the delegates decided, to anticipate political division, so they drew boundaries for counties and gave them names. Many of those hastily drawn lines later were accepted after the territory was formed. But the suggested names did not fare as well—St. Helens, Steilacoom, and Simmons among them.

The memorial to Congress was long—1,500 words—and Chapman made it evident in the first paragraph that he was the author: "The Committee...have directed me to report...to Congress." He gave numerous reasons for dividing Oregon Territory and listed some outstanding complaints. Distances were so great that it cost more and took longer for a Puget Sound resident to visit a clerk's office or judge than for a man to travel by horseback from St. Louis to Boston and back. With many harbors and an abundance of water power, the northern part would make a fine state. Because of the Hudson's Bay Company, there were comparatively few American settlers—in fact, immigrants had been "until this day literally excluded from the Northern Territory of Oregon." Even so, said the memorial in an expansive tone, "there are now about three thousand souls north of the Columbia."

It continued: "Territorial officers, located 300 miles away, seldom visit the northern area and generally neglect it." The only judge lived in Cathlamet, far down the Columbia valley. No Indian agent had been seen north of the river since Joe Lane, the original agent, had gone east to assume new duties as Oregon's territorial delegate. Despite all these difficulties, the memorial stated, immigrants were arriving with regularity, emphasizing the need for a new territory. Moreover, the document was exact about the desired designation, specifying that "the name of Columbia is most especially solicited and required."

Agreeing to meet again in May in Olympia, the Cowlitz Landing Convention closed after adopting two more resolutions. One implored the federal government to halt the practice of outsiders sending ships into Puget Sound with crews who helped themselves to timber along the shores. Another asked the newspapers in southern Oregon to publish the deliberations of the convention. The *Oregon Spectator* and the Portland *Oregonian,* both of which had some circulation in Washington, D.C., acceded to the request and printed the proceedings.[3]

The Cowlitz Memorial had misspellings, exaggerations, and some inaccuracies that did not escape Oregon Delegate Joe Lane's notice when he received it, probably in October 1851, since the convention was held in late August. Mail in this era went by a steamer or sailing ship down the coast in successive jumps to Panama, across the isthmus by horse-drawn vehicle, then by steamer across the Caribbean and up the East Coast. Lane understood the situation in the Northwest quite well, having been appointed the territory's first governor in 1848. He left that position when elected to succeed Oregon's first territorial delegate to Congress, missionary Samuel Thurston, who became ill and died while traveling through Mexico. The petition simply did not persuade Lane that it was desirable to divide the territory, so he handed the Cowlitz Memorial to the clerk of the House Committee on Territories, where it was effectively buried.

The Cowlitz Convention delegates had scheduled another meeting at Olympia in May 1852 to consider Chapman's ambitious proposal for a "statehood" movement. However, the settlers concluded it would be futile to discuss statehood when they had failed to even get a congressional hearing on territorial status. The issue did not fade away, however, nor were residents any less dissatisfied with their plight or less eager for change. They remained convinced that the realization of their aspirations would bring economic development, population growth, and, eventually, a place in the Union as a state.

Olympia's Fourth of July orator in 1852 was John R. Bigelow, another young lawyer newly admitted to the practice. He was as eager as John Chapman to display his speaking talents and enthusiasm regarding the predominant issue of the day. In doing so, Bigelow expressed visionary views that often were repeated for the next century as successive generations awaited fulfillment of this far corner's economic greatness. Oregon Territory, he said, though weak and dependent,

> occupies a commanding and important position. It is the frontier of the Republic in the Northwest. Fronting on the Pacific with its facilities for commerce, it seems to stretch out one hand to China and the east Indies and the other to the States. The two great harbors of the Pacific Coast are San Francisco and Puget Sound. Our colonization westward must for a time here be checked, but the force of our example and the advancement of free principles will not stop; it will still go on and illuminate the islands of the sea, and exert such a powerful influence that benighted China will wake up from her sleep of ages and take strides forward in civil freedom.

A visitor who may have heard Bigelow's oration was Thomas Jefferson Dwyer, who six months earlier had begun the *Weekly Oregonian* in Portland. Northerners had persuaded Governor John P. Gaines to visit the northern part of the territory and Dwyer decided to accompany him, possibly because he had also been invited. It was somewhat of an exploring adventure for both, involving arduous travel by boat, canoe, and horseback over several days.

In Olympia, several prominent citizens, including Lafayette Balch, who founded Steilacoom; George A. Barnes, an Olympia merchant; and Elmer Sylvester, a large property owner at the Olympia townsite, approached Dwyer with a proposal. They handed him a statement which read:

> The undersigned, believing that the interests of that portion of Oregon north of the Columbia River demand the establishment of a Newspaper in that part of the Country, do agree to donate the several sums of money set opposite our respective names for the purpose of establishing a Newspaper at some prominent point on Puget's Sound, to be called the *Columbian*.[4]

The statement went on to specify that the proposed newspaper should promote the interests of northern Oregon and be neutral in matters of religion and politics.

The pledges totaled $572, enough to induce Dwyer to heed the request. Back in Portland, he decided to send two of his employees, Thornton F. McElroy and James W. Wiley, to Olympia to start the newspaper. McElroy, then 27 years old, had come north from the California gold fields where he had not done well, and went to work at a trade he knew—typesetting. Wiley, at 32, had some legal training and writing skills. Dwyer assigned him to do the editing while McElroy would handle production and business matters. Dwyer also furnished the equipment, which included a small Ramage hand press on which the *Oregonian* had first been printed, several fonts of type, and enough paper to print 300 or so of several four-page editions.[5] No mention of Dwyer's ownership or the financial support of local businessmen appeared in the *Columbian*, probably because the backers felt that an apparently independent newspaper, vigorously supporting the move to divide the territory, would have more influence than one known to be owned by and indebted to private citizens.

The *Columbian* made it quite plain in its first issue on September 11, 1852, that it would give rousing support to the division of Oregon—it printed Bigelow's Fourth of July oration in full. The *Columbian* started with an announced circulation of 350—a figure that may have been somewhat exaggerated, like population estimates—but it was the first and only newspaper published north of the Columbia and was thoroughly and widely read. The published list of places where it had agents indicates that its thin editions covered a large area—Monticello, Whidbey Island, Port Townsend, Steilacoom, Nisqually, Cowlitz farms, Chlickeeles (Chehalis), New York (later known as Seattle),[6] New Dungeness, Oregon City, Jackson's Prairie, Poe's Point, and Washington City (D.C.). The last listing shows that the *Columbian* had some readership in the national capital.

In the September 25 issue, Major H.A. Goldsborough, concealing his identity by using the pseudonym "ELIS" (the ancient symbol for Olympia), led off column one of the front page with a lengthy "Fellow Citizens" exhortation intended to stir more enthusiasm for the cause. Oregon Territory contained five times as much area as Missouri, he reminded readers, and six times as much as Illinois. Oregon was seven times the size of New York and had 550 miles of coastline, altogether too much for one territory or one state. Much of the vast area lay north of the Columbia River, where the number of voters actually entitled it to four rather than the mere two representatives now in the 25-member assembly in Salem.

When the fall session of the district court was held at Jackson's Prairie in October 1852, so many citizens showed up that Goldsborough called an impromptu meeting. More than a year had gone by since the Cowlitz Landing meeting and there still was no word from Delegate Lane about the possibility of congressional action on a division of Oregon Territory. Goldsborough told those who gathered around him at John R. Jackson's log house that a new start needed to be made.

The others agreed and immediately convened a formal meeting, selecting F.A. Chenowith of Clark County to preside. A resolutions committee made up of Jackson, Goldsborough, and Quincy Adams Brooks composed a call for every settlement and precinct in northern Oregon to send delegates to a general convention at Olympia in November. In the discussion that followed, however, the advocates agreed to hold the meeting instead at Monticello at the mouth of the Cowlitz River.

The *Columbian* began at once to enthusiastically promote the forthcoming convention. It raised its editorial voice to a shout with the biggest type it had:

CITIZENS OF NORTHERN OREGON!

It behooves you to bestir yourselves to claim your independence for the territorial authority exerted over you by the Willamette Valley. Call meetings in your several precincts; memorialize Congress to set us off; exhibit our grievances both in omission and commission under which we have suffered from all departments of government and that body will be compelled to regard your prayer?[7]

Editor McElroy realized that travel at any time was difficult and, in November, the trail south would likely be deep in mud. Travelers would proceed south on foot or by horseback to Cowlitz Landing. They would rest there, then move on down the twisting course of the Cowlitz River for another 30 miles by canoe or bateaux to Monticello. The latter settlement consisted only of Darby Huntington's place, part home and part hotel; Olson and Mahan's store; two old HBC warehouses; and the houses and barns of L.P. Smith and Royal Smith. The *Columbian* urged everyone to help the delegates as they made their way to the convention, and

inasmuch as dollars are not plentiful in this region…and as many of our delegates will have to incur considerable sacrifice in order to attend the convention, it is to be hoped that the good people along the routes—Warbassport, etc., instead of desiring to turn the necessary means for reaching Monticello at a profit, on the contrary…will endeavor to make the expenses of the delegates from the interior as light as possible.[8]

Whether E.D. Warbass, who owned the wayside hotel at Cowlitz Landing (also known as Warbassport) and who later established a store at Monticello, complied with the suggestion that he provide delegates free services was not recorded, but he may have done so, since he was himself a delegate.

The *Columbian* was determined that attendance at Monticello be substantial, realizing that the more names on a petition to Congress, the more attention it was likely to get. Under the heading "PREPARE! PREPARE!" McElroy and Wiley explained why the meeting was to be held at Monticello, far down on the Columbia River, a hundred miles from Olympia. They said that the desire for independence from the southern part of Oregon Territory was unanimous among those living between Whidbey Island and the Cowlitz River, but those along the Columbia were close to the Willamette Valley and might have divided feelings about a separation. If the convention were held in Olympia, they said, people from Vancouver, Monticello, Cathlamet, and Cascade City might not send many delegates.

According to accepted procedure, said the *Columbian*, voters should meet in every precinct to elect delegates and alternates. Instead of limiting the number, the *Columbian* urged, "let all be appointed who can possibly attend." Numbers were more important than protocol. And the newspaper, referring to lack of action after the Cowlitz Convention, warned that, "if we should fail again," the southern part of Oregon might achieve statehood before a third attempt at separation could be made. In arranging the new state's boundaries, "serious encroachments" might be made in the area "which nature designed should be incorporated with our own." Therefore, the newspaper declared: "We must be vigilant and active in arranging matters for the crises before us. Again we say 'PREPARE! PREPARE!'"[9]

The tone of the editor's exhortations in the following issue reflected the apprehension that poor attendance at the convention would make an unfavorable impression on Delegate Lane and his congressional colleagues. "TURN OUT! TURN OUT!" shouted the headline. "ACTION! ACTION!" Time was growing short; delegates must be elected without delay. The great concern, the *Columbian* explained, was that the Willamette region would receive all the favors from the federal government because all the territorial officers lived there, and because even the existence of northern Oregon might be over-looked in the national capital. Only through action at Monticello could that eventuality be avoided. "Rally! Rally!" exclaimed the *Columbian* in its issue of November 20. "On to the convention!" By then some of the delegates were indeed on their way, including some who only the year before had settled at two new places on Puget Sound—New York (Seattle) and even more distant Port Townsend.

Those farthest north made their way down the Sound in canoes to Olympia, then by horse along the slow land route to Cowlitz Landing. One of the travelers, Quincy Brooks, was surprised to find at the landing a young man he had known in the East, Edward J. Allen, then 22 years old. Allen had arrived in the territory earlier in the year, worked as a logger near Vancouver, and then decided to go north, driving three yoke of oxen. Unaware of the impending meeting at Monticello, he had taken the opposite side of the Cowlitz River and plodded on to Cowlitz Landing, where he was resting when the party of delegates from the north showed up.

Brooks explained their mission and urged him to leave his own oxen at the landing and accompany the group down the Cowlitz to take part in the convention. Allen demurred, saying he could hardly qualify as a citizen of Oregon, having just arrived. But Brooks assured him that this made no difference; numbers were needed at Monticello, not merely delegates bearing credentials. So, to be obliging, or not wanting to miss the excitement, Allen went along.

At Monticello, the delegates found shelter wherever they could and gathered for their meetings in Darby Huntington's large home. Forty-four were counted as delegates. Conventioneers elected a Puget Sound man, H.G. McConaha, afterward president of the first territorial legislature's upper house, as chairman, and Dr. R.J. White as secretary. Quincy Brooks moved for the appointment of a 13-member committee to undertake the all-important task of drafting the memorial to Congress. Those selected besides Brooks, who served as chairman, were Seth Catlin, known as the "sage of Monticello," D.C. (Doc) Maynard of Seattle, W.W. Plumb, Alfred Cook, John R. Jackson, Eugene L. Finch, A.F. Scott, Fred A. Clarke, C.S. Hathaway, E.H. Winslow, Nathaniel Stone, and the young man who just happened by, Edward Allen.

Allen left the only recorded account of anything other than official business at Monticello.[10] His description of the social activities in a lamp-lit, crowded attic—probably in Darby Huntington's house—the night before the convention deliberations began tells much about the character of the delegates gathering at Monticello that rainy November in 1852. They all looked like middle-aged to Allen, but most were in their 20s and 30s. A few—Catlin, Huntington, Dr. Nathaniel Ostrander, and Simon Plamondon among them—were more than 40. Their entertainments were simple ones. They talked a great deal, drank some whiskey, smoked pipes, and were filled with feelings of nostalgia when someone sang, "Oh, Don't You Remember Sweet Alice, Ben Bolt?" Festive occasions were rare on the Northwest frontier, as were gatherings of such size, so the evenings of socializing turned out to have some of the characteristics of a pleasant stag party for those who had come to conduct serious business.

The Monticello Memorial to Congress, drawn up and promptly adopted, was considerably shorter than the one devised at the Cowlitz Convention the year before, and was far better written. The actual author may well have been Allen, putting into words what Brooks and the others advised him to write. Addressed to the House and Senate, the memorial "respectfully represents" that northern Oregon be set apart as a new territory to be called Columbia. The Columbia River should be the border on the south and east, the 49th parallel to the north, and the Pacific Ocean on the west. This proposed 32,000-square-mile area did not even approximate the vast sweep of land that Congress would eventually designate as a new territory in due time.

Numerous reasons were given to support the petition. Oregon as it stood was far too big. The regions north and south of the Columbia were economic rivals and always would be. With most of the voters living in the southern part, those in the north were not getting a fair share of congressional appropriations. The seat of government in Salem was an exaggerated 400 miles from those living on the Puget Sound. And, the petition concluded:

> Northern Oregon, with its great natural resources, presenting such unparalleled inducements to immigrants and with its present large population constantly and rapidly increasing by immigration, is of sufficient importance, in a national point of view, to merit the fostering care of Congress, and its interests are so numerous, and so entirely distinctive in their character, as to demand the attention of a separate and independent legislature.

No mention was made of the exact population.

Quincy Brooks had gone to the convention with a prepared speech and insisted on giving it—repeating again the many reasons for a new territory—even though there were none to argue with him. The entire convention, the *Columbian* reported, was held in a "spirit of harmony and agreement."

All 44 delegates signed the memorial to Congress. Copies were made and entrusted to the uncertain mails on December 3, 1852. On January 31, 1853, two months later, Delegate Lane wrote to Brooks acknowledging receipt. Meanwhile, two months previously, on December 6, Lane *already* had decided to take the action he had been urged to take a year before—he had introduced a resolution calling for the creation of Columbia Territory.

The news that Lane had introduced a Columbia Territory bill, however, did not reach the Northwest for almost three months, leaving the northern Oregon settlers to wonder if their efforts had been in vain. On March 2, 1853, the *Columbian* echoed the generally felt discouragement when it editorialized: "Even the most active and enthusiastic supporter of these movements [perhaps referring to the editor himself] did not think that either of the memorials would have the desired effect on Congress."

In the next issue, "Agricola" urged in a letter that a meeting be held in Olympia to keep the separatist movement alive and proposed that a fund be raised to send an elected delegate from northern Oregon to Congress, even though he would have no official status when he arrived. But before another meeting could be held, the mails brought the welcome report of Lane's introduction of the Columbia Bill (presented in Congress, December 6, 1852).

Several early historians, including Clinton A. Snowden, Hubert Howe Bancroft, Elwood Evans, and Edmond S. Meany, mistakenly attributed Lane's action directly to the Monticello Memorial document itself. Meany, however, later corrected this discrepancy when he realized that the convention report, which was sent east on December 3, could not possibly have reached Lane in the nation's capital by December 6, 1852.[11]

So what prompted Lane to act? It could hardly have been the Cowlitz Convention Memorial, which he had received and buried in committee a year earlier.

Actually, the historians that Meany corrected, including himself, were only partly wrong about the Monticello Convention's influence on Lane. True, he had not received the petition by December 6, 1852, but he knew it was coming and he knew what it would say. He knew this because he had read about it in the issues of the *Columbian* that he had received. The newspaper had stirred up public sentiment in favor of a new territory beginning with its first edition, and Lane could not but notice that no opposition was being expressed in any quarter, even in southern Oregon.

Furthermore, Lane received pressure from some prominent individuals. Isaac N. Ebey, a settler on distant Whidbey Island who had been elected as one of the northern area's two delegates to the Oregon territorial legislature, had earlier written to Lane on January 23, 1852, "at the request of Col. [Michael] Simmons and other citizens of Oregon." After commenting on the then-burning issue of the territorial capital's location—whether at Oregon City or Salem—Ebey said that it made little difference "so far as the north side of the river is Con curned." Then, backtracking self-consciously, he undertook to please the incumbent delegate, whose term was about up, by saying, "I speak the sentiments of the people when I say they are almost unanimous in favor of Con tinu ing you as their delegate." But, he added:

> This statement is subject to some qualification, as there are two or three would appeares to be emisaries of the Salem Clique; and certain Gentleman, adventurer, from your native State [Indiana] John B. Chapman, who

appears ambitious to be considered the head and front of the movement in favor of divideing the Territory.

Chapman, Ebey suggested, would like to run for the office of territorial delegate himself. Ebey considered Chapman to be one of a

> hoste of political adventurers who came up the rough and rugged Cowlitz River…with pack on there back, seedy fashionable dress, & delicate white hands, trudgeing their weary way on foot; Olympia gained, there toils ended, there comfortably ensconced on board of a ship, or more comfortable situated behind a desk, quill in hand, and folio before them in a nice comfortable office.

He was referring particularly to men sent out to fill federal jobs when a customs district was created. Writing as a "sincear, though humble friend," Ebey concluded by urging Lane to run for reelection and "to give the subject of the proposed division of Territory your careful consider ation. That question must sooner or later be the absorbing question in this Territory."[12]

Delegate Lane, as the elected representative of all of Oregon Territory, simply responded to the wishes of a sizeable number of his constituents when he introduced his measure. As evident in stories he saw in newspapers from the Northwest, the movement, started a year earlier, was gathering momentum and finally deserved his attention.

A further consideration was the political situation in Oregon, where the so-called "Salem Clique" of Lane's fellow Democrats firmly controlled the territorial government. It is not difficult to believe that Lane's political allies in Oregon urged him to bring about the division. Northern Oregon was gaining more new population than the south, now that the treaty with Britain finally had been signed. There was more free land north of the Columbia for new settlers to claim. Voter strength could grow in northern Oregon to such an extent that those in power in Salem would be threatened. It might be better to let the northerners go off and form their own government. Southern Oregon was large enough for a state anyway.

The Oregon legislature, with the two northern representatives—F.A. Chenoweth and Isaac Ebey—in attendance, convened in Salem only 10 days after the Monticello Convention adjourned. Although neither representative had been at Monticello, they too were strongly for division and Ebey introduced a memorial to Congress supporting that proposition. It noted that in the four-and-a-half years since Congress had authorized Oregon Territory, population had spread north of the Columbia River, and the people of the area "labor[ed] under great inconvenience and hardship, by reason of the great distance to which they are removed from the present territorial organizations…Communication between these two portions of the territory is difficult, casual and uncertain."

The memorial declared that the Columbia River was a natural dividing line, adding that "experience has proven that when marked geographical boundaries, which have been traced by the hand of nature, have been disregarded in the formation of local governments, that sectional jealousies and local strife have seriously embarrassed their prosperity and characterized their domestic legislation."

Therefore, the memorial approved by the Oregon legislative assembly concluded, "the time has come…to establish a separate territorial government for all that portion of Oregon Territory lying north of the Columbia River and west of the great northern branch of the same, to be known as the Territory of Columbia." The Oregon house adopted this document on January 14, 1853, and the upper house on January 18.

Allowing a month for mail to reach Washington, it must have been mid-February 1853 before Lane received it. Like the earlier Monticello Memorial, this petition could hardly have influenced Lane when, on December 6, 1852, he had introduced his bill to create Columbia Territory. But it is very likely through the mail, territorial leaders in the Northwest had urged Lane, in November or earlier, to take action, or at least had indicated that they would not object if he initiated legislation to divide the territory.

Lane's bill came out of the House Committee on Territories with a favorable recommendation on February 8, 1853. It was one of several territorial measures, including those pertaining to Nebraska and Wyoming. None had completely smooth sailing. Lane's bill could have foundered on the issue of Indian land titles or whether the relatively small population of northern Oregon justified the expense of setting up another territorial government. Representative Daniel Jones of Tennessee was against Lane's proposal because of the north's meager population. Jones' motion to table the bill was followed by some parliamentary maneuvering, and then Lane made a speech, forcefully arguing for the creation of Columbia Territory, repeating much of what was included in the Cowlitz and Monticello memorials.

At one point Representative Charles Skelton of New Jersey interrupted Lane, asking how many people lived in northern Oregon. Lane was ready with a skillful though evasive answer—as many as the whole of what Oregon Territory had when it was established in 1848. The answer seemed to satisfy the questioner. And well that it did, for if Lane had been forced to state a number, and had been honest about it, he would have said that there were only about 3,000 white citizens north of the Columbia River.

In his remarks, Lane persuasively emphasized that the regions on both sides of the Columbia River were essentially the same—heavily forested with much good soil for farming. Each area, he said, would make a fine state. Congress had invited people to move west when it passed the Oregon Donation Land Law of 1850. Now it had an obligation to provide adequate government for those responding to the invitation.

Lane's effective speech injected a new unexpected issue into the proceedings. Suddenly the question was not whether the new territory should be created, but what name it should be given. Representative Richard Stanton of Kentucky moved that the bill be amended by striking the word "Columbia" wherever it occurred and substituting "Washington." Lane, perhaps sensing that this would give his colleagues new reason to vote for the bill—to give honor to the first president—without hesitation said, "I shall never object to that name."

Representative Jones persisted in his tabling motion, but Representative Edward Stanley of North Carolina interrupted him, making a short speech favoring the name Washington. "There is something very appropriate about it," Stanley said. "And it is a little singular that this same idea should have occurred to others at the same time." He had suggested it to his seat mate moments before, but he realized it "might lead to trouble" if some day there should be a city of Washington in a state by that name. "Washington, Washington," would hardly do. Nevertheless, the House then voted favorably on the motion to substitute Washington for Columbia. That detail taken care of, the House set aside consideration of the bill itself while it debated a measure to create the Territory of Nebraska.

When Lane's bill came up for discussion again, one congressman made an attempt to restore the name Columbia to the Washington bill. Representative Alexander Evans of Maryland agreed that George Washington deserved to be honored, but, he said:

> Our geographical nomenclature has become such a mass of confusion that [it] is almost impossible, when you hear the name of a town, to know in what part of the world it is, much less to know what part of the United States it may be found. We have perhaps in this country one hundred counties and towns of the name Washington.

Evans suggested giving northern Oregon "one of the beautiful Indian names which prevail in that part of the country." But it was too late. The name Washington already had been substituted for Columbia all through the bill, and that is the way it passed the House. On March 2, 1853, the proposal went before the Senate where it quickly gained approval with no debate. "It is one of the old fashioned territorial bills," one senator explained, and so needed no discussion.

The *National Intelligencer,* a leading Washington, D.C., newspaper of that time, was not happy with the name for the territory on the West Coast because it "contributes fresh confusion to our already confused nomenclature [and] will have to be changed." But it was never changed, and the confusion that the *Intelligencer* foresaw did materialize and grow more bothersome with the years, often making it necessary for Washingtonians on the West Coast to add the word "state" to differentiate their home from the city on the Potomac River. Historian Julian Hawthorne commented in 1893 that "it would have been far better to have retained the name first selected...But as all things yielded to... [George Washington] in 1776, so the name Washington appears to have been equally irresistible in 1853."[13]

Harvey Scott, a pioneer Oregon editor and historian, blamed the name change entirely on Representative Stanton, noting that he had been born in the national capital. Stanton surely was aware of several failed attempts to fund the preservation of Mount Vernon, George Washington's estate on the lower Potomac. Many considered these failures a slight to the first president. Naming a territory after him would help atone for allowing his home to decay. Still, it was unfortunate, Scott said, that Congress rejected the name preferred by those who lived in the new territory.[14]

The fact remained that Congress had taken away half of Oregon Territory and made it into Washington Territory. The dividing line was the Columbia River from its mouth to the point where it crosses the 46th parallel near today's Tri-Cities. The boundary then extended eastward along that parallel to the summit of the Rocky Mountains, and then north to the Canadian border. It was a huge area. (Oregon Territory yet remained relatively large, too, retaining essentially all of what is now southern Idaho until Oregon's statehood in 1859.)

News that the House had passed the bill and changed the name to Washington reached Olympia in early April. The size of the favorable vote, 128 to 29, made the *Columbian* confident that the measure would soon gain Senate approval. Referring to the name change, the newspaper remarked:

> Although Washington is not the name with which we prayed that our infant might be christened, yet it is certainly a very beautiful one. Nevertheless this novelty has met with some distaste among many of our citizens, whilst with others it met with enthusiastic applause. It will be remembered that our Memorial prayed for the name "Columbia"—this the House refused to grant us. Be it so. Even if the name "Columbia" had our preferences, we would not

cavil at a name when principles are at stake. It is a mere difference in taste, and the people of northern Oregon are not sticklers for trifles.[15]

The settlers were obviously so pleased that their efforts were succeeding that they did not want to risk delaying or impending final approval by objecting to the designation the House had chosen, much as they preferred Columbia.

A few days later, the *Columbian* reported, a mud-spattered horseman rode into Olympia and reined up in front of one of the principal houses of entertainment—meaning a saloon.

> His appearance was that of deepest melancholy...Contagion spread among the people—consternation reigned...everyone ran out and all hurried to throng around the stranger, the center [from] whence emanated all the new-born dismay. "What news? What news?" all asked. Then the stranger spoke up saying, "All is lost, Congress...[has] adjourned, the new territorial bill did not pass the Senate, and I am sorry to bring you such tidings."
>
> The crowed sighed and turned sorrowfully away to cogitate upon their blasted prospects. "We are in Oregon yet," said one. "Confound the luck..." Conversations of this kind were held in gloomy little parties throughout the community...[T]hen a kind hearted understanding few undertook the work of consolation. Wait until Congress meets again, they urged, saying, "All's well that ends well."[16]

Then the mail came from Portland, and fortunately there was nothing to confirm what the bearer of bad news had said. Congress, indeed, had not adjourned at the time reported, and a week later the *Columbian* was able to publish the final good news:

> The Territory of Washington is a fixed fact...henceforth northern Oregon has an independent existence, and a destiny to achieve separate and distinct from that of her southern neighbor. She has been baptized by the Congress into a new name—a name Glorious and dear to every American heart. Everywhere, throughout the length and breadth of the Territory the news will be received with joyful acclamations...The separate organization which the citizens of northern Oregon with earnestness, and, may we say, entire unanimity, have ardently wished and labored for, has been triumphantly achieved.[17]

Thus, Washington Territory came into being. It was something of a political phenomenon, considering that in 1846 only a small handful of Americans lived north of the Columbia River. When northern residents launched the movement for separation in 1851, the population had only reached 1,000, and a census in mid-1853 gave the new territory 3,965 persons, of whom 1,682 were voters. The boundaries of the new territory encompassed far more area than the Monticello delegates had requested. It included all of what is now Washington, plus northern Idaho and the part of Montana lying west of the Continental Divide. Control of that vastness would, of course, only endure until the early 1860s, when the great Idaho and Montana gold rushes occurred.

One can speculate on how different the course of Pacific Northwest history might have been with only a few slight changes in events. The western one-third of present-day Washington could well be part of Canada, if the HBC had taken colonization more seriously by offering better inducements for Canadians to come west and settle in the Puget Sound region, and if the company had successfully discouraged Americans from entering there. Under such circumstances—with numerous British subjects living and farming a land governed for two decades by a paternalistic company—the British government might well have taken a firmer stand on the Oregon Question.

As it was, the Michael T. Simmons party of 1845, and those Americans who followed—the ones who soon decided that they must have self-government—found themselves in the right place at the right time for a showdown with Great Britain over who would gain this land. It would be American, the newcomers decided. Thus they displaced the relatively few British that were there, which was one of the reasons the American settlers bestirred themselves at the very outset to seek the destiny they desired.

One can also speculate about whether there would have been a Washington had the settlers not aggressively sought division, or if a newspaper had not started publishing in Olympia in 1852—a newspaper that could take the lead in generating enthusiasm for a successful separation movement. Other newspapers already existed in Portland and Salem, and they helped spread the news of the original meeting at Cowlitz Landing. But it was the appearance in September 1852 of the *Columbian* that made the great difference. Its enthusiasm was infectious. The *Columbian* convinced the doubters with repeated argument and exhortation that separation need not be just a dream.

Delegate Lane in Washington, D.C., grasped the temper of the populace by reading editions of the *Columbian* in late October and November 1852, learning that a second formal petition from the people would soon reach him. When Lane had received the Cowlitz Memorial a year before, he had buried it. Now he knew another memorial would be forthcoming, but rather than wait for its arrival, he swung into action. When the actual Monticello document did arrive—during congressional debate over Lane's resolution—he had the clerk read the text of it to the assembled House of Representatives.

If the first settlers had been content to remain citizens of Oregon, would Washington ever have been created? It might be contended that because

Oregon Territory was so large, it likely would have eventually been divided anyway. But it is noteworthy that California was large and did, in fact, remain intact. The building of roads and the development of steamboat transportation, with the resulting improvement of mail service, would have advanced communications so much that a main reason for dividing Oregon—the distances between the northern and southern parts—soon would have faded. Thus, the timing appears important. If the settlers had decided to be patient, much more of the original, vast Oregon Territory might have remained whole at Oregon's statehood.

Washington came into being when division was feasible. It might have been more difficult later—when governmental institutions in Oregon became more firmly and widely established, when there were more voters, and when it would become laughable for a mere handful of men to gather at a riverbank settlement to claim themselves as spokesmen for all those living within a vast region.

As it was, no discernible opposition developed. The political leaders in the Willamette Valley, firmly in control of the Oregon territorial government, and seeing in their acrimonious capital location dispute the seeds of continuing north-south contention, not only did not oppose giving up half of the territory, they actually gave it their blessing.

Because 36 years went by before Washington achieved statehood, it might be contended that the new territory came into being prematurely. Nevertheless, later generations of Washingtonians may well admire those pioneer Americans for their audacity, persistence, and foresight—they laid the foundation for what eventually became one of the nation's great sovereign states.

Bibliographical References

Few primary sources regarding the origins of Washington Territory have come to light. If any of the Cowlitz or Monticello pioneers besides Edward Allen were diarists, their written accounts have yet to be discovered. Nor have any extensive records for the meetings in 1851 and 1852 surfaced. Even manuscript copies of the Monticello Memorial defied discovery during a diligent search made a half-century ago in the state and national capitals, although one convention delegate is known to have kept a copy.

Territorial newspapers of the time, plus the *Congressional Globe* (now the *Congressional Record*), provide the chief published source material. The Olympia *Columbian*, of course, carried particularly useful information, as did the Portland *Oregonian*.

The relative scarcity of primary sources could be due to the non-controversial nature of the movement to create a new territory. No opposition developed on either side of the Columbia. Though delegate Joseph Lane was slow to act on the request for a division, he never expressed opposition. There must have been correspondence between Lane and political leaders in Oregon before he finally introduced legislation to create a new territory, but, if so, such letters have not been found among the Joseph Lane Papers in the Indiana University Library, Bloomington; while only one letter is in the Oregon Historical Society collections.

Nevertheless, published secondary sources on the political events and the westward movement that set the stage for Washington's creation are extensive. Some of the more useful include: Melvin C. Jacobs, *Winning Oregon: A Study of an Expansionist Movement* (Caldwell, Idaho: Caxton, 1938); Adam Thom, *The Claims of the Oregon Territory Considered* (London: Smith, Elder, 1844); John D. Unruh Jr., *The Plains Across: The Overland Emigrants and the Trans-Mississippi West, 1840–60* (Urbana: University of Illinois Press, 1979); Frederick Merk, *The Oregon Question: Essays in Anglo-American Diplomacy and Politics* (Cambridge, Massachusetts: Harvard University Press, 1967); these works by Hubert Howe Bancroft—*History of the Northwest Coast*, 2 vols. (San Francisco: A.L. Bancroft, 1884), *History of Oregon*, 2 vols. (San Francisco: History Co., 1886, 1888), and *History of Washington, Idaho, and Montana, 1845–1889* (San Francisco: History Co., 1890); Clinton A. Snowden, *History of Washington: The Rise and Progress of an American State*, 5 vols. (New York: Century History Co., 1909–1911); and the publications of the Hudson's Bay Record Society. Pertinent manuscripts of this period include the Elwood Evans Papers in the Bieneke Library at Yale University, and the journal of Peter Crawford in the Bancroft Library at the University of California, Berkeley.

Notes

1. Some Britons and Canadians were never quite reconciled to the boundary settlement. A modern Canadian historian, James R. Gibson, bitterly commented in *Farming the Frontier: The Agricultural Opening of the Oregon Country, 1786–1846* (Seattle: University of Washington Press, 1985), 205: "Present-day Canadians have valid reasons for regretting and even resenting the Oregon settlement, since the British claim to the territory north of the Columbia-Snake-Clearwater river system was at least as good as, if not better than, that of the United States... Canadians should not forget that they were dispossessed of part of their rightful Columbia heritage, a heritage whose economic potential in general and agricultural

possibilities in particular were initially and successfully demonstrated by the Hudson's Bay Company."

2. Quoted in Barbara Cloud, *The Business of Newspapers on the Western Frontier* (Reno: University of Nevada Press, 1992).

3. For the text of the Cowlitz Memorial and an evaluation of it, as well as the same for the later Monticello Memorial and the petition for separation passed by the Oregon legislature, see Edmond S. Meany, "The Cowlitz Convention: Inception of Washington Territory," *Washington Historical Quarterly* 13 (January 1922):3–19.

4. Cloud, *Business of Newspapers*.

5. This printing press is preserved at the School of Communications, University of Washington, Seattle. Newspapers were fairly easy to establish on the frontier since the only equipment required were several fonts of foundry type, a press, and a few reams of paper. Columns of type, locked in an iron frame, were laid on the bed of the press, inked, and a sheet of paper laid on top. Then the platen of the press was lowered by a lever arrangement to bring the sheet against the type and cause it to pick up the inked image.

6. In 1852, the settlement on Elliot Bay was called New York; the name later was changed to Alki and eventually to Seattle.

7. *Columbian*, October 16, 1852, p. 3.

8. Ibid., November 13, 1852, p. 2.

9. Ibid., November 6, 1852, p. 3.

10. See Clinton A. Snowden, *History of Washington: The Rise and Progress of an American State*, 5 vols. (New York: Century, 1909–1911), 3:206–10.

11. Ibid., 3:210; Hubert Howe Bancroft, *History of Washington, Idaho, and Montana, 1845–1889* (San Francisco: History Co., 1890), 60–61; [Elwood Evans,] *History of the Pacific Northwest: Oregon and Washington,* 2 vols. (Portland: North Pacific History Co., 1889), 1:348–49; Edmond S. Meany, *History of the State of Washington* (New York: Macmillan, 1909), 156–58, and his article, "The Cowlitz Convention," 3–19.

12. Isaac N. Ebey to Joseph Lane, January 23, 1852, Ms. 1146, Joseph Lane Papers, Oregon Historical Society, Portland (original spelling, spacing, and punctuation kept in the quotations here). Ebey, while serving as collector of customs, was able to have the customs office established at Port Townsend, just across Admiralty Inlet from his land claim on Whidbey Island. On the night of August 11, 1857, a band of northern Indians beached their war canoes on Whidbey Island, planning to murder Ebey. They were seeking revenge for the shooting deaths of 23 Indians eight months earlier by a federal government vessel, the *Massachusetts*, near Port Gamble. After killing Ebey, who they considered to be a "white Tyee" or chief, they severed his head and vanished into the night. Two years later, the head was recovered by a HBC fur trader in a native village far to the north.

13. Julian Hawthorne, ed., *History of Washington, the Evergreen State: From Early Dawn to Daylight,* 2 vols. (New York: American Historical Publishing Co., 1893), 2:22.

14. Harvey Scott, *History of the Oregon Country,* 6 vols. (Cambridge, Massachusetts: Riverside Press, 1924), 2:190–91.

15. *Columbian*, April 12, 1853, p. 1.

16. Ibid., April 23, 1853, p. 3.

17. Ibid., April 30, 1853, p. 1.

IV
Statehood:
Symbol of a New Era

Howard R. Lamar

*T*HE PROSPECT OF ADMITTING *the four Omnibus States—Washington, Montana, and North and South Dakota—to the Union in 1889 caught the imagination of Americans as an important turning point in history, not only in constitutional terms, but also in many other ways.*

Reformers saw it as an opportunity to replace corrupt local political systems with new honest and efficient ones; others saw the chance to enact the kind of social reforms later associated with the Progressive period; imperialists believed that the new State of Washington and the port of Seattle provided a base from which the United States could further dominate the Pacific and capture more of the Far East trade.

In fact, national discussions of the Omnibus Bill often became a paradigm for regional, national, and even international concerns of the day, and thus are valuable in revealing the mood of the nation in the late-19th century.

If historians are asked what the United States was like when Washington, Montana, and the two Dakotas were seeking admission to the Union in the late 1880s, some would respond that it was a terrible time. It was the Gilded Age, a period when robber barons like Jay Gould and Jim Fisk flourished, when everyone both admired and hated John D. Rockefeller and his Standard Oil Company for proving just how powerful and successful an aggressive limited-liability corporate monopoly could be. In fact, the heartless new spirit of the business world was captured in a reputed remark by J.P. Morgan: "I like a little competition, but I like monopoly better."

Other historians would disagree, offering the counter argument that it was an age of great expectations, speculative dreams, and financial and industrial breakthroughs, when inventive businessmen became more prominent than politicians. It is probably true that by the 1880s Americans knew more about

Rockefeller, Morgan, Collis P. Huntington, Henry Villard, and James J. Hill than about some of the senators and congressmen of their home states.

As indicated by the persons just named, it was an age of railroads. Huntington was associated with the Union Pacific and the Southern Pacific, Morgan dominated New York and Southern railway systems, Henry Villard controlled the Northern Pacific for a time, and Hill was the builder of the Great Northern. At one point, Jay Gould held sway over a system of tracks stretching across the nation. The railroads enabled firms such as Standard Oil and United States Steel to succeed, partly because they allowed the industrial giants to serve a national market and partly because the lines gave favored customers rebates on charges. To express this point another way, because of railroads, business began to think nationally rather than regionally. Indeed, our forebears had railroads on the brain, for they had learned that this new form of transportation could make or break them, whether they ran a store, raised wheat or cotton, mined coal, refined oil, or shipped manufactured merchandise.

The citizens of Washington Territory were especially sensitive to the need for railroads. Listen to the cry of the *Walla Walla Watchman* before any of the transcontinentals had reached the Pacific Northwest. "Give us a railroad!" the newspaper exclaimed. "Though it be a rawhide one with open passenger cars and an iron sheet boiler; anything on wheels drawn by an iron horse! But gives us a railroad!"

So intimately connected was a railroad to agricultural success in the 1880s—as Charles M. Gates has noted—farmers moved ahead of Henry Villard's Northern Pacific construction crews into the Palouse country of the Columbia Basin. Once the railroads arrived, the Yakima Valley blossomed under irrigation—which the railroads helped to introduce. Partly because of such inducements, some 95,000 people came to Washington between 1887 and 1889.

The completion of the Northern Pacific, observes Gates, meant that "in 1889 Washington rode to statehood on the crest of an economic boom."[1] Thus one can safely assume that Washington eagerly embraced railroads, the arch symbols of modernity in Gilded Age America. The focus on railroads meant, among other things, a preoccupation with materialism and quick wealth. This led Vernon Louis Parrington to call it "The Great Barbecue"— "a world of triumphant and unabashed vulgarity without its like in our history."[2]

It was also in 1889 when President Benjamin Harrison yielded to the unceasing pressure of white settlers, speculators, and railroad promoters by opening a vast land reserve in Indian Territory. The famous Oklahoma land run of that year riveted the nation's attention on not only that parcel of land, but others in Indian Territory—which led to subsequent rushes. Almost inevitably, in 1890 Congress established another potential state when it created Oklahoma Territory.[3]

There was certain glory as well as a certain horror associated with these events. People believed they needed land regardless of whom they displaced or hurt. At the time, one cynical Oklahoma Indian leader remarked that his land's chief beauty in the white men's eye lay in the fact that "they have no right to it." Henry George and others described the public land system, and especially the abuses of the Homestead Act, as often a cruel mockery—benign in intent, but a "speculator's dream."[4]

Given these selective examples of the Gilded Age, was there still a sense of patriotism, a spirit of national unity, and evidence of political statesmanship? Had not a half-million men died in the Civil War to preserve the Union and to end black slavery? So far as the 1880s are concerned, the answer is disturbing. A leading historian of the Gilded Age, H. Wayne Morgan, has observed that despite the Constitution, the Civil War, and patriotic ideals, the United States emerged from the war "a collection of regions varying in age, economics, populations, and social attitudes."

There was so much variation, in fact, that phrases like Yankee, Southerner, and Westerner held deep and often hostile meanings for some citizens. As Morgan himself asks: Could Duluth, Minnesota, and New Orleans be in the same country? On a lighter level, clever humorists such as Petroleum V. Nasby, Artemus Ward, and Josh Billings used distinguishing sectional or hayseed language in their jokes and writings.[5] After his election as president in 1888, Benjamin Harrison visited Atlanta to discuss his "probable Southern policy"; later the *New York Times* ran headlines when rumors circulated that Harrison would consider two "Westerners" (from Iowa and Minnesota!) for his cabinet.[6]

This sense of deep division in the country was also symbolized by the fact that while the Republicans had successfully elected presidents throughout the Gilded Age, the Democrats had controlled eight out of ten sessions of Congress during a 20-year period. Republicans supported protective tariffs and industrial development, while Democrats backed low tariffs and a weak, almost negative government. With memories of the Civil War still vivid, there continued to be confrontations in Congress between Southern Democrats and Northern Republicans, or even between Northern and Southern Democrats.

It was in this time of greedy materialism, robber barons, sectional biases, and a Congress separated from the executive branch by partisan politics that

Washington Territory, along with the territories of Dakota, Montana, Idaho, Wyoming, New Mexico, and Utah, sought admission to the Union as states. Because it seemed likely that even the creation of some of these states would unsettle the current political balance of power in Congress, the reluctance of that body to admit them long after they had met the usual population requirements is understandable. In addition, senators and congressmen greatly enjoyed controlling federal offices in the territories. This was one way to reward faithful party members who had lost an election, or to provide jobs for needy relatives.

Even so, there is another side to the Gilded Age that many historians would stress; for despite all the bad things, it was also an age of hope and reform. It was a time filled with intelligent proposals for bettering American life. One thinks of the Farmers' Alliance, the Populists, the passage of the Civil Service Act, the creation of the Interstate Commerce Commission, and the woman suffrage movement, to name only a few.[7] Generally speaking, the nation not only exhibited some sense of fair play and justice, it showed strong signs of rising above sectionalism to achieve a new nationalism.

By the 1880s, daily newspapers had become common and were at a high point of influence. Aided by the new technology of wire services, local papers could and did cover national and international news. Moreover, people read these newspapers and avidly discussed their contents. During the 1880s, citizens still voted in huge turnouts on election day. Some 3,000 journals and magazines benefited from broad circulation provided by new national transportation services (achieved by standardizing the width of rails and by connecting competing lines). Consequently, the United States began to enjoy a national popular culture.

Many Americans of that generation read Louisa May Alcott, Ralph Waldo Emerson, and Nathaniel Hawthorne. Charles Dickens was never more popular.[9] Both rural and urban audiences heard talks on the Chautauqua circuit from famous persons such as Andrew Carnegie and Mark Twain. Many people also watched Joe Jefferson, Edwin Booth, and Sara Bernhardt perform on stage, or at least knew of them. The mining town of Butte, Montana, for example, was on a national vaudeville circuit.[10]

At the same time, the nation could boast that it had now produced such famous writers as Emerson, Twain, William Dean Howells, Stephen Crane, and Henry James. Moreover, it was exporting its first fully trained professional American mining engineers to other countries. Meanwhile, a host of educated American scientists and lay persons tried to persuade their fellow citizens to accept Darwinian evolution.[11] There was, in all of this ferment, a desire for resolving old problems, for closing down the Civil War hatreds once and for all, for regulating outrageous business practices, and for defining a new and modern America.[12]

Similarly, there was a sense of closing the old frontier. Geronimo, a dramatic symbol of fierce last-ditch Indian resistance to white authority, was captured and sent to prison at Fort Sill, Oklahoma, in the 1880s. By giving Indians homesteads, the Dawes Act of 1887 tried to make them into Jeffersonian yeomen and thus end tribalism. In 1889, Senator George Franklin Edmunds of Vermont joined Congressman John Randolph Tucker of Kentucky to pass a bill that forced Mormons in Utah to abandon their sanction of polygamous marriage. The opening of some 11-million acres of Sioux lands in 1890, along with the provision that more tracts in Oklahoma would be accessible to whites, meant that no more unbroken frontiers of free land existed in the nation. That same year, the last major Indian-white battle occurred at Wounded Knee. Three years later, historian Frederick Jackson Turner called attention to the end of the frontier in his famous address, "The Significance of the Frontier in American History."[13]

One of the themes of this essay is that the national debate over the admission of Washington and other territories to the Union revealed the "state of mind" of the country in a remarkable way—almost as if someone had put the nation on the psychiatrist's couch and persuaded it to confess its collective hopes and fears.

A second theme is that the passage of the Omnibus Bill of 1889, by which North Dakota, South Dakota, Montana, and Washington were admitted, was the result of a statesmanlike compromise in Congress that signified a turning away from the old sectionalism that had persisted in national politics since the Civil War. Indeed, the passing of the Omnibus Bill may well have been the fourth and last great compromise in settling national crises about the size and nature of the Union. There had been a crisis when Missouri sought admission in 1820; a second one when California became a state and Utah and New Mexico became territories in 1850; a North-South political compromise in 1877 after the contested presidential election; and then in 1889, when the Southern states finally abandoned the idea of "matching" or pairing states to keep the existing sectional balance in Congress.[14]

Further, there is evidence that by rounding out the Union in the Northwest, Congress felt it had created a solid tier of states all the way to the West Coast that could provide a new connection tapping the trade of the Orient. That objective coincided with a rising interest in overseas trade generally, the securing of coaling stations in the Pacific, and a new desire for an interoceanic canal.[15] And finally, the passage of the Omnibus Bill in 1889 broke congressional resistance to admission of the remaining territories, for between 1890 and 1912 nearly all the rest came in, leaving only Alaska and Hawaii in territorial status.

One way of fathoming the mind of the country is to ascertain the image the American public had of the future Omnibus States. It seems that the most favorable impressions were of Dakota Territory—a vast square on the map, diagonally bisected by the Missouri River—an expanse so large that the public felt, along with most Dakotans, that it must become two states. Americans saw it as an exceptionally prosperous land, with bonanza wheat farms in the northeast quadrant, gold mining in the Black Hills, smaller farms to the southeast, and a potentially great ranching region west of the Missouri. Moreover, the Dakotas had a key ingredient—its railroads—with the Northern Pacific reaching across the northern half, and the Chicago and Northwestern tapping the southeast part. Dakotans were seen as solid, safe, backbone-of-the-nation types.[16] Despite unsettling blizzards in 1886–1887 and drought, the area was viewed as a new Iowa or Minnesota.

Americans regarded Montana as a large mining community that, while regrettably dominated by big business, had developed enough for statehood. Idaho was seen as less developed, but still nearly ready for statehood, as was even more relatively unpopulated Wyoming. Utah and New Mexico, however, were believed to be flawed—the first by Mormon rule and the practice of polygamy, and New Mexico by the fact that its Spanish- and Mexican-Indian inhabitants did not yet know English, were Catholic, and did not fully accept American institutions.[17]

In contrast to the latter areas, the American public viewed Washington as a gem. The territory contained fantastic resources—forests, coal, and a rich variety of agricultural lands. Promoters boasted that it had the scenery of Switzerland, a benign climate, the best type of settlers, and two transcontinental rail connections—soon to be three with the expected arrival of James J. Hill's Great Northern. The potential of trade for its ports was so great, one orator declared, that Puget Sound would become a second Adriatic.

Washington also benefited from extremely intelligent, factual, and effective propaganda put out by the Territorial Bureau of Immigration and the railroads. The bureau's brochures, issued in the 1880s, made Washington seem enormously attractive. One of the enduring comparisons portrayed Washington as the "Pennsylvania of the West" because of its splendid variety of resources, rich soils, and temperate climate. In addition to brochures crammed with statistics, a bevy of talented orators (both before and after statehood) enchanted eastern audiences with glorious accounts of the "Evergreen State." Typical was Henry B. Clifford's descriptions of the wealth of western Washington: "It is so mild that when snow does fall it rests as lightly as a bashful kiss and then melts away through warm passion of mother earth."[18]

Seattle was described as having a good population and a high civilization. Local people, aware of Seattle's heavy-drinking on Skid Road, might have rephrased it to say that the city had a "high" population that need some "good" civilization. Spokane would certainly become a second Minneapolis and St. Paul. An 1888 brochure declared: "North of the Snake in the Palouse Country settlers are of the farming classes, steady and industrious, and have brought with them a love of churches, schools, and social development rather than a spirit of adventure and speculation."

In short, by 1889 the national perception of Washington was hardly one of a rough frontier, but rather of a region full of active, educated, yeoman farmers and churchgoers. Indeed, another immigration pamphlet stated that the "vast majority came from the older settled east and brought with them their eastern college education, the eastern culture; they have lost nothing but the narrow pride of section which arises from a lack of knowledge of all that lies beyond the narrow limits of that section in which they were born or raised."[19]

Such broadly optimistic statements obscured complex political and economic situations with which the region grappled in the late 1880s, as a look at the statehood drive both in Washington Territory itself and in the nation's capital will reveal. For example, while various territorial politicians had proposed statehood over the years, a majority of voters did not approve a call for a constitutional convention until 1876. That body actually met in Walla Walla and drew up a document the voters approved, but that Congress opposed in 1878, saying the population was too small. In 1882, Thomas H. Brents, the territorial delegate, got a favorable House vote on a statehood act, but the bill never made it to the Senate. In 1886, a similar measure passed the Senate, but was defeated by the House.[20] One of the reasons given for the defeat was that, upon admission, Washington would become a Republican state, a possibility that the Democratic majority of the House did not want.

The Senate debate of 1886, however, provides the first of many insights into the thinking of congressmen about larger issues, among them the real implications of statehood for Washington. This occurred when Senator John Tyler Morgan of Alabama delivered a major address favoring the admission of Washington.[21] Given the rumor that Washington would be a Republican state and the fact that the North and the South still did not trust one another, why was Morgan outspokenly for the admission of the Pacific Northwest territory? The senator revealed his reason when he stated that the future of American prosperity lay in the Pacific trade. A hundred years hence, he predicted, the value of commerce with Asia would be "$10 for every one" that came from Europe.

To capture that trade, explained Morgan, Americans must compete successfully with Great Britain, and especially with British Columbia, where Vancouver business interests, and the Canadian Pacific Railroad (then being completed), posed a major threat to American aspirations. Furthermore, Victoria boasted a powerful British naval station, whereas the United States had built no major docks or defense posts in Washington Territory. As Morgan noted:

> Sir, if there is a place on the American continent where all of the best power we have got under our form of government ought to be concentrated, it is in Washington Territory. It is an indispensable thing for the national security to say nothing of the progress that her people ought to make and must make in that quarter.

Senator Morgan voiced both the old hope of effecting a Passage to India that would allow the establishment of an empire based on trade, while acknowledging the new fact of aggressive imperialism that European nations already practiced in Africa and the Pacific. Another senator, California's Leland Stanford, had earlier warned that Victoria now had fort-nightly steamers plying between that city and Hong Kong. Echoing Stanford, Morgan said that the United States must have Pacific coaling stations: "Commerce it is that rules the world at this hour. Armies and navies are servants of commerce today."

His imperial vision truly expansive, Morgan went on to praise Secretary of State William H. Seward for buying Alaska, urged American exploitation of Pacific fisheries, and declared that the United States must have Hawaii as an "outpost of the sea." He also called upon his countrymen to build an Isthmanian canal, although his own preference was for a passageway through Nicaragua. For California to develop its iron ore depositors, he said, it must have Washington coal and then both could build ships on the West Coast so that Americans could command the Pacific. To realize this dominance, Morgan envisioned a self-sufficient West Coast, a key to which was Washington's geographic position and strategically important resources.

Morgan's desire for a new American imperialism coincided with Leland Stanford's more immediate concern that the completion of the Canadian Pacific to Vancouver would threaten American trade with the Orient, and thus adversely affect the Union Pacific. Both men anticipated a Northern Pacific Railroad advertisement of 1887 which, after having praised the Pacific Northwest, went on to say that man's highest callings were "commerce, trade and manufacturing."

Several years later, Henry B. Clifford, in a speech to an audience of 3,000 at the Boston Music Hall, echoed these themes about the enormous promise of a new State of Washington. Among other things, he urged reciprocal trade treaties with every country in the Pacific, for "trade with a foreign land is like love—it is not successful unless in a measure returned." Clifford, who was probably interested in railroad promotion, hoped that the United States would divert most of the trade of China, Japan, and Siberia through Puget Sound.[22]

Morgan and Clifford's riding of the new wave of sentiment for an overseas economic empire reflected James G. Blaine's ardent belief in trade with Latin America. Already known for his support of reciprocity treaties, one of Blaine's first acts when he became Secretary of State for the second time in 1889 was to hold the first Pan American trade conference, which laid the basis for the Pan American Union.[23] Yet, for all his grand imperial vision, Senator Morgan (so his biographer tells us) wanted Cuba, Puerto Rico, and Hawaii annexed as states, "believing them Southern in politics."

Thus, the old idea of balancing sectional power in Congress that had led to the compromises of 1820 and 1850 still simmered. At the same time, Morgan was acutely aware that the older internal frontier was at an end. Land exhaustion and the decline in available areas for homesteading, he noted, had led "inquisitive and hungry men" to surround the territory of Oklahoma "almost three deep." Using what was to be Frederick Jackson Turner's classic safety valve theory, he said that the cities were overloaded with poor tenement populations and that Washington State could be one outlet for the surplus.[24]

By the time of the 1888 presidential election, agitation to admit at least some western territories as states was so great that both parties endorsed the idea. The Republicans made it one of the key planks in their platform. Western political leaders and the railroad propagandists had done their work well. They had created such attractive images of Washington and Dakota that the public had become quite favorable to statehood for both territories.

Nor was it an accident that the Republicans especially focused on this issue in their platform. Their candidate, Benjamin Harrison, had chaired the Senate Committee on Territories and had been on record for four years as having tried to get statehood for South Dakota.[25] Patronage appointees from his home state of Indiana occupied positions in perhaps a dozen key territorial offices across the West. Knowing that the territories would be states one day, he had cultivated the Republican leaders in each of them. A cousin, Dr. Frank Harrison, conveniently living in Utah, reported to him personally about territorial events there and elsewhere.[26] Benjamin Harrison also had secured a civil government for Alaska Territory.

Until 1888, the Democrats opposed admission of the western territories in order to retain control of the House and Senate. They were certain that North and South Dakota would be Republican and they thought Washington might be as well. They believed Montana could be a Democratic state, but were not sure. No party in its right mind would knowingly welcome into Congress six and possibly eight new senators belonging to the opposite party. (Although they assumed New Mexico and Utah could be lured into the Democratic column, these were two flawed territories with little national popular support for admission.)

Facing the inevitable fact that sooner or later the northwest tier of territories would be states, the Democratic strategy initially planned to minimize the number of admissions. Illinois Congressman William McKendree Springer, Democratic chairman of the House Committee on Territories, advocated admitting Dakota as only one state; having just two Republican senators was better than having four. This proposal infuriated both northern and southern Dakotans, who wanted a division of the territory into two states. The future South Dakota had voted for separation overwhelmingly in 1885.

Nevertheless, Springer proposed an omnibus bill whereby three states would come in—Dakota, Montana, and Washington—with the expectation that the latter two might stir up enough support to pressure Dakotans to accept only single-state status. To satisfy the South, Springer urged Democratic officeholders in New Mexico to create a statehood movement there. Similar Democratic efforts also appear to have been made in Utah. Suspicious of the motives for Springer's bill, the *Chicago Tribune* later called the omnibus proposal: "Springer's How-Not-To-Admit Bill." Ironically, the *Tribune* employed Springer's own tactic when it suggested that the only way to get New Mexico into the Union was to join it to neighboring Arizona.[27]

While it seems Springer was sincere—if overly clever—in his efforts to admit western states, he kept meeting obstacles that threatened his version of admission. In the 1888 election, for example, not only did Harrison win, but the Republicans took over both houses of Congress. Moreover, the Republicans regarded this as a mandate to admit new and safely Republican states. When the lame duck Congress met in December 1888, Democrats were in a quandary. If they refused to admit the northwestern territories, they would be denounced in all of these prospective states. The question was how to retain some popularity. Meanwhile, the Republicans already were threatening to call a special session to round out the Union.

It was in this atmosphere that Representative Springer presented the final version of this three-state omnibus bill. After a motion to include New Mexico failed, the measure passed. The Republican Senate, on the other hand, not only wanted admission for Washington and Montana, but wanted Dakota to come in as two states. Furthermore, the Senate Republicans called for South Dakota, which already had passed and approved a state constitution four years earlier, to be admitted at once. The House rejected the Senate's proposal.

Thus, the Senate had refused to accept the Democratic proposal, and the House in turn rejected the Senate's plan to admit South Dakota at once. South Dakota now was required to again ratify the 1885 constitution, and conduct a new vote for the division of Dakota into two states.[28] After years of waiting and enduring various sets of itinerant political officials, however, the territories were ready to express serious protests.

Tempers grew short, as demonstrated by the remarks of Delegate Joseph K. Toole from Montana, who said the territories were being held in bondage just as Britain was holding Ireland against its wishes. Using heavy-handed biblical satire, Toole stated that President Garfield in the early 1880s, when he assigned territorial appointments, had believed wise men came from the East. Toole claimed that his current Republican friends had determined that history should repeat itself—a jab at all the nonresident brothers-in-law and cousins of congressmen being foisted on the territories as federal officials. Then President Cleveland beginning in 1884, Toole continued, claimed wise men came from the South, which meant that Southerners should run the territories.

In the case of Montana, he said: "There was only one remedy for the evil—a star on the flag, a vote, and a voice in both branches of Congress. Without this, there…[will be] nothing but political insomnia and unrest." Toole ended by declaring that home rule in the territories "lay bleeding at the foot of despotism."[29]

A day later, Delegate Charles S. Voorhees of Washington voiced the demand of his territory's people for admission into the Union, and "expressed extreme regret and profound indignation, which he, in common with his constituents, felt at the apathy exhibited by Congress to that demand in the past."[30]

Congressman S.S. Cox of New York State—a man so flamboyant and eloquent that after a particularly florid description of a sunset, his fellow politicians gave him the nickname "Sunset" Cox—emerged from the divided Congress as just the compromiser the Northwest needed to gain admission. Originally a Union Democrat and admirer of Illinois compromiser Stephen F. Douglas, Cox had entered Congress during the Kansas-Nebraska crisis (serving then as an Ohio representative). Always a believer in moderation, he was a peace Democrat during the Civil War. Once the fighting had ended, Cox advocated amnesty for high-ranking ex-Confederates and the forging of a new national unity. By then he had moved to New York City; there he served as a congressional representative for the next 20 years.[31]

Cox had watched the omnibus bill debates with growing concern. Seeing that the Democrats could ruin themselves by a retreat into sectional obstinacy and filibusters, he and a fellow New York congressman, Charles S. Baker, laid down a set of binding conditions that would govern the House and Senate Territorial Conference Committee. Cox appears to have been supported by Senator Matthew C. Butler of South Carolina in these efforts. The stipulations decreed that all states would be admitted on the basis of the same rules; that is, all were to have new constitutional conventions. The one exception was South Dakota, where the 1885 document could stand, provided it was updated. However, South Dakota, like the others, had to elect new state officials. Thus Cox, a Democrat, rose above party loyalties to make sure the new Omnibus States would have justice. That Cox was sincere there can be no doubt. He firmly believed that every territory except Utah should be in the Union.[32]

Accepting the guidelines, the House passed the "Omnibus Bill" on January 18, 1889, with New Mexico included, but, on February 14, that body voted to exclude the Southwest territory. Fourteen Democrats joined the Republicans in this latter vote. And, when the issue arose of permitting South Dakota to come in with an old constitution, eight Democrats joined the Republicans to carry it, with all these Democrats being from the northern or north-central states.[33]

Congressman Joseph C.S. Breckenridge of Kentucky, a former Confederate who had been with Jefferson Davis on his flight from Richmond at the end of the Civil War, used several parliamentary tricks in an attempt to defeat the Omnibus Bill or to have New Mexico included. Despite Breckenridge and others, the bill finally passed the House on February 20, and the Senate concurred. By this time, the spirit of inevitably and compromise proved so strong that the only real discussion in the House-Senate conference arose when woman suffrage advocates from Washington Territory pleaded that a suffrage clause be written into the bill. Some 22 senator endorsed the request.

However, Senator Platt of Connecticut, chairman of the Senate Territorial Committee, said the conferees wanted to wait and see what the Supreme Court ruled regarding an appeal emanating from the Washington territorial courts, which recently had denied women the right to vote.[34]

Washington, like Utah and Wyoming, had been the scene of early agitation for female suffrage—women in Washington had voted and served on juries for two years before the law allowing them to do so was ruled invalid. Significantly, Washington was in the forefront of a progressive new age, debating a suffrage reform issue that would not reach the national level until the early-20th century.

A minor crisis marked the final hours before Congress enacted the Omnibus Bill, when, at the last moment, a move to change the name of Washington to Tacoma was quashed.[35] Suddenly it was all over. A combination of Democrats and Republicans in a Democratic House and a Republican Senate had voted to admit four states. The bill was rushed to Grover Cleveland, the Democratic president, who signed it on George Washington's birthday in honor of the new state named after the first president. It was, said the strongly Republican *New York Herald Tribune,* "a graceful action."[36]

On February 23, the national wire services reported on the Omnibus Act's provisions—for constitutional conventions to be convened on July 4, 1889, in the four states; a vote of ratification to take place in October; and for admission in November. The newspapers were intrigued at the prospect of having 42 stars in the national flag by December 1889. Crowed the *New York Herald Tribune*: "The event is unique. Never before has so great a number of Commonwealths been admitted at one time," nor had previous states been as fully qualified as these four, which entered "by right and not by suffrance."

Two days later, after the truth about the new states had sunk in, the *Herald Tribune* carried an editorial titled "Growing Nation," which noted that, with the new admissions, the center of political power had moved west to Indiana. The Northwest and other newer states could now elect a president without New York! With a bittersweet sense of loss, the editorial concluded: "So true it is that the west has become the ruling power in the Republic." Echoing the *Tribune,* on July 3 the *San Francisco Bulletin* claimed the Omnibus States were new weights to shift the center of political gravity away from the slums of New York to the purer air of the West.[37]

Ironically, the *Tribune* and *Bulletin* predicted the rise of the West only four years before Frederick Jackson Turner lamented the demise of the frontier. As a matter of fact, the western states would continue in financial colonial servitude until World War II, when they finally became economic and political powers in their own right. But in 1889, Washington and the other Omnibus States, indeed, served as early symbols of a new progressive America in which the voice of the West would be heard.

The political action now shifted to the territories, where elected delegates convened in constitutional conventions in their respective capitals—in Washington at Olympia on July 4, 1889. That convention probably had the most distinguished presiding officer of all four state bodies in the person of J.B. Hoyt, an ardent advocate of woman suffrage. Hoyt had served as house speaker of the Michigan legislature, governor of Arizona Territory, and a judge on the Washington territorial supreme court.

Washington's convention was made up of 43 Republicans, 26 Democrats, 4 labor representatives, and 2 independents (different sources give slightly variant break-downs of these affiliations). Of the 75 delegates, there were 22 lawyers, 17 farmers, 3 miners, and 33 "other." Of the 63 delegates born in the United States, 46 were from the North and 17 from the South (with Missouri furnishing 10). A relatively large number of the Washington delegates, 12, were foreign born.[38]

The state convention reflected trends of the times. Historian John D. Hicks has written that the nation was so ashamed of its political corruption—of which the territorial governments had been disgraceful examples—that the delegates paid special attention to the national cry for reform and the government regulation of railroads and other public services. The delegates also wanted better control of state government by the people, justice for labor, protection of women, and child labor provisions. Meanwhile, the public followed the proceedings with enormous interest.

Some delegates proposed to submit all special laws to popular vote. They also wanted to do the same for other additional laws, if one-third of the legislature so desired it be done. These sentiments later grew in the Progressive Era, when the movement for the "initiative, referendum, and recall" would become especially associated with the Pacific Northwest. Also, as historian Herman J. Deutsch noted, the Washington convention reflected early Populist sentiments in its "deep-seated suspicions of corporate enterprise." Indeed, by 1896 that disaffection would give the state a Populist governor.[39]

Ardent advocates of woman suffrage, as well as equally ardent opponents, stirred up especially deep emotion in Washington, which had allowed women to vote for a short period, only to see that right struck down by the courts. At the time of the convention, Seattle had drawn up a petition supporting woman suffrage bearing 25,000 names, but the Seattle fire of that year destroyed it.[40]

The story of hope and failure in the Washington woman suffrage movement is poignantly encapsulated in the history of the Walla Walla Women's Club. Founded in 1886, the club had as its original purpose the promotion of self-improvement and a mutual exchange of ideas. Its 22 members discussed such topics as, "The Authenticity of Shakespeare," "Are We Anglo-Saxon?" "China Speaks for Herself," and "English as She Is Taught," as well as other literary themes. But soon the emphasis shifted to "Suffrage for Women," and "A Biblical View of Women's Suffrage." Disagreements over the selection of topics and the organization's purpose must have surfaced, because in 1889 the club disbanded and a new one, called the Equal Suffrage League, succeeded it.

Guided by the women of the Isaacs family of Walla Walla, the new group lobbied for the constitutional convention to grant women the vote. A strong suffrage movement had sprung up throughout the Pacific Northwest, with Abigail Scott Duniway of Portland being the most prominent but certainly not the only important voice. It seems likely that the Walla Walla Equal Suffrage League cooperated with a larger group that held a suffrage conference in Olympia on July 3, 1889, on the very eve of the constitutional convention.[41]

Despite the urging of convention president J.B. Hoyt and two other members, the delegates did not approve a women suffrage clause. The convention did allow a separate article or clause granting suffrage to be submitted to Washington's (male only) electorate. In Washington's October election, it lost by an overwhelming vote of 34,500 to 16,500.[42] It would be 1910 before Washington again granted women the right to vote. Although the outcome of the 1889 suffrage fight was not a happy one, the seriousness with which delegates debated indicated that the issue was alive and well in Washington.

In October 1889, Washington voters ratified the constitution, elected the popular Elisha P. Ferry as governor, and defeated prohibition as well as woman suffrage. Then, in November, President Harrison signed the proclamation of statehood for Washington and the other Omnibus States.[43] Clearly—for America—the old era of maintaining an internal western colonial empire was beginning to end. In 1890, Idaho and Wyoming also came into the Union, and Utah, having declared itself Republican and non-polygamous in 1890, gained admission as well in 1896. By 1912, Oklahoma, Arizona, and New Mexico also won admission. Congress would not admit any other states until 1959, when Alaska and Hawaii entered the Union.

Notes

1. Charles M. Gates, "A Historical Sketch of the Economic Development of Washington since Statehood," *Pacific Northwest Quarterly* 39 (July 1948):214. Frustration with the Northern Pacific's slow arrival and its choice of Tacoma over Seattle as its western terminus led many citizens to feel that the line was their "archenemy" rather than their salvation. Dorothy M. Johansen and Charles M. Gates, *Empire of the Columbia: A History of the Pacific Northwest*, 2nd ed. (New York: Harper and Row, 1967), 308.

2. Vernon L. Parrington, *Main Currents in American Thought*, 3 vols. (New York: Hancourt, Brace, 1927, 1930), 2:210.

3. See Arrell M. Gibson, *Oklahoma: A History of Five Centuries* (Norman, Oklahoma: Harlow, 1965), 288–94, and also *The West in the Life of the Nation* (Lexington, Massachusetts: D.C. Heath, 1976), 512. An eyewitness account of the 1889 Oklahoma land rush by *New York Herald Tribune* reporter Harry Hill can be found in "Library of *Tribune* Extras," July 1, 1889 (New York: Tribune Association, 1889), in the Yale University Western Americana Collection; hereafter cited as YWA.

4. "Oklahoma," *New York Herald Tribune*, February 23, 1889; Henry George and George W. Julian, quoted in Henry Nash Smith, *Virgin Land: The American West as Symbol and Myth* (Cambridge, Massachusetts: Harvard University Press, 1950), 190–91, 199.

5. H. Wayne Morgan, "Toward National Unity," in his edited volume, *The Gilded Age*, 2nd ed. (Syracuse, New York: University of Syracuse Press, 1970), 2–3; Robert Falk, "The Writers' Search for Reality," ibid., 280–81.

6. *Atlanta Constitution*, January 12, 1889; Homer E. Socolofsky and Allen B. Spetter, *The Presidency of Benjamin Harrison* (Lawrence: University of Kansas Press, 1987), 25, state that Harrison's first choice for secretary of the treasury was Senator William B. Allison of Iowa, but for political reasons he chose William Windom of Minnesota. These were his "Western" candidates.

7. Earl S. Pomeroy, "Carpetbaggers in the Territories, 1861–1890," *Historian* 2 (1939):53–64; Morgan, *The Gilded Age*, chaps. 4, 5, 8.

8. Ibid., 6–7. A random sampling of four newspapers for the years 1888–1889—the *New York Herald Tribune*, *New York Times*, *Atlanta Constitution*, and *Chicago Tribune*, plus consultation of local papers such as the *Sioux Falls Argus Leader*—support the statement as to national and international coverage.

9. Michael McGerr, *The Decline of Popular Politics: The American North, 1865–1928* (New York: Oxford University Press, 1986); Madeline B. Stern, *Louisa May Alcott* (Norman: University of Oklahoma Press, 1950). In 1879, no less an author than Henry James wrote a biography of Nathaniel Hawthorne; an edition of Hawthorne's *Complete Works* appeared in 1883. In addition to Emerson's own works, two biographies appeared in the 1880s. Robert R. Roberts, "Popular Culture and Public Taste," in Morgan, *The Gilded Age*, 276, states that "more copies of Dickens were sold in the 1880s than in the 1860s and his influence was strong." See also, ibid., 281.

10. "In 1878 Chautauqua started a Literary and Scientific Circle that was the first American book club. The list of contributors to Chautauqua lecture platforms and book publications was virtually a Who's Who of the times…Chautauqua helped make rural areas part of the Nation": Max J. Herzberg, ed., *The Reader's Encyclopedia of American Literature* (New York: Thomas Y. Crowell, 1962), 169. See also Victoria Case and Robert Ormond Case, *We Called It Culture* (New York: Doubleday, 1948), and Henry P. Harrison, *Culture under Canvas: The Story of Tent Chautauquas* (New York: Hastings House, 1957).

11. Clark C. Spence, *Mining Engineers of the American West* (New Haven: Yale University Press, 1970); Cynthia Russett, *Darwin in America: The Intellectual Response* (San Francisco: W.H. Freeman, 1976). See also Paul F. Boller Jr., "The New Science and American Thought," in Morgan, *Gilded Age*, 239–44, 257.

12. These are basic themes in Morgan, *Gilded Age*; C. Vann Woodward, *Origins of the New South, 1877–1913* (Baton Rouge: Louisiana State University Press, 1951); Robert H. Wiebe, *The Search for Order, 1877–1920* (New York: Hill and Wang, 1967).

13. Robert M. Utley, *The Indian Frontier of the American West, 1846–1890* (Albuquerque: University of New Mexico Press, 1984), 197–201; Wilcomb E. Washburn, *The Assault on Indian Tribalism: The General Allotment Law (Dawes Act) of 1887*, America's Alternatives Series (Philadelphia: J.B. Lippincott, 1975); Leonard J. Arrington, *Great Basin Kingdom: An Economic History of the Latter-day Saints, 1830–1900* (Cambridge, Massachusetts: Harvard University Press, 1958), 360–69; Herbert T. Hoover, "The Sioux Agreement of 1889 and Its Aftermath" *South Dakota History* 19 (Spring 1989):56–94; Frederick Jackson Turner, "The Significance of the Frontier in American History," American Historical Association, *Annual Report 1893* (Washington, 1894).

14. In 1886, during congressional debates over the admission of the Dakotas and Washington, Benjamin Harrison urged the Senate to "get rid of this old and disreputable mating business…It grew out of slavery." Harrison to Senate, January 27, 1886, in "Dakota, Her Claims to Admission as a State," p. 9, YWA pamphlet. The Autumn 1987 (vol. 37) issue of *Montana: The Magazine of Western History* launched "The Centennial West," a series of articles devoted to centennial themes concerning Washington, Montana, North Dakota, South Dakota, Idaho, and Wyoming. The series, in consecutive fall issues, emphasized politics (1987), economics (1988), society and culture (1989), and the arts and architecture (1990), and should be consulted for additional information on several of the topics suggested in this essay.

15. United States concerns in the Pacific are discussed in Earl S. Pomeroy, *Pacific Outpost: American Strategy in Guam and Micronesia* (Stanford, California: Stanford University Press, 1951). See also analyses of the roles of both James G. Blaine and Benjamin Harrison in articulating and advancing United States overseas expansion in the 1880s and 1890s, in Socolofsky and Spetter, *The Presidency of Benjamin Harrison*, 109–23.

16. John E. Miller, "The Way They Saw Us: Dakota Territory in the Illustrated News," *South Dakota History* 18 (Winter 1988):214–44; Howard R. Lamar, "Public Values and Private Dreams: South Dakota's Search for Identity, 1850–1900," ibid., 8 (Spring 1978):140–41.

17. Gibson, *The West in the Life of the Nation*, 509, asserts that Congress was "completely unresponsive to the [earlier] statehood appeals from Montana Territory." Doubt about Montana's readiness were voiced by the *New York Herald Tribune*, November 11, 1889, and the *New York Times*, November 11, 13, and 16, 1889, when they castigated Harrison for admitting the state without cleaning up its political corruption. Idaho, with a population of only 90,000 in 1890, and Wyoming, with just 63,000 people that year, were seen as gaining admission because of the popularity of the statehood idea rather than because of readiness. See Gibson, *The West in the Life of the Nation*, 505. In an editorial, the *New York Times*, February 21, 1889, declared that "New Mexico is utterly unfit for Statehood, and is likely to remain so for some time." Other remarks were even harsher: "It was the un-American Greaser Territory," opined the *Chicago Tribune*, January 23, 1889.

18. *Washington the Evergreen State and Seattle Its Metropolis* (Seattle: Crawford and Conover, 1890), 52. The Washington Immigration Board was directed by Mrs. A.H.H. Stuart. See for example: *Historical and Descriptive Reviews of the Industries of Seattle, Washington Ter-*

ritory, 1887 (Seattle, 1887); Oregon Immigration Board, *The New Empire: Oregon, Washington, Idaho* (Portland, 1888); *The Resources and Attractions of Washington for the Home Seeker, Capitalist, and Tourist,* compliments of the Passenger Department, Union Pacific Railroad (St. Louis, 1883). The quotation is from *Masterly Address of Henry B. Clifford on the Resources and Future of the State of Washington,* delivered at the Boston Music Hall, January 14, 1890 (Boston: Northern Syndicate for New England, 1890), 6–7. All brochures in YWA.

19. W.H. Ruffner, *A Report on Washington Territory* (New York: Seattle, Lake Shore and Eastern Railway, 1889), 172–74; Oregon Immigration Board, *The New Empire,* 5, 28.

20. Edmond S. Meany, *History of the State of Washington* (New York: Macmillan, 1909), 266–69; Johansen and Gates, *Empire of the Columbia,* 334–39; Paul L. Beckett, *From Wilderness to Enabling Act: The Evolution of a State of Washington* (Pullman: Washington State University Press, 1968), chap. 3; Keith A. Murray, "The Movement for Statehood in Washington," *Pacific Northwest Quarterly* 32 (October 1941):381; John D. Hicks, "The Constitutions of the Northwest States," *University Studies* 23 [Lincoln: University of Nebraska] (January-April 1923):16–17.

21. The following statements by Senator Morgan can be found in *Speech of Hon. J. T. Morgan of Alabama in the Senate of the United States, April 1, 1886* (Washington, 1886). Pamphlet in YWA.

22. *Historical and Descriptive Reviews of the Industries of Seattle,* 44; Clifford, *Masterly Address,* 8.

23. Both Blaine's and Harrison's roles as imperial expansionists are discussed in Socolofsky and Spetter, *The Presidency of Benjamin Harrison,* 109–23, 125–56.

24. "John Tyler Morgan," *Dictionary of American Biography,* vol. 13 (New York: Scribner's, 1934), 180–81.

25. Howard R. Lamar, *Dakota Territory, 1861–1889: A Study of Frontier Politics* (New Haven, Connecticut: Yale University Press, 1956), 256–59, 262, 264.

26. Arthur C. Mellette of Indiana, a friend of Harrison's for many years, had gone to Dakota Territory as a federal land officer in the 1870s. He was active in the statehood movement, was appointed the last territorial governor by Harrison, and then was elected the first governor of South Dakota. David B. Miller, "Dakota Images," *South Dakota History* 19 (Spring 1989):133. See also *New York Herald Tribune,* January 21, 1889.

27. *New York Herald Tribune,* January 19, 1889; *Chicago Tribune,* January 21, 1889.

28. Ibid., January 19, 1889.

29. Delegate Joseph K. Toole was quoted in ibid., January 16, 1889, as well as in other papers.

30. *Atlanta Constitution,* January 17, 1889.

31. Ibid., January 28, 31, February 4, 1889; David Lindsay, *"Sunset" Cox: Irrepressible Democrat* (Detroit, Michigan: Wayne State University Press, 1959), 252–54.

32. *Chicago Tribune,* January 16, 1889. Cox and Baker's activities are covered in detail in [Elwood Evans,] *History of the Pacific Northwest: Oregon and Washington,* 2 vols. (Portland: North Pacific History Co., 1889), 2:chap. 59, pp. 56–59.

33. *New York Herald Tribune,* February 15, 1889.

34. "The Omnibus Bill Passed," ibid., February 21, 1889.

35. *Atlanta Constitution,* February 21, 23, 1889.

36. *New York Herald Tribune,* February 23, 1889.

37. Ibid.; Hicks, "Constitutions of the Northwest States," 23 ff.; *New York Herald Tribune,* February 24, 1889; *San Francisco Bulletin,* July 3, 1889, as quoted in Hicks, "Constitutions of the Northwest States," 149.

38. Ibid., 29, 27n, 28, 30, 30n; Meany, *History of the State of Washington*, 280 ff.
39. Herman J. Deutsch, "A Prospectus for the Study of Government of the Pacific Northwest States in Their Regional Setting," *Pacific Northwest Quarterly* 42 (October 1951):283–84, 295–99.
40. Hicks, "Constitutions of the Northwest States," 136.
41. Nelson A. Ault, "The Earnest Ladies: The Walla Walla Women's Club and the Equal Suffrage League of 1886–1889," *Pacific Northwest Quarterly* 42 (April 1951):123–37; Ruth Barnes Moynihan in *Rebel for Rights: Abigail Scott Duniway* (New Haven, Connecticut: Yale University Press, 1983), 182–84, 214, details the early suffrage fights in Washington and lists its leaders.
42. Ibid., 135–37.
43. Meany, *History of the State of Washington*, 287.

V

A Matter of Context:
The Pacific Northwest
in World History

Kenneth S. Coates

T HE ACCOUNT IS A FAMILIAR ONE: a frustrated gold miner, unsure of local prospects, in contemplation turns his eye toward the future. Then, as though manna from heaven, news arrives:

> Everyone seemed to be Klondike mad with excitement, and the newspapers were looked for eagerly to get the latest news from the field and the number of tons of gold already produced and the number of boats that been sent down the Yukon from Dawson City laden with gold and also the latest gulches found and the number of tons of gold taken from the Discovery Claim. I amongst the rest was getting a bit excited, and it only wanted a few more good reports to start me going, the excitement was just about up to fever heat…I was Klondike mad sure enough.[1]

What makes the case of William Sharman Crawford Nicholl stand out a bit from the crowd of Klondike stampeders who responded to the call of northern gold in 1897 is his point of departure. Nicholl was living near Waihi, at the southern end of New Zealand's Cormandel Peninsula. Although that mining camp showed signs of promise, the lurid tales of Klondike fortunes proved overwhelming and Nicholl set off in New Zealand's spring of 1897 (October) for Vancouver, British Columbia, and the Yukon gold fields. Only a few months after news of the Klondike discovery shocked and amazed North America, miners thousands of miles away were setting their course for the Yukon.

Gold rushes are unique events, unusually dramatic, and stimulating the most base of human emotions—greed and the search for adventure. Perhaps Nicholl's situation, and that of the Klondike Gold Rush generally, is best considered a special case, and not a useful starting point for a consideration of a vital element in the history of the Pacific Northwest. However, to overlook the implications of the excitement at Waihi—tucked between verdant forests and sandy beaches on New Zealand's North Island—about developments in a sub-Arctic wilderness, thousands of miles, numerous degrees of latitude, and many degrees of temperature removed from New Zealand, is to miss one of the more important elements in the evolution of the Pacific Northwest.

Consider a second example, that of Kang Youwei, a Chinese migrant to the West Coast of North America. Kang arrived via Japan from Hong Kong, where he had fled in 1898 after Empress Dowager Cixi dramatically ended attempts to reform the monarchy in China. Numerous reformers were ordered arrested, and executed; Kang Youwei escaped before these fates befell him. Having reached British Columbia, he passed on to the United States, moved next to England, and then returned to Victoria. Once back in the Pacific Northwest, he founded *Bao Hunang Hui* (the Save the Emperor Society, or the Chinese Empire Reform Association), which soon emerged as the first mass political party in China.

The reform association, while focusing on political structures in China, was strongly influenced by British Columbian developments. The experience of the Guangdong merchants in Canada, where they learned the importance of cultural self-defense and used their exclusion from local and national government to create institutions that gave them control over their own destiny, influenced the *Bao Hunang Hui* and therefore had a significant impact on the evolution of Chinese politics.[2] While the little-known connection between British Columbia and Chinese political development was not of profound impact within the Pacific Northwest, it provides a second, and very different example of the importance of understanding local developments within an international and global context.[3]

Oregon's Hood River Valley is an unlikely place to consider the social and economic impacts of the Meiji era in Japan, but the life and career of Matsuo Yasui provides an important window on the connections between the internal dynamics of Japan, and ethnic and business developments in the Pacific Northwest. Yasui's father was raised in the midst of the Meiji transformation of Japan, when the country abandoned its isolationist policies and embraced international trade and cultural connections. His father, struggling with high land taxes in Japan, was attracted to the United States, as were many Japanese at that time.

Matsuo Yasui, who remained behind with his mother until he was older, discovered that Japan offered few opportunities for social mobility; the United States, in contrast, appeared to provide limitless options. The Japanese government, anxious to protect its citizens from the racism and hostility experienced by Chinese migrants in America, screened Matsuo Yasui and thousands of others for literacy, character, and suitability.[4] Yasui passed the test, migrated to the Pacific Northwest, and worked variously on the railway, in an Astoria salmon cannery, and in Portland, before moving to the Hood River valley where he set up a store to serve the Japanese in the area.[5] Matsuo Yasui's story is not particularly bold or dramatic, but it is a single example, drawn from thousands, of the relationship between transformations and crises in Japan and patterns of migration, work, and settlement in the Pacific Northwest.[6]

However much the Pacific Northwest exists as a region, it also is an integral part of a complex and ever-changing global web of economic, social, political, cultural, and environmental relationships. It is not a singular pattern. In some instances, as in the case of the Klondike Gold Rush, regional economic developments have had international impact. In others, as with Japanese migration, social trends in far distant lands end up having a direct affect on the Pacific Northwest. In still other instances, broad international intellectual currents have washed across North America or the Pacific, and affected public and political thinking in the region.[7] And, more often than one might suspect, the Pacific Northwest itself has seen its ideas and concepts picked up, and sometimes transformed, in the process of spreading to distant corners of the globe.

My call to historians for a larger context in the writing of regional history is not new. W.L. Morton, a leading historian of the Canadian West, long held that regional historians had to pursue a "delicate balance" between region and nation. Although himself a passionate western Canadian, Morton did not support or practice the parochialism, chauvinism, and boosterism that often crept into the writing of regional history—this latter perception of regional bias, in fact, has made it far too easy for "national" historians to by-pass regional scholarship and to relegate it to the background of the historical profession.[8] Along these lines, British Columbian labor historian Mark Leier repeated a long-standing criticism of regional history when he argued, "regional history is only useful and exciting when it treats the region as a case study, as a field of investigation in which theory can be applied, tested and criticized." Leier goes too far, suggesting that regional history has limited merit on its own, and finds purpose and substance only when it addresses questions of broader significance. But there is a germ of truth in his observation: "By focusing on the region rather than on the larger issues, we risk turning our gaze inward and becoming less interesting, less creative, and more inclined to find out more and more about less and less."[9]

The Pacific Northwest, in fact, has for many years struggled to find its own historiographical identity. Numerous borders—national, territorial, state, and provincial—have stood in the way of developing a strong and logical sense of the evolution of regional society and of the interconnections between the various political jurisdictions that make up the area.[10] The region's many historians, indeed, have worked largely within the confines of national, state, and provincial boundaries. Increasingly, however, thematic connections in labor, cultural, women's, and economic issues have created some cross-border historians, who have helped to clarify the influence of the national boundary on regional developments. These scholars have begun to identify the nature and structure of a trans-boundary regional order. This loosening of national blinders, through a series of borderlands projects, has increased academic interchange between Canada and the United States. Thus, a growing sense of common cause in the contemporary era has prodded scholars, particularly those relatively new to the field, to examine developments that transcend national boundaries, traditional historiographies, and conceptual structures.[11]

The search for global characteristics and patterns that sits at the heart of the emerging field of world history *might* seemingly call on historians to eschew local and regional exclusivity. The lively discussions among world historians, obviously, cover the broad themes of history—modernization, cultural encounters, economic integration, and market relationships—and local developments might appear as little more than footnoted examples. World history is historical inquiry on the widest possible scale—rather more like painting a house with an industrial paint-sprayer than the intricate landscapes of the regional scholar. World history seems then, at first blush, to be the antithesis of regional scholarship, a rejection of the idea that there are unique characteristics that set regions such as the Pacific Northwest off from world events.

Few world historians, however, would be comfortable with such a view of their work—an emerging sub-discipline sees its contribution as providing and adding context and perspective to regional historical work that otherwise might fall short of its potential. The writing of world history is not about knowing the whole world—and even the most arrogant scholar would shy away from such a robust claim—but rather about being alert to the global influences that impinge upon regional developments, and to the potential international implications of experiences within a confined setting. As Jerry Bentley suggested:

> Historians have become increasingly aware of some inherent limitations in historical writing focused on national communities. At the same time, they

have recognized the challenge and promise of a historical perspective that transcends national frontiers. Many powerful historical forces simply do not respect national or even cultural boundary lines, but work their effects instead on a regional, continental or global scale. To name but a few, these forces include population movements, economic fluctuations, climatic changes, transfers of technology, the spread of infectious and contagious diseases, imperial expansion, long-distance trade, and the spread of religious faiths, ideas, and ideals. In their efforts to analyze and understand these forces, scholars have generated a body of literature increasingly recognized as world history—historical analysis undertaken not from the viewpoint of national states, but rather from that of the global community.[12]

Regional historiography, particularly of the Pacific Northwest variety, indeed has started to overcome the traditional approaches of the broader Canadian and American scholarly profession. The balance of covering region and nation that Morton sought has, in the hands of a number of fine Pacific Northwest historians, been achieved. Margaret Ormsby, the author of *British Columbia: A History*[13] and a strong promoter of regional history, saw herself as a national historian, who also worked on regional projects. Her studies of British Columbia were rich in their understanding of national influences. Works by other recent historians of the Pacific Northwest have integrated national developments with regional realities, and illustrate the vital interplay between internal and external factors. As Brian Dippie asserted, regional histories "are predicated on the assumption that there are meaningful differences between local and national developments."[14] But Stephen Ceron also makes the case: "The recent history of the western states still makes more sense when it is prefaced by the history of conquest, colonization, and capitalist consolidation of the continent, which under the republic moved basically from east to west."[15]

Regional history, of course, is not in crisis—the abundant scholarship regarding Western and Pacific Northwest history and the expanded output of first-rate historical essays and books provide convincing evidence of the strength and growing complexity of regional historical writing.[16] And it would be wrong, in the extreme, to accuse the region's historians of parochialism. Much recent work is strongly founded in national contexts, and rooted in contemporary theoretical and conceptual developments. Sarah Deutsch has particularly captured the complexity and energy of the New Western historical writing:

> The West is a messy place. The experience of both majority and minority groups occurred in the context of multiracial and multicultural dynamics. Any larger historical narrative of the region must partake of an interactive multifaceted model. It must allow the constant interaction and diversity

within and between groups itself to become the story. In doing so, it builds a framework within which we can understand the continual tensions created by forces that simultaneously erode boundaries and re-create them.[17]

While the Pacific Northwest does not yet sit at the center of national historiographies in either Canada or the United States—and while British Columbia is largely separated from the historical writing focusing on the prairies that attracts more national attention, and the American Northwest seem only weakly connected to the ongoing debates about the "New" Western history—regional scholars nevertheless now are acknowledged for their many and significant contributions to North American history.[18] Studies of Pacific Northwest indigenous peoples and of native-newcomer relations, for example, have illustrated native resistance to government policies, their responses to economic transitions and immigrations, and the devastating impact of European diseases on local populations.

Likewise, a growing understanding of working class life and of the social and economic roots of labor radicalism in the Pacific Northwest—a region noted for the extremism and ideological intensity of its trade union movements—has done much to help historians elsewhere to understand the complexity of working class culture and political activism. Carlos Schwantes' *Radical Heritage: Labor, Socialism, and Reform in Washington and British Columbia, 1885–1917* is an excellent example of this trend. Overall, this body of work illustrates the connections that stretched across the international border and connected workers in the Pacific Northwest to a broader world—as one unionist argued, there was "no 49th parallel of latitude in Unionism. The Canadian and American workingmen…joined hands across the Boundary line for a common cause against a common enemy."[19]

Efforts to understand Pacific Northwest history, however, have rarely taken into account a global perspective, although individual Pacific Northwest historians have successfully focused their local studies within some broader social, economic, political, and cultural contexts. Regional history teeters between the nuts and bolts of historical analysis—an abundance of local sources and the search for an appropriate context or framework for understanding. Placing regional developments within the sweeping setting of world history, and searching for interconnections with distant lands and peoples, can seem like an ambitious, even unreasonable challenge for scholars, who seek to explain unique elements of regional character and root developments within a specific local context. But placing the Pacific Northwest within world history presents new opportunities for regional historians to assess the significance of well-known international and global developments, and to begin the process of recognizing the impact of the Pacific Northwest on other regions and nations.

The early story of the Pacific Northwest provides several key illustrations of the region's global connections. Indeed, the initial human occupation of the area thousands of years ago, still hotly debated by anthropologists attempting to explain the origins and timing of the arrival of the first peoples, is in itself an element of the world's most important migrations.[20] Waves of indigenous peoples from Asia, and also perhaps from elsewhere, were drawn by population pressures behind them and opportunities lying in front, and moved across to North America and advanced over the continent—the first grand example of the connections between the Pacific Northwest and distant lands.

Many millennia later, European maritime exploration in the late-18th century biologically connected the Pacific Northwest to Europe, Asia, and other parts of North America with the introduction of alien microbes, plants, and animals from those places.[21] Indigenous peoples faced depredations from hitherto unknown diseases, particularly suffering significant depopulation from smallpox epidemics in the late-18th and early-19th centuries—although the scale is still the subject of debate—and found their natural world substantially transformed. The Pacific Northwest had become incorporated into a global ecological order.[22]

The assertion of European sovereignty—i.e., the division of the Pacific Northwest between Britain, Spain, Russia, and eventually America and Canada—offers another illustration of world influences. The first explorations along the Northwest coast were part of European attempts to find a new route between Europe and Asia for international commerce, endeavors to advance world geographic and scientific knowledge, and, most pertinent to the Pacific Northwest, to extend colonial empires.[23] Consequently, the political boundaries that have long influenced, shaped, and bedeviled events and development in the Pacific Northwest were not determined by natural geographic features or obvious social and economic groupings.

In 1825, for example, the assigning of the 141st meridian as the principal boundary between Russian America and British North America followed the classic colonial model of European diplomats—they drew boundaries on the map that bore little relationship to local conditions. Their reliance on less than precise geographic demarcations along the Alaska Panhandle created much subsequent confusion, and in the late-19th century provided the foundation for Canada's intense but ill-founded claims for access to the sea during the Alaska boundary debates with the United States.

The establishment of colonial boundaries also eventually bifurcated the entire region into its American and British/Canadian elements in 1846, and in so doing tied the respective areas to separate national systems. The expansion of U.S. and later Canadian hegemony into the Pacific Northwest seemed to sound a death-knell for the prospect of future unity in the region, and set the different areas onto divergent paths.[24]

The resource industries upon which the Pacific Northwest has long based its enviable prosperity have, from the earliest time, been strongly influenced by international markets and investments. National businesses have supplemented, sustained, and enriched local entrepreneurs, companies, and industries, while global prices and demand often have played a vital role in underpinning economic development in the Pacific Northwest. This has been the case since the early days of the coastal fur trade, when sea otter pelts were fed into a complex trading web that connected America, Britain, China, and Russia.[25] The dynamic and exploitative coastal fur trade rested as much on the seemingly endless Chinese demand for expensive pelts as on British and American rapaciousness.

Similar arrangements continue in modern times as minerals from British Columbia, the Yukon, and Alaska feed industries in Germany, Japan, and other countries. When the first export market for coastal salmon was developed in Hawaii in early times, it stimulated a small but notable migration of Hawaiian workers to the Pacific Northwest. Global trading connections also underlay the building of the western intercontinental railways in the late-19th and early-20th centuries.

And so it has gone, with developments and decisions in other parts of the world creating opportunities or, at times, crises in the Pacific Northwest economy. The completion of the Canadian Pacific Railway in the late-19th century sparked an expansion of Canadian trade by steamship with Asia. In 1914, the city of Vancouver sought to capitalize on the opening of the Panama Canal and to position itself as a major export center, a theme illustrated at the Vancouver Exhibition (precursor to the Pacific National Exhibition).[26] Seattle also strived, through such efforts as the Alaska-Yukon-Pacific Exposition (1909) and the Century 21 World's Fair (1962), to position itself as an international city.

The recent flurry of activity and encouragement of greater trade with Japan, China, and the growing economies of Southeast Asia is, therefore, not a new phenomenon, but rather a continuation of an old approach to trade development. Few question the significance of the international economy in determining the prosperity of the contemporary Pacific Northwest, but far less attention has been paid to the historical origins and the ongoing importance of global trading networks (be it of the early fur traders, or the Hong Kong Chinese), international trade (from the development of markets for Pacific coast salmon, to selling Boeing aircraft in Asia),[27] and global competition (for regional minerals in the late-19th century, to the unsettling and expanding rivalries between American and Canadian fruit producers, farmers, and forest products companies).

Historians have overall, it is important to note, been very good at identifying the global connections of the "early western" economy.[28] For example, Keith Bryant's 1994 essay concerning the American West in this regard was appropriately titled "Entering the Global Economy." As Bryant observed, in a manner attaching rather lesser regard to indigenous people:

> Europeans occupied "free land" in North and South America, Asia, Africa, and the South Pacific throughout the nineteenth century. A treasure trove of minerals spurred that process. The movement of peoples into the trans-Mississippi West introduced both material progress and concepts of liberty even as it destroyed those non-European indigenous cultures that resisted. Technologically superior Europeans simply overwhelmed less-sophisticated societies. Transportation and communication accelerated this expansion as peoples of low skill levels were pushed aside. These "frontiers" quickly joined a world-capitalistic core market centered in western Europe. Maturation beyond self-sufficiency brought rising levels of participation in the world economic order to peripheral areas like the American West. As the French historian Fernand Braudel has shown, capitalism is an identifying theme for studying the modern world, for it provides structure and organization for examining relationships within a society. Capitalism emerged as the prevailing force in world history by the nineteenth century and as an all-pervasive aspect of American life, especially in the West.[29]

The human face of the Pacific Northwest—originally indigenous, then substantially European, later augmented by Asian migration, and recently enriched by influxes of African Americans and Hispanics—provides evidence of the global demographic and cultural tapestry that has been woven in this region. In the late-19th century, Japanese and Chinese migrants, drawn by the seemingly endless wealth of the West Coast—what the Chinese called "Gold Mountain"—flooded into the Pacific Northwest. So many came and so many more wished to come that non-Asian residents protested openly and insisted on restricting immigration. As part of the British Empire, British Columbia was an attractive and seemingly automatic point of entry for thousands of East Indians who sought access to North America. When the governments of the United Kingdom and Canada, anxious to stem xenophobic outbursts, passed restrictive measure to keep the "foreigners" out, East Indians persisted, sending a ship, the *Komagata Maru*, to Vancouver in 1914. Authorities blocked the vessel from landing, and Vancouverites gathered by the thousands to watch the stand-off in English Bay. The *Komagata Maru* was forced to leave without letting off its would-be immigrants.

New waves of migrants have always continued to enter the region—Greeks, Italians, and Eastern Europeans alternately fleeing difficult conditions in their home countries or drawn by the prosperity and natural beauty of the West Coast; impoverished Southeast Asians escaping Vietnam or Cambodia; and wealthy Asians fleeing unrest and political change in Hong Kong. At the broadest level, the settlement of the Pacific Northwest was part of the process of establishing "neo-Europes" in the New World, a lengthy, remarkably successful development of transcendent global significance. It also is part of the outward migration of Asia, a pattern seen in its early decades as an irritant to the host countries, but which has emerged in recent years as a potent economic force in its own right.[30] As Gail Nomura observed in calling for greater attention to context in the study of Asian American history:

> It is impossible to view Asian American history without understanding the "far Eastern" context. Asian American history connects the United States West to the global experience of the diaspora and interchange of people and ideas from the colonial to the post-colonial era, to transnational labor migration, to international assembly lines in Asia, and to multi-racial financial and corporate structures in the Pacific Rim...envisioning the United States West as a vital component of the Pacific Basin we challenge the Eurocentric focus of both western and national United States history.[31]

Nomura is far from alone in recognizing the international connections that have influenced and shaped Pacific Northwest history. The settlement history of the region is the sum of thousands of individual stories—heroic, tragic, frightening, ennobling, common, exceptional—and often is best understood at the personal and family level. These stories begin not in the Pacific Northwest, but in the social, cultural, economic, and political ferment of home countries from Eastern Europe, Central America, to India and the Far East.

Domestic turmoil, visions of North American riches, the dynamic pull of gold rushes, frontier opportunity, the experiences of other migrating community members, and additional influences pushed and forced tens of thousands into the heart-wrenching decision to migrate. For some, the journey to the Pacific Northwest brought hardship, pain, destitution, and a retreat to the home country; for most, however, it brought at least an acceptable measure of opportunity and prosperity, even if the reception from the English-speaking majority often has been less than welcoming.

The cumulative impact of global settlement, with waves of migrants from the east, west, and south, was to provide the Pacific Northwest with tangible evidence of personal human connections that bind this region to the rest of the world. Networks maintained by the individual migrants with their families, communities, and business contacts in their homelands proved to be vital conduits for knowledge, commerce, subsequent migrations, and the maintenance of Old World cultural traditions.

Italian migrants, many of them poor, unskilled laborers drawn to work in the hard rock mines, illustrate the connections that tied the Pacific Northwest to Europe. Many of the Italian migrants first came to Canada, and subsequently moved across the border. The Corsinis, a large Italian family, initially moved to Extension, British Columbia. While four of the children remained in the area, one daughter moved to San Francisco with her husband, and another two relocated in Seattle. In Canada, the Italian immigrants of the early-20th century maintained strong ties to their homeland, operating an Italian-language newspaper (*L'Italia nel Canada*), a network of social and cultural clubs, a mutual aid society (*Società Mutuo Soccordso Figli d'Italia*), and often lived together in small residential enclaves.[32]

Over time, the multi-cultural population of the Pacific Northwest assumed a North American social character—with sufficient differences in the Canadian and United States sections to justify the rhetoric of both regional chauvinists and cultural nationalists. But as contemporary developments have made clear, the migrants' historic ties to their home countries have provided them with the cultural strength sufficient to over-ride decades of assimilation, maintaining a sense of their unique history and a continuing connection to their country of origin.

Global economic expectations, too, provide strong evidence of the international influences that have shaped Pacific Northwest history. The Klondike Gold Rush of 1897–1900 started with discoveries on Rabbit Creek and leapt into wild prominence when successful prospectors arrived in Seattle and Portland in 1897. Most of the stampeders who then headed to the Yukon came from the Pacific Northwest, raising Canadian fears that "lawless" Americans would overwhelm the small Canadian presence in the area. While the American dominance in the Klondike was a key, even central, part of the story, the reality is more complex. The rush for gold rests, itself, in the ancient and persistent infatuation with the precious metal that is present in many cultures around the world.

The Klondike stampede was not a solitary event, but rather the culmination of a process in 19th-century North America that had moved steadily across the continent from Georgia, reaching California, Nevada, and Colorado, and then turning northward through Oregon, Washington, British Columbia, Idaho, Montana, South Dakota, and Alaska, before culminating in the Yukon rush. As David Goldman wrote, "Given the tendency toward national aggrandizement, historians too often have ignored the larger imperial story which spawned those mining frontiers."[33]

More broadly, Klondike gold hit a special global nerve, generating tremendous interest in many corners of the world. Stampeders flocked from England, Europe, Australia, New Zealand, and other countries, flushed with the prospect of instant riches. Most were soon disappointed by the bitter realization that the vast majority of the gold-bearing fields had been claimed long before the would-be miners reached the district. Today, the Klondike lives on in world historical memory—perhaps the only event in Canadian history that is known around the globe—as a historical metaphor for the excitement, potential, and disappointment that was an integral part of the frontier experience.[34]

A less precise, but no less important, illustration of global influences on Pacific Northwest development rests in the world of cultural concepts and ideas. Tracing international connections in this regard may be more difficult than establishing the paths of miners to the gold fields, but there is little doubt about the importance. When Europeans first arrived in the region and established relations with indigenous populations, they saw these peoples through the filter of existing values and images.

British experiences with Polynesians, Spanish understandings of South and Central American societies, and Russian views of indigenous Siberian peoples colored their impressions and expectations in the Pacific Northwest. Perhaps the best illustration of this was the tendency of newly arrived European explorers and traders in the late-18th century to assume that all the native people were cannibals. Expecting to see extensive cannibalism, they took a large number of indigenous acts and customs to be evidence of this "fact," when the actual cultural situation regarding limited cannibalism was much more complex than they assumed.[35]

A century later, much the same was true of the reaction to Asian immigrants. Ingrained American and Canadian mental images of Asians shaped the local response to the Chinese, Japanese, and East Indians coming into the region. Many of the recent European migrants to the Pacific Northwest, too, maintained prejudicial stereotypes and assumptions. The result, as Peter

Ward wrote of British Columbia's reaction to the Chinese, was often a legacy of discrimination and antipathy:

> "John Chinaman" was what they usually called him, though sometimes they also dubbed him the "heathen Chinese" or "the almond-eyed son of the flowery kingdom." These were names nineteenth-century North Americans commonly gave the Chinese immigrant. They were part of the rhetoric of race of white America. Essentially the names were terms of derision, not as disparaging as the twentieth century's "Chink," but with heavy overtones of mockery and contempt. Together they revealed something of the animus with which both Canadians and Americans greeted the Oriental immigrant who touched the Pacific margin.[36]

Relationships and contradictions between other locally held mental visions and the broader patterns of thoughts and concepts also affected the region—e.g., the competing political traditions of American republicanism versus British parliamentary democracy, and a variety of reform and protest movements, including women's and workers' rights, socialism, utopian sentiments, and the like. Origins for these can be traced to a variety of national and world-wide intellectual influences.

For example, the region's 1919 general strikes, while shaped by the actions and ideas of hundreds of local labor organizers, politicians, and business and community leaders, owed much to the intellectual currents of socialism and communism, and the counter-currents of anti-communism, that were sweeping the western industrialized world. Indeed, significant numbers of industrial workers were, in the early years of the 20th century, caught up in the international rhetoric of class war, and Northwest organizations such as the Industrial Workers of the World caused special alarm among government officials and business leaders.

A good case in point is the 1903 strike in Vancouver by the United Brotherhood of Railway Employees that lasted four months and resulted in more than 2,000 laborers laying down their tools. Other workers, meanwhile, responded with sympathy strikes and work-stoppages. Many community leaders blamed the strike on American-inspired intrigue and a "socialist" conspiracy.[37] Many of the men who struck in 1903, like those who brought on the turmoil of 1919, were tied to broader organizational and intellectual developments, seeing their local situation through the lenses of an international class struggle. Thus, regional strikes in Canada, America, or cross-border reflected the force of ideas then sweeping across the industrial world.

While historians have well documented the spread of disease in the period of initial indigenous and European contact, less attention is generally paid to the ongoing epidemiological relationship between regional populations and the world as a whole. While the AIDS epidemic of recent decades illustrates this pattern, so do key developments in earlier times. In 1918, on the heels of the military mayhem of World War I, a great influenza pandemic swept around the world.[38] The so-called Spanish Flu exacted an enormous toll and disrupted life throughout the Pacific Northwest:

> None knew how best to combat the new scourge. Some people thought laundering money—literally—might help; others tried staying away from crowds. Thanksgiving festivities had to be canceled in some parts of the region because of bans on public gatherings. Various communities required people to wear gauze masks in public, deferred any type of public meetings, or closed theaters. The pandemic, which subsided in December and then made a brief comeback in early 1919, ultimately took a higher toll of life than the war itself: 500,000 to 700,000 Americans died of influenza, whereas the combat toll was 50,000. The influenza killed between 20 million and 40 million people worldwide.[39]

The military history of the 20th century demonstrates, once again, the multifaceted connections that bound the Pacific Northwest to the broader world. In World War I, imperial and national decisions committed first the Canadian West and, three years later, the western American states into the largely European conflict. Thousands of soldiers headed for the Western Front; many more residents supported the war through war bond drives and, less voluntarily, through rationing programs and by suffering through war-induced shortages. While, particularly in British Columbia, western businesses did not fully share in the war-time industrial boom that accompanied World War I, some fortunate corporations (the best known, Boeing) used military contracts as the basis for post-war expansion and profitability.

World War II and the Cold War that followed had an even more profound impact on the Pacific Northwest. The prospect of a Japanese invasion convinced the U.S. government to finance a series of defense projects designed to protect the far Northwest and Alaska, and spurred Canadian and American officials to jointly plan for the defense of coastal regions. Although military developments on the Pacific front soon rendered many of these preparations unnecessary, the highways, telephone lines, and other extensive projects undertaken during the war would have a lasting impact on development patterns in Washington, British Columbia and Alaska.

During World War II, American military spending had a much more pronounced western dimension than in World War I, fueling the rapid industrialization of the Pacific Northwest—in airplane manufacturing, shipbuilding, nuclear weapons development, and constructing military facilities and infra-structure. This provided a strong foundation for an industrial and military economy in the post-war era.[40] The economic impact north of the border was less evident, as the national government directed most military spending to established factories in central Canada, with a focus on the European war. Overall, the Canadian government needed to direct much less attention to the Japanese than did the Americans, who were carrying the great brunt of military action across the Pacific toward Japan.

War with Japan generated other reactions, however, including an out-pouring of hostility directed at Japanese-Canadians and Japanese-Americans, and culminating in their incarceration in government-run internment camps away from the coast.[41] This sad chapter in West Coast history carried over into subsequent decades, perpetuating debate over tolerance, assimilation, and racism. Considerable partial resolution of this injustice later was achieved in the courts and by government.

The military economic pattern continued through the Cold War era, as the region found itself deeply immersed in the affects of Soviet and Free World rivalry. Carlos Schwantes provided an excellent description of the regional fall-out from Cold War rhetoric:

> In the late 1940s and 1950s, the Cold War haunted the imaginations of Pacific Northwesterners even as it took tangible shape in defense-related products such as atomic bombs and long-range aircraft and in the parade of troops shipping out from the docks of Seattle to fight a grim new hot war with Communism in Korea. Closer to home the media was filled with talk of Communist conspiracy. Schools ran atomic-bomb drills along with fire drills, and a Boy Scout "Family Be Prepared Plan" of 1951 admonished people to stockpile food and to keep doors and windows shut during an atomic attack, advice better suited to the dangers of World War II than to the realities of the 1950s.[42]

The economic impact was particularly noticeable in Alaska, which became something of a U.S. armed forces dependency in this period, and around Puget Sound, now a major location for Navy, Army, and Air Force bases and military-oriented industries. In Canada, however, Cold War activity was largely limited to the establishment of numerous radar facilities along the Mid-Canada, Pine-Tree, and Distant early-warning lines, to detect a possible Russian bomber attack across the polar region. There was, however, additional military development in the Queen Charlotte Islands (a high technology listening post targeted at the Soviet Union) and Victoria (a major West Coast naval base).

Today, in a reverse pattern with the demise of the Soviet Union, combined with ongoing military technological changes, reductions have occurred in West Coast military spending. This has substantial future economic and social implications for the region.

The Pacific Northwest has, as well, played an important role in the development of both a global social consciousness and environmental awareness. First Nations groups in British Columbia and the Yukon, and Indian groups in Washington and Alaska, have for several decades been at the forefront of indigenous rights movements, largely in the realm of new ideas and progressive perceptions. Regional leaders, particularly George Manuel of British Columbia, were instrumental in establishing the World Council of Indigenous Peoples.[43] The first meeting of the organization, held on Vancouver Island, brought attention to the desperate conditions and serious political crises affecting many indigenous communities in other parts of the world.

A similar pattern evolved with the environmental movement. While the roots of contemporary environmentalism are deep and broad, the Pacific Northwest has long held pride of place in the field. It was one of the first regions to politically internalize a conservation ethic (at least in the urbanized coastal areas; developments in the interior and to the North tended to follow a separate path). The founding of Greenpeace, as a result of a Canadian protest over an American action, is perhaps the best illustration of the world environmental movement's Pacific Northwest connection. Greenpeace International has explained its origins as follows:

> Greenpeace was conceived in 1971 when members of the Don't Make A Wave Committee in Vancouver, Canada, renamed their organization the better to proclaim their purpose: to create a green and peaceful world. Greenpeace today adheres to the same principle that led 12 people to sail a small boat into the U.S. atomic test zone off Amchitka in Alaska in 1971: that determined individuals can alter the actions and purposes of even the most powerful by "bearing witness," that is, by drawing attention to an abuse of the environment through their unwavering presence at the scene, whatever the risk.[44]

For decades now, the political struggles over old-growth forests, the establishment of national parks and wilderness areas, the attempts to set limits on resource exploitation in valued natural areas—the Alaska National Wildlife Refuge (ANWR) campaign being a good example—plus other environmental efforts have attracted regional, national, and international attention. British Columbia's seemingly endless battles between protectionists and developers—over Clayoquot Sound, the Stein River, the Windy

Craggy mine project, the Kemano Completion project, etc.—were all tied into international networks of supporters.

Environmentalists tried (and on occasion, succeeded) to organize European boycotts of British Columbia pulp, paper products, and lumber as a means of protesting against clear-cut logging. At one point, British Columbia Premier Glen Clark referred to the environmental activists as "enemies" of British Columbia. These intense battles juxtaposed over the development or the protection of regional resources are generally seen in domestic terms, which has obscured the degree to which these intellectual and political movements are connected to forces extending far beyond the Pacific Northwest.

There is, perhaps, no better example of the interconnections between the region and the world than the modern re-conceptualization of the term "wilderness," and its stimulation to the tourism industry.[45] The Pacific Northwest is known globally for its beautiful natural settings and for a comparatively limited despoliation of much of its physical environment.[46] Regional tourism promotion—much of it handled collectively in cross-border cooperation—capitalizes on a fascination with "wilderness" in European and Asian populations.

The concept of "wilderness" has evolved dramatically over the past century. In earlier times, undeveloped regions in the Pacific Northwest were seen only as wasteland or potential industrial-resource extraction areas. In the post-World War II era, however, the Pacific Northwest has been a major focus for the re-examination of the meaning of wilderness, preserving the wild, and the marketing of the outdoors to national and international tourists. This has, over the past several decades, emerged as a vital element in regional economic planning, the foundation for thousands of jobs, and, just as importantly, the underpinning of the Pacific Northwest identity.

Today, the Pacific Northwest's active role in the contemporary world is in little doubt—ranging from Vancouver's development as the North American outpost for Hong Kong,[47] to Seattle's contribution to the global marketing of cappuccino/espresso. The region holds a prominent place in the computer revolution, not only as the home of the global Microsoft empire, but also due to scores of other companies on both sides of the border contributing to the evolution of computer and telecommunications capabilities. There are countless examples of the influences of the global economy—the international orientation of Pacific Northwest-based consultants and advisors, the continued global competition for local extractive resources, and high-profile Asian investments in major regional assets.[48] Seattle and Vancouver have, in particular, emerged as important global centers, linked by commerce, airlines, and technology, especially to the fast-growing Asia-Pacific economy.[49]

With the vast expansion of Asian trade in recent decades, the lumber industry also became strongly tied to the world's fastest growing economic zones. By 1988, for example, 3.6 billion board feet of raw lumber was shipped from Oregon and Washington to Japan alone. That year, three-quarters of regional timber production was sold overseas at prices 40 percent higher than in the domestic market. The Weyerhaeuser Corporation exported 40 percent of its product.

In 1989, half of the wheat crop in the American sector of the Pacific Northwest was sold to China, Japan, Russia, Korea, and Egypt. In northern British Columbia, perhaps as much as one-quarter of the local economy was now directly tied to Japan, in ownership and joint-ownership of sawmills, contracts for coal, the purchase of sea products from the Prince Rupert area, the marketing of pine mushrooms, and in the development of the world's largest chopstick factory in Fort Nelson.

In conclusion, there is a vital congruence between world history and the contemporary changes affecting the Pacific Northwest. That the region is now part of an integrated, globalizing economy is accepted as a given.

The struggle to come to terms with globalization, however, frequently has been difficult, and is typically presented as an issue with a complicated present and an unknown future, but without a significant past. As the region searches for an understanding of the present and future, it urgently requires the context and perspective offered by scholars regarding the "past" from a world history perspective.

Notes

1. W.S.C. Nicholl, "The Thames Today and as It Opened 60 Years Ago," typescript, (1927), p. 9. Graciously provided by Philip Hart, Department of History, University of Waikato, Hamilton, New Zealand.
2. T. Stanley, "Chinamen, Wherever We Go: Chinese Nationalism and Guandong Merchants in British Columbia, 1871–1911," *Canadian Historical Review* 77, no. 4 (1996):475–503.
3. For a broader context regarding the Chinese in British Columbia, see E. Wickberg, ed., *From China to Canada: A History of the Chinese Communities in Canada* (Toronto: McClelland and Stewart, 1982).

4. Mitziko Sawada, "Culprits and Gentlemen: Meiji Japan's Restrictions of Emigrants to the United States, 1891–1909," *Pacific Historical Review* 15 (1991):339–60.

5. Lauren Kessler, "Spacious Dreams: A Japanese American Family Comes to the Pacific Northwest," *Oregon Historical Quarterly* 94 (1993):141–66.

6. For a Chinese women's perspective in Canada, see Midge Ayukawa, "Good Wives and Wise Mothers: Japanese Picture Brides in Early Twentieth Century British Columbia," *BC Studies* 105/106 (1995):103–18.

7. One of the best studies regarding the spread of ideas throughout the region is Carlos Schwantes, *Radical Heritage: Labor, Socialism, and Reform in Washington and British Columbia, 1885–1917* (Seattle: University of Washington Press, 1979).

8. See W.L. Morton's essays in A.B. McKillop, ed., *Contexts of Canada's Past: Selected Essays of W.L. Morton* (Toronto: Macmillan, 1980).

9. Mark Leier, "Whither Labour History: Regionalism, Class, and the Writing of British Columbia History," *BC Studies* 111 (1996):61–75.

10. There is no general consensus on what constitutes the boundaries of the Pacific Northwest. While Washington, Oregon, and British Columbia are almost automatically included in the public and tourist conception of the region, historians rarely venture across national boundaries. Adjoining areas—Idaho, the Yukon, and Alaska—are often ignored, dismissed as too marginal, too distant, or too historiographically unconnected to be included. For the purposes of this essay, I have defined the Pacific Northwest in broad terms, encompassing the four American states in the Northwest—Washington, Oregon, Idaho, and Alaska—and including British Columbia and the Yukon in Canada. I would argue that the failure to fully understand the historical interconnections of this region has resulted in uncertainty about the definition of the region. David Emmons gives further perspective on boundaries in his analysis of what comprises the overall American "West": "More than a few of the respondents, however, excluded all or parts of California, Oregon, Washington, Hawaii and Alaska. These areas were, presumably, 'West of the West,' too new, too urban and sophisticated, too well-watered and too economically favored. All of this suggests that the 'true' West must be rural, semi-primitive as well as semi-arid, and broke." David Emmons, "Constructed Province: History and the Making of the Last American West," *Western Historical Quarterly* 25, no. 4 (1994):437. See also, Edward Ayers, et al., *All over the Map: Rethinking American Regions* (Baltimore: Johns Hopkins University Press, 1996).

11. It is important to note that comparative history, which has contributed substantially to the study of the American and Canadian Wests, is a different form of historical analysis. For an introduction to this approach, see Walter Nugent, "Comparing Wests and Frontiers," Clyde Milner II, et al., eds., *The Oxford History of the American West* (New York: Oxford, 1994), 803–33.

12. Jerry Bentley, "A New Forum for Global History," *Journal of World History* 1, no. 1 (1990): iii.

13. Margaret Ormsby, *British Columbia: A History* (Toronto: Macmillan, 1964).

14. Brian Dippie, "American Wests: Historiographical Perspectives," in Patricia Nelson Limerick, et al., eds., *Trails: Towards a New Western History* (Lawrence: University of Kansas Press, 1991), 122.

15. Stephen Ceron, "From Frontier to Region: Frederick Jackson Turner and the New Western History," *Pacific Historical Review* 64 (1995):479–502.

16. One useful study that takes a different approach designates the North Pacific as the region of analysis. See Walter McDougall, *Let the Sea Make a Noise: A History of the North Pacific from Magellan to MacArthur* (New York: Basic, 1993).

17. Sarah Deutsch, "Landscape of Enclaves: Race Relations in the West, 1865–1990," in William Cronin, et al., eds., *Under an Open Sky: Rethinking America's Western Past* (New York: W.W. Norton, 1992).

18. Regarding British Columbia historiography, see Robin Fisher, "Matter for Reflection: BC Studies and British Columbia History," *BC Studies* 100 (1993–94):59–77. See also, Jean Barman, *The West beyond the West: A History of British Columbia* (Toronto: University of Toronto Press, 1991).

19. Quoted in Bryan Palmer, *Working Class Experience: The Rise and Reconstitution of Canadian Labour, 1800–1980* (Toronto: Butterworth, 1983), 149.

20. Brian Fagan, *The Great Journey: The Peopling of Ancient America* (London: Thames and Hudson, 1987).

21. Cole Harris, "Voices of Disaster: Smallpox around the Strait of Georgia in 1782," *Ethnohistory* 41 (1994):591–626; Robert Boyd, "Commentary on Early Contact-Era Smallpox in the Pacific Northwest," *Ethnohistory* 43 (1996):307–32; R.M. Galois, "Measles, 1847–1850: The First Modern Epidemic in British Columbia," *BC Studies* 109 (1996):31–43.

22. Alfred Crosby, *Ecological Imperialism: The Biological Expansion of Europe, 900 to 1900* (Cambridge: Cambridge University Press, 1986), provides an excellent introduction to this theme. For the cultural underpinnings of this transformation, see Richard Mackie, *The Wilderness Profound: Victorian Life on the Gulf of Georgia* (Victoria: Sono Nis Press, 1995).

23. Among the vast exploration literature, some useful studies to consider include Carlos Schwantes, ed., *Encounters with a Distant Land: Exploration in the Great Northwest* (Moscow: University of Idaho Press, 1994); Robin Fisher and Hugh Johnston, eds., *From Maps to Metaphors: The Pacific World of George Vancouver* (Vancouver: University of British Columbia Press, 1993); James Ronda, *Revealing America: Image and Imagination in the Exploration of North America* (Lexington: D.C. Heath, 1996); Barry Gough, *The Northwest Coast: British Navigation, Trade, and Discoveries to 1812* (Vancouver: University of British Columbia Press, 1992); H. Beals, ed., *Juan Pérez on the Northwest Coast: Six Documents of His Expedition in 1774* (Portland: Oregon Historical Society, 1990); Graham MacDonald, "The Exploration of the Pacific," *Journal of Interdisciplinary History* 24, no. 3 (1994):509–16.

24. Ken Coates, "Boundaries and the Pacific Northwest: The Historical and Contemporary Significance of Borders in Western North America," in Lars-Folke Landgren and Maunu Häyrynen, eds., *The Dividing Line: Borders and National Peripheries* (Helsinki: Renvall Institute, 1997).

25. J.R. Gibson, *Otter Skins, Boston Ships, and China Goods: The Maritime Fur Trade on the Northwest Coast, 1785–1841* (Seattle: University of Washington Press, 1992).

26. David Breen and Ken Coates, *Vancouver's Fair: A Political and Administrative History of the Pacific National Exhibition* (Vancouver: University of British Columbia Press, 1982).

27. For a broad view of world trade, see Peter Hugill, *World Trade since 1431: Geography, Technology and Capitalism* (Baltimore: Johns Hopkins University Press, 1993).

28. See, in particular, Bill Robbins, *Colony and Empire: The Capitalist Transformation of the American West* (Lawrence: University of Kansas Press, 1994).

29. Keith Bryant Jr., "Entering the Global Economy," Clyde Milner III, et al., eds., *The Oxford History of the American West* (New York: Oxford, 1994), 196.

30. John Naisbitt, *Megatrends Asia* (New York: Simon and Schuster, 1996).

31. Gail Nomura, "Significant Lives: Asia and Asian Americans in the History of the U.S. West," *Western Historical Quarterly* 25, no. 1 (1994):69–88.

32. Patricia Wood, "Borders and Identities among Italian Immigrants in the Pacific Northwest, 1880–1938," in Ken Coates and John Findlay, eds., *Parallel Destinies: Canadian-American Relations West of the Rockies* (Seattle: University of Washington Press, 2002).

33. David Goldman, *Gold Seeking: Victoria and California in the 1850s* (Stanford: Stanford University Press, 1994).

34. Douglas Fetherling, *Gold Crusades: A Social History of Gold Rushes, 1849–1929* (Toronto: Macmillan, 1988) provides the best analysis of the global nature of the gold rushes. On a more limited scale, see James Drucker, "Gold Rushers North: A Census Study of the Yukon and Alaskan Gold Rushes, 1896–1900," in Steve Haycox and M. Childers Mangusso, eds., *An Alaska Anthology: Interpreting the Past* (Seattle: University of Washington Press, 1996), 219.

35. Robin Fisher, *Contact and Conflict: Indian-European Relations in British Columbia* (Vancouver: University of British Columbia Press, 1977).

36. Peter Ward, *White Canada Forever: Popular Attitudes and Public Policy toward Orientals in British Columbia* (Montreal: McGill-Queen's University Press, 1978).

37. Patricia Roy, *Vancouver: An Illustrated History* (Toronto: Lorimer, 1980).

38. Alfred Crosby, *Epidemic and Peace, 1918* (Westport, Connecticut: Greenwood Press, 1976).

39. Carlos Schwantes, *The Pacific Northwest: An Interpretative History* (Lincoln: University of Nebraska, 1996), 360.

40. For an overview of Northwest defense projects, see Ken Coates and W.R. Morrison, *The Alaska Highway in World War II: The U.S. Army of Occupation in the Canadian Northwest* (Norman: University of Oklahoma Press, 1992). For a more U.S.-focused study, see Heath Twichell, *Northwest Epic: The Building of the Alaska Highway* (New York: St. Martin's Press, 1992). On the impact of World War II on the economy of the western United States, see Gerald Nash, *The American West Transformed: The Impact of the Second World War* (Bloomington: Indiana University Press, 1985).

41. For the Canadian side of this story, written from an interesting Japanese and Canadian perspective, see Pat Roy, et al., *Mutual Hostages: Canadians and Japanese during the Second World War* (Toronto: University of Toronto Press, 1990). On the American side, see Roger Daniels, Sandra Taylor, and Harry Kitano, eds., *Japanese Americans: From Relocation to Redress*, rev. ed. (Seattle: University of Washington Press, 1991).

42. Schwantes, *The Pacific Northwest*, 425.

43. Peter MacFarlane, *Brotherhood to Nationhood: George Manuel and the Making of the Modern Indian Movement* (Toronto: Between the Lines, 1993). See also, Paul Tennant, *Aboriginal Peoples and Politics: The Indian Land Question in British Columbia, 1849–1989* (Vancouver: University of British Columbia Press, 1990).

44. The quote is taken from the historical overview on the Greenpeace World Wide Web Site.

45. See William Cronin, ed., *Uncommon Ground: Toward Reinventing Nature* (New York: Norton, 1995).

46. The *Pacific Historical Review* devoted a special issue (vol. 65, no. 4, November 1996) to the study of tourism in the American West; see, M. Shaffer, "See America First: Re-Envisioning Nation and Region through Western Tourism," 559–83.

47. Jim Simon, "Uncertain Canadians," *Pacific Magazine*, February 23, 1997, 10–15.

48. See Schwantes, *The Pacific Northwest*; and Carin Holroyd, "The Japanese Presence in the Northern British Columbia Economy," *The Northern Review* (1997). On the global aspect of the modern logging industry, see Patricia Marchak, *Logging the Globe* (Montreal: McGill-Queen's University Press, 1995), and "For Whom the Tree Falls: Restructuring of the Global Forest Industry," *BC Studies* 90 (1991):3–24.

49. For an interesting analysis of why Seattle has emerged as an important global center and why Portland has not, see Carol Abbott, "Regional City and Network City: Portland and Seattle in the Twentieth Century," *Western Historical Quarterly* 23, no. 3 (1992):293–322.

Section Two

People

VI

The American Indian and Freedom of Religion: An Historic Appraisal

Alvin M. Josephy Jr.

*A*MERICAN HISTORIANS RECOGNIZED *as early as 1907, when J. Franklin Jameson made it the subject of a presidential address before the American Historical Association, that religion has played an important role in the nation's social and cultural development. Jameson declared that any scholar wanting to understand the American character could "provide himself with data representing all classes, all periods, all regions, [and] may find in the history of American religion the closest approach to the continuous record he desires."*

For many citizens, religion had drawn more universal attention than literature, philosophy, music, art, or even politics. It was true, Jameson conceded, that the main concern of the masses always had been the daily struggle to make a living, but history must be concerned "with more than mere economic matters."

Even though white Americans have long realized the importance of religion in their own culture, they have been reluctant to extend this same acknowledgement to Indian beliefs. Early Protestant missionaries, such as the Whitmans and Spaldings, were quickly given a place in the pantheon of Pacific Northwest history. Likewise, the diligent labors of the Catholic fathers, such as François Norbert Blanchet and Peter John DeSmet, did not go unnoticed by scholars. Yet many modern-day Americans view Indian spiritual systems as something less than valid, and force Native Americans to continue to struggle for their religious freedoms.

By examining Indian-white history in the Pacific Northwest, Alvin M. Josephy Jr. shows that Indian spiritual systems had been largely ignored as key motivating forces in Indian life and in their relations with whites. The result has been a legacy that in large measure continues to denigrate the true nature and role of traditional native religions.

On August 11, 1978, Congress passed the American Indian Religious Freedom Act. Most of the non-Indian U.S. population was unaware of its passage.

Indeed, if a large publicity splash had been made about it, many might have wondered why such legislation had occupied the mind and time of Congress in a nation that for almost two centuries had taken pride in possessing a constitutional guarantee of religious freedom. However, to Native Americans, including those in the Northwest, and to whites who were knowledgeable about their affairs, the need was clear.

Most Americans, indeed, have long recognized—as in the case of the Mormons and others who from time to time have known intolerance—that elements of the population have not always lived up to or enforced the constitutional guarantee. But in the case of native groups, as late as 1978—and even continuing today—most Indians have been unhappily aware that a majority of the rest of the population has sanctioned a widespread interference with, and even a trampling on, their traditional beliefs. As corroborated by current fishing and other conflicts and by accumulating court cases, society and government have failed on numerous occasions to understand traditional native religions or regard them as being protected by the Constitution.[1]

The testimony has been heard in the courts, in public discussions, hearings before Congress, and in the media. In Washington, Oregon, and Idaho, as well as the Great Lakes states, many whites, including state and federal officials, readily grasped the economic competitiveness of Indian fishermen, who demand the observance of their treaty fishing rights. But whites have cynically greeted Indian assertions that these rights also have a deep and continuing religious significance to native people. Somewhat begrudgingly under court decisions, government has apportioned fish to the treaty tribes for "ceremonial use"—the ceremonies, in the public mind, usually conveying the image of being a tribal civic or social event, rather than a genuine and meaningful religious experience.

In a similar vein in another part of the country, the long fight of the Taos Pueblo Indians in New Mexico to regain title to their sacred Blue Lake and the forests around it—the fountainhead of their centuries-old religion—was opposed until 1970 by whites, who could see no visible religious shrines in the area and therefore charged that the Indians' religion was a fraud being used to hide the tribe's desire to economically exploit timber.[2]

A good deal of this attitude stems from history and continues as a legacy of innocence, a lack of knowledge, and stereotypic thinking, exemplified by the early Washington settler and writer George Gibbs, who in 1854 informed the U.S. government that the Klickitat tribe "in common with the other Oregon tribes, seem to have had no distinct religious ideas previous to those introduced by the whites…Their mythology consists of vague and incoherent tales."[3]

Some of this, too, is a holdover of cultural arrogance. Whatever may be the contemporary reasons for such thinking, the mounting litigation and persistent pressure and testimony of Indians before congressional committees in the 1970s, seeking protection for various aspects of their spiritual life, persuaded Congress that neither the government nor the general public had yet accorded traditional native religions the validity and legal rights that were entitled. And this was a century after the close of the wars against the tribes, and a half-century after Indians had been recognized, in 1924, as full citizens of the United States.

Despite its passage, the 1978 Religious Freedom Act had rather little initial impact on the long heritage that it was meant to overcome and reverse. Introduced by James Abourezk of South Dakota, Democratic chairman of the Senate's Select Committee on Indian Affairs, it stated: "Henceforth it shall be the policy of the United States to protect and preserve for American Indians their inherent right of freedom to believe, express, and exercise the traditional religions of the American Indian, Eskimo, Aleut, and native Hawaiians, including but not limited to access to sites, use, and possession of sacred objects and the freedom to worship through ceremonials and traditional sites."

The Act called for consultations with Indians, and government hearings were conducted around the country to "determine appropriate changes necessary to protect and preserve Native American religious cultural rights and practices." The grievances expressed by Indians at those hearings were numerous and varied, including resentments over the desecration of cemeteries and sacred sites, lack of access to such sites and to materials needed for holy purposes, and interference with ceremonies and rituals.

One hearing was held on the Colville Reservation at Nespelem, Washington, June 14–15, 1979. Tribal members from throughout the Northwest listed a host of complaints—the dwindling supply of salmon and other fish necessary for religious purposes; the halting of ceremonial fishing at certain sites and the lack of access to other spiritually important locations; the desecration and destruction by loggers and others of traditional sacred areas; the disinterment of Indian remains by highway and dam builders, and the failure to rebury them (storing the remains instead in museums and other public buildings); the vandalism of Indian burial sites; the inability to secure eagle feathers and animal and vegetable products needed for religious purposes; the interference by customs officials on the U.S.-Canadian border with the transfer of religious objects between tribal groups in the two countries; the breaking up of religious ceremonies of Indian college students by local police; and the denial of the right of Indian prison inmates to practice their native religions and use sweat baths, traditional religious objects, and the ministrations of native religious teachers.[4]

The Act unfortunately had no teeth. Its policy—expected only to serve as an educational stimulus for the general public—was intended to be observed in both principle and action by the three branches of the federal government. Some agencies of the executive branch, including divisions of the Justice and Interior departments, made efforts to satisfy or ameliorate certain of the Indians' expressed grievances. These ranged from helping to provide tribes with eagle feathers and other natural objects and materials required for spiritual purposes, to exercising greater care than before in considering threats to Indian religious and cultural sites in government-prepared environmental impact statements regarding affects on land holdings.

But, by and large, little else changed. The awareness and attitudes regarding Indian religions held by state governments and the general public were largely unaltered, and the court cases continued on. Even federal agencies, when it has suited their purposes, defeated Indian attempts to make the Act effective. In Tennessee, for example, the Cherokees after 1979 were unable to prevent the TVA's Tellico Dam from flooding a host of their most sacred sites, and, in Arizona, a Navajo appeal for the protection of holy shrines at Rainbow Bridge was rejected by the Bureau of Reclamation and by federal courts.[5]

Today, the Indians' struggle for equality in religious freedom that would match that enjoyed by all other Americans has a particular relevancy for non-Indian historians. In the quest to understand the nature of present-day conflicts with Indians, we must fall back on the roots of those differences, examining how well we know what led from there to here. In doing so, it becomes clear that in the past we have largely ignored or underemphasized a key and often decisive element in Indian-white relations—the strong, pervasive force of spirituality in Indian life.

Relying heavily on white witnesses and their testimony and documentation—often being the most extensive and readily available sources—we have focused on what have seemed to be essentially political and economic motives in confrontations regarding Indians and whites. Though we have shown an appreciation for the existence of cultural differences and misunderstandings, we have only rarely given adequate attention to the role of native spirituality as a motive for actions and reactions, nor have we generally appreciated the impacts of white activities on Indian spiritual life. While we have acknowledged that, among whites, religious motives were frequently intermingled with materialistic aims—as with the Puritans in New England, and various missionaries in the Northwest—we have failed at the same time to recognize that, among Indians, political and economic thought and actions often flowed directly and naturally from the profound religious context of their group and individual lives.

This dereliction, recognized today more by Indian scholars than by their white peers, has resulted not only in a partial distortion of history, but also in a legacy that continues to denigrate native religion so thoroughly that most whites still know little of its actual nature or role. Being uninformed, moreover, the general public continues to accept the old popularized image of traditional Indians—furthered by generations of cheap fiction, movies, and television—as not religious at all, but instead being led by backward and outmoded "medicine man" superstitions and, as Gibbs wrote, by "vague and incoherent tales."

Though most Americans are at least benign enough to feel indifferent about what spiritual beliefs and practices Indians wish to embrace for themselves, they remain skeptical about this religious validity—viewing sweat bathing, for instance, as a picturesque custom, and sun dances as being largely social entertainment—and will not suffer Indian religious-based claims to interfere with construction projects and other land-altering activities or the wants of the dominant non-Indian society. As a result, Indian religions, when clashing with non-Indian interests over land use, the taking of fish, or other matters, are still often deemed unworthy of protection under the First Amendment.

Historically, our attitude finds roots in patterns established by the early Spanish, French, and English explorers, settlers, and entrepreneurs who came to what is now the United States. If they learned anything about Indian religious life, as some of them did, they found it strange and alien, and judged it as inferior, heathenish, malevolent, and usually unworthy of tolerance. A vast literature exists on the efforts, everywhere in this country, to convert the tribes to the religion of the whites. What is less familiar is what the tribes were being converted from.

In the Pacific Northwest, as in all parts of the Americas, there was no single Indian religion. Spiritual ideas, practices, and systems varied from one native group to another, sometimes profoundly, sometimes only in details. In view of the American reactions to these beliefs, however, it was ironic that traditional beliefs everywhere were relentless and pervasive. The fact of the matter is that Indian religions always have been the skein that held native life together, from morning till night, from day to day, from year to year. All of these beliefs had evolved through the centuries to help ensure the unity and perceived well-being of the different peoples, and, as all religions seek to do, to provide individuals and groups with answers to such fundamental questions as: "Who am I?"; "Where did I come from and where am I going?"; "What are the meaning and purpose of my existence?"; and "What is my relationship to others, to my group, to the rest of creation, and to the unseen world?"[6]

Most, if not all, of the Northwest native religions, as elsewhere, taught that everything in the universe—trees, winds, rocks, living creatures, and man himself—possessed spiritual power, or a life force, and that all of these spiritual forces, together with those of the unseen world, were interconnected in a delicate, harmonious balance that allowed individuals and their groups to survive and enjoy well-being. Much as we talk today of the need to maintain ecological systems, so the native religions taught that individuals, by errant thoughts or deeds, could disrupt the harmony, balance, and order of the world's spiritual and natural network and imperil themselves and their communities. All behavior and conduct, and all actions, reactions, and decisions, therefore, took into account impacts in either maintaining or disrupting a group's harmonious relationship with various elements of the spiritual realm and the land.

Some of the religions' systems appeared relatively simple in outward form, resting essentially on long-defined relationships between Indian groups and their shamans, both men and women, who had strong spiritual powers that enabled them to communicate or intercede with the supernatural world for purposes either good or bad. Usually, shamans assisted the people as mediums, bringing about desired aims, as foreseers of the future, or as curers. However, whites termed them derogatorily as "witch doctors," "wizards," or "medicine men," despite the fact that shamans often combined psychology and psychosomatic treatments with the use of plants and other natural products on which modern-day medicine relies.

Other aspects of the spiritual systems were far more complex, combining numerous intricate levels of concepts, beliefs, prayers, and rituals that, under the trained guidance of leaders and teachers, united the group with the universe and oversaw the maintenance of harmonious bonds with the supernatural and the forces and creatures of nature. Even the smaller and simpler societies were rich in legends, ceremonies, songs, dances, and arts, for these were integrated parts of their spiritual systems, serving to hold their societies together by instructing people about right and wrong behavior, personal positions and obligations within a group, and what the group expected of each of its members.

During the 19th century, many Pacific Northwest Indians informed whites that they shared a belief in a single all-powerful Creator, or Creative Spirit, above all other spiritual forces. This Creator Spirit, however, often was actually viewed by them as a vague entity, remote from the daily events of people's lives. More important was each individual's own "guardian spirit"—in the Columbia Plateau, usually sought for and acquired in solitary vision quests to remote locations while the seeker was still a youth. Preparations for these quests, and follow-up rituals, were conducted under the supervision of a shaman or an elder. A guardian spirit—which could be an eagle, dragonfly, bear, or other natural thing in spiritual guise—guided, counseled, and assisted an individual throughout his or her life.

Other important aspects of native religious systems included increasing a people's collective spiritual power by adding those from allied groups, and in relying on prophecies made public by persons with strong spiritual powers. From time to time—particularly in periods of sustained anxiety or calamity—prophecies ordained additions or changes in religious systems, such as new ceremonies, songs, special conduct, and even in beliefs. Frequently in the far West after the 1780s, apprehensions over the coming of the whites and from disastrous epidemics sometimes led to the emergence of full-blown prophetic cults.

In addition, most of the religious systems, stemming basically from origin myths, united the people with great emotional and spiritual attachment to the land on which they lived, and from which they secured their livelihood. Many legends of the Northwest tribes told of a day before humans, when the world was inhabited only by animals or, in some cases, by powerful cannibal monsters. At some point, a Changer or culture hero appeared—coyote to the Nez Perces, mink to the Quilleutes, fox to the Puget Sound tribes. Each had all the attributes, both good and bad, of humans, but also in many ways were superhuman. It was they who finally brought forth the first humans and the different tribes, giving people the lands on which they were thereafter to live.

To the different native groups, such legends—usually repeated by grandparents in stories told in wintertime lodges to grandchildren—inherently held all the force that Scripture possesses for devout whites. In other parts of the country origin myths differed. They often told of a Creator or supreme spiritual power, rather than a culture hero, who gave a particular area of the earth to a tribe. Whatever the story, the binding of people to their homeland was sacred. Landmarks and particular places on their terrain were revered, because they were markers of the tribe's universe and associated with spiritual events and concepts, or with the bones and souls of departed ancestors.

In truth, this brief treatment does not give full justice to an understanding of Native American religions, but enough is noted to provide the beginning of new perspectives on Indian-white relations in which three points should be emphasized—

First, the most important consideration of Indian groups—whether families, villages, bands, or tribes—was the survival and well-being of the people. This was achieved basically by adhering to traditional religious practices and beliefs—i.e., by keeping the universe in balance through harmonious relations with spiritual forces, and avoiding anything that might disturb them.

Second, this adherence made religion a daily aspect of life and conduct for every individual. The worst thing that could happen would be to imperil the welfare of the group; spiritual beliefs thus became as much a part of an individual as his or her skin. The attachment of a person's guardian spirit to the broad spiritual universe was more than an article of faith; it was being.

Third, this attachment to the rest of creation made much of the earth sacred. The destruction of it, or the forced separation from it, would be a soul-searing, emotional ordeal with the coloration even of death.

With all this in mind, let us examine a few episodes of Pacific Northwest history as we know it from the non-Indian point of view. The earliest whites on the coast and in the interior were essentially explorers, fur traders, and trappers. Among them were the Astorians, an American fur company with both Canadian and American personnel. Two anecdotes during their sojourn at the mouth of the Columbia and in the Oregon country in the period 1811–1814 are instructive.

On August 26, 1813, the Astorian clerk, Alfred Seton, who had gone up the Willamette River, noted in his journal that he had met the Calapooya Indians. "They have not many articles of white men among them," he wrote, "are clothed in Dear skin robes, which, with their bows and arrows form all their riches; these are a miserable wandering set."[7] Like Lewis and Clark and others, Seton and the Astorians observed and judged the tribes they met solely on materialistic and physical perceptions. It was the traditional way white men judged Indians, and which, for the most part, continues today. The Astorians and other early whites also compared the outward appearances of the lower Columbia and coastal Indians with those of the interior Columbia Plateau or Basin, and found the former wanting.

Yet it is unlikely to believe that the Calapooyas would have been regarded as inferior or judged "miserable" if Seton had been aware that they, like the upriver Indians, had other wealth—a rich and satisfying spiritual life that enabled them to live in harmony and balance with their homeland. Without this concern for the religious factor, we have the legacy today of largely unflattering, stereotypic images of the Calapooyas, Chinooks, Clatsops, Cowlitz,

Chehalis, and other lower Columbia peoples that does not do justice to the sophistication of their religions, and the strength, dignity, and richness that their spiritual systems endowed to their societies.

Again, referring to the Astorians, we find them regularly observing, but rarely adequately understanding. On one occasion, when the Chinook chief Comcomly refused to let the whites handle the first fishes caught at the commencement of a salmon run, the Astorians were amused; they ascribed it to superstition or whim. But Comcomly's action was a Chinook article of faith, as important to them as an injunction in the Bible might be to whites. The Chinooks, like many other Pacific Northwest tribes, believed that salmon actually were humans, who lived in a dwelling under the ocean and annually assumed the guise of fish in order to provide food for the Indians. The first salmon, after being caught and ceremonially thanked, were cut up and treated, and then the Chinooks put their bones back in the water to return them to their homes, once again as humans, in order that they might return the following year as food for the Indians. This was the Chinooks' understanding of the marvelous life cycle of salmon, but they also knew that if they offended the first, or chief, fish—with whose spirit their own was interconnected—by failing to thank him, by improper treatment, or crippling him by not carefully returning all of his bones to the river, then the salmon might not return again.[8]

To this day, the lives of Northwest fishing Indians gain strength and security from association with salmon and steelhead. Though the scientific facts of the salmon's life cycle are now known, ceremonies continue and have important religious meaning for all the fishing tribes. How sad, though, that the white man's history did not prepare us for a better appreciation and understanding of a people, who still, deep down, dare not fail to honor and thank the spiritual life force of fish, to which they have for millennia been so closely attached.

After the fur men came the missionaries. We are familiar with the white men's recorded histories of Daniel and Jason Lee, the Whitmans and Spaldings, and all their contemporaries and successors residing among many of the Pacific Northwest tribes. But can we grasp, from the Indian viewpoint, the enormity of the affects that these representatives of the white men's religions were attempting to accomplish? Far from simply bestowing white beliefs and practices, missionaries tried, in truth, to *convert* Indian people from their ancestral faith and trust in everything that held their life together and gave meaning to existence, and which bound Indians to the seen and unseen world, and that gave safety and security to the continuance of the group and ensured survival and well-being for parents, wives, children, relatives, and friends. Indians were asked to cut their links with the spirit world upon which their ancestors, for untold generations, had relied, and in which they themselves had been instructed since childhood not to offend. Those links were as much a part of their being as their physical features and personality. In a sense, it was not only like asking them to shed their skin for a new one, but, in doing so, to imperil their universe.

An appreciation of this perspective adds new breadth and depth to our understanding of the relationship between missionaries and the tribes. From the tribal viewpoint, it is quite true that many Indians, including village, band, and tribal headmen, and even shamans, had eagerly sought knowledge of the white men's religion, welcomed the missionaries, and accepted what they taught. But what the Indians actually were doing, or trying to do, was to acquire an understanding of additional—and seemingly very powerful—spiritual forces that could be added to their own systems to enhance their individual and collective existence. They did not intend to abandon their traditional spiritual life, only to enhance it.

The missionaries seem not to have fully comprehended this, and thus were doomed to frustration and heartsick defeat. Despite their years of laboring during the 1830s–1850s, missionaries of all denominations, including the Whitmans and Spaldings, did not make a single convert in the sense of weaning any Indian totally away from still pervasive native beliefs. Henry Spalding's most prominent converts, the Nez Perce headmen Tamootsin and Tuekakas, known to whites as Timothy and Old Joseph respectively, added Christian teachings to their spiritual inheritance, but in time Joseph found reason to abandon, not his ancestors' religious system, but rather the additions that Spalding had led him to accept.

Even individuals originally welcoming the missionaries with eagerness, such as the Nez Perces' Tackensuatis and Lawyer, the Yakama's Kamiakin, and various Cayuse headmen, were not convinced to give up their ancestral understanding of their relationship to the supernatural, which had guided them in their interactions with, and perceptions of, fellow humans, nature, and indeed, all of creation. In March 1854, Gibbs's report to the government, transmitted through Washington Territorial Governor Isaac I. Stevens's subordinate, George B. McClellan, noted that Kamiakin possessed "the greatest influence" among the Yakama, but that he, in turn, was "much under the influence of the missionaries, with whom he lives altogether."[9] Yet a year later, Kamiakin was in revolt against the whites. His decisions and actions were still based on his native spirituality that continued to bind him to his people and the land.

Similarly, the Cayuses by the 1850s—among whom Marcus and Narcissa Whitman had worked so diligently, and a people who had learned much about Christianity from fur traders and Iroquois trappers long before the Whitmans arrived—had shown not a single sign of having shed the spiritual beliefs of their ancestors. Even Lawyer, the steadfast Nez Perce friend of missionaries and whites, who in supporting the acceptance of Christian teachings and the material goods and means underlying the white men's power, could not and would not crusade for the abandonment of the Nez Perce spiritual system and religious beliefs. It was basically on a materialistic path—in the matters that were Caesar's, so to speak—that he chose to follow, which separated him most notably from the traditionalists. It is significant that, not until November 1871, was Lawyer baptized by Spalding and formally enrolled as a Christian convert. By that time, the original cultural foundations of Nez Perce life were about to be thoroughly undermined, as the structure of Nez Perce society was going through profound and fundamental changes caused by the overwhelming impact of white settlement in the Northwest.[10]

In the stormy period of tribal treaties, hostilities, and dispossession that followed the missionary era, we see, perhaps more clearly than at any other time, the deep wounding of Indian religious sensibilities, which generally was not appreciated by whites in those times and scarcely taken into account even today. At each of the treaty sessions conducted by Governor Stevens in 1854 and 1855, first with the Puget Sound and coastal peoples, and then with those in the interior, the tribes were persuaded, cajoled, and pressured not merely into giving up much of their traditional economic base, but the very center of much of their spiritual universe. Whites saw it practically all in economic terms—trading so many acres of land for so much goods, services, and annuities. The tribes saw it differently, in much broader terms, and said so.

At treaty sessions on Puget Sound at Medicine Creek and Point Elliott in December 1854 and January 1855, the Nisqually, Puyallup, Duwamish, and other tribes, bowing to the inevitable, not only ceded a majority of their ancestral lands to the government—afterward concentrating their populations on reservations or reduced plots of land—but were separated from many traditional sites that meant so much to their spiritual well being. This caused sufficient turmoil that the treaties eventually were amended and reservation boundaries were altered to include more traditional sacred and fishing locations. Even so, armed conflict broke out between the whites and a portion of the Indians in 1855–1856, resulting in the defeat of those spiritually driven small groups of tribes people who chose hostilities. Another eventual result was the execution of one of the key traditional and spiritual native war leaders, Leschi, amidst deep pro and con arguments over this action in the white community.

In the interior, Governor Stevens, Oregon Indian Superintendent Joel Palmer, and other white negotiators had a rather vague understanding of the deep spiritually based objections raised at the 1855 Walla Walla treaty sessions, as the tribes agonized over ceding lands and places to which they were religiously interconnected. The council minutes overflow with passionate pleas by native spokesmen regarding those localities where individual bands felt an unbreakable symbiotic relationship to the terrain—where humans and the earth were inextricably combined in the spiritual and physical worlds.

"I wonder if this ground has anything to say?" asked Tauitau, the Young Chief of the Umatilla Valley Cayuses:

> I wonder if the ground is listening to what is said?...I hear what this earth says. The earth says, God has placed me here. The earth says that God tells me to take care of the Indians on this earth...The water speaks the same way: God says, feed the Indians upon the earth. The grass says the same thing: feed the horses and cattle...The earth says, God has placed me here to produce all that grows upon me...God on placing them on the earth...said, you Indians take care of the earth and do each other no harm.

And from Owhi, a Yakama: "God made our bodies from the earth...What shall I do? Shall I give the lands that are a part of my body?" Owhi also was "afraid of the laws of the Great Spirit" should the Indians cede lands.

Another Cayuse leader, Stickus, said his "heart" was in the Grande Ronde, Touchet, and Tucannon river valleys.[11]

But Stevens and Palmer were impatient. Palmer could not understand what more information the Indians needed. He told them, they would get sawmills, gristmills, teachers, and annuities. "We don't come to steal your lands," he added. "We pay you more than it is worth." Howlish Wompoon, a Cayuse, glared at Palmer, and stated, "I cannot think of leaving this land. Your words since you came here have been crooked. That is all I have to say."[12] Stevens and Palmer, of course, had their way, though it finally tipped the region's long-term Indian-white tension to war in 1855–1858 involving portions of the interior tribes. The ultimate outcome of the white victory forced the Indians to accept their land cessions in the signed treaties and their required acceptance of the Yakama, Umatilla, and Nez Perce reservations.

These same sorts of confrontations in councils, however, continued in following years. Smohalla, a leader among one of the peaceful bands still independently occupying the mid-Columbia area, arose to spread the

"Dreamer Religion" among many demoralized Northwest native groups and communities. White settlers, the military, and local and federal officials saw it as a plot to unite the Indians in renewed hostilities, but, rather, Smohalla was giving voice to the traditional bonds between Indians and all creation—bonds that white pressure and influence were discrediting and stamping out:

> You ask me to plow the ground! Shall I take a knife and tear my mother's bosom?
>   Then when I die she will not take me to her bosom to rest. You ask me to dig for stone! Shall I dig under her skin for her bones? Then when I die I cannot enter her body to be born again. You ask me to cut grass and make hay and sell it, and be rich like white men! But how dare I cut off my mother's hair?"[13]

Such highly charged religious and emotional perceptions increased the pain and agony of ceding lands. To understand the spiritual depth of this injury is to recognize why a number of bands determinedly resisted ceding places where their ancestors were buried. Prime examples are several "non-treaty" Nez Perce and Palouse groups led by Chief Joseph, White Bird, Toohoolhoolzote, Hahtalekin, and others. During the Idaho and eastern Oregon gold rush years—as waves of miners entered Indian lands—a majority of Nez Perce leaders had signed an 1863 agreement reducing the size of their reservation (originally established in the 1855 Stevens' treaty at Walla Walla). Most of the Indian signatory parties to the revised treaty, however, still largely retained their own bands' Clearwater River home sites. On the other hand, several excluded groups—mostly in southern Nez Perce territory and including the Joseph band—would lose their homes and refused to sign. By not coming onto the much reduced reservation, they risked years of confrontation (and eventually war) in their struggle to stay where they were.

No meeting was more moving than that between General O.O. Howard and the non-treaty bands at Ft. Lapwai, Idaho, in May 1877. At that time, Howard presented the non-treaty Indians with an ultimatum to leave the Wallowa country and other areas along the Snake and Salmon rivers, and come onto the Clearwater reservation. In facing Howard, Toohoolhoolzote, a spiritual leader and Snake River headman, spoke for all the non-treaty Indians, including Chief Joseph, who were at the meeting. "The earth is part of my body," Toohoolhoolzote told the general. "I belong to the land out of which I came. The earth is my mother."

Howard did not appreciate the whole point. He wrote in his reminiscences:

Toohoolhoolzote, the cross-grained growler, had the usual long prelimi-
nary discussion about the earth being his mother, that she should not be
disturbed by hoe or plough, that men should subsist on what grows of
itself, etc., etc...He was answered: "We do not wish to interfere with your
religion, but you must talk about practicable things. Twenty times over you
repeat that the earth is your mother...Let us hear it no more, but come to
business at once."[14]

The true climax of the great tragedy that followed—the 1877 Nez Perce
War—was not Joseph's powerful surrender speech at the Bear Paws in Montana, so often celebrated by whites, but Joseph's long struggle thereafter for
his people's right to return to their sacred Wallowa homeland—a right never
granted. In the nation's capitol on January 14, 1879, Joseph, who had come
from his place of exile in Oklahoma, tried to persuade the government to return
his people to the Pacific Northwest. He made this most eloquent plea:

> Let me be a free man—free to travel, free to stop, free to work, free to trade,
> where I choose, free to choose my own teachers, free to follow the religion
> of my fathers, free to think and talk and act for myself—and I will obey
> every law, or submit to the penalty.[15]

This appeal and other passionate requests were denied. Joseph's people
were not returned to the Pacific Northwest until six years later—part of them
to reside on the Nez Perce Reservation, and part, often the most dedicated
traditionalists, to live on the Colville Reservation in northeast Washington.
Descendants remain at both places today.

In the following decades, religious freedom was banned among all American
Indians by federal government regulations, which were vigorously enforced
by agents, missionaries, and other officials (this policy was not reversed until
passage of the Indian Reorganization Act in 1934 as part of President Franklin D. Roosevelt's New Deal). When Joseph died in 1904 on the Colville
Reservation, probably due to a heart attack, a sympathetic local physician
reported that the chief had succumbed to "a broken heart." Joseph had still
spiritually yearned for the spirits of the mountains, meadows, canyons, and
grasslands of the beautiful Wallowa Valley, which he had only briefly visited
again in 1899 and 1900.

Following this brief historical appraisal, two points remain to be summarized
and made clear—

First, beyond any question Indians did, indeed, individually and collectively often pursue political, economic, or materialistic goals, in addition

to spiritualistic considerations. To imply otherwise would be incorrect and misleading. But, at the same time, it has not been adequately recognized that such goals often did include spiritual components and motivations. The history of Indian-white relations, as the white man knows it, has placed too great a stress on equating the driving forces in Indian cultures with those of the whites. If historians in the future give greater regard to traditional Indian spiritual beliefs, we will acquire fuller, truer, and sometimes different readings of history than we now have. No longer will stories of the Nez Perce, Yakama, Coeur d'Alene, Klickitat, or Chinook be written with blinders, largely ignoring the affects that traditional spiritual systems have had on events, actions, and relationships.

Secondly, many individual Indians and even entire native groups, in the course of their histories, have not only become nominal but also practicing adherents of Christianity. Significant numbers also have abandoned their native religious systems altogether. Historically, however, this generally followed utter social collapse by the late-19th century, affecting traditional native systems of belief and collective organization. In the case of the Chinooks and a number of tribes west of the Cascades, Old World diseases had decimated their settlements by the mid-19th century, killing a majority of their people, including, of course, many religious, civil, and war leaders, and leaving a handful of demoralized survivors. Other groups, including a number in the interior, also lost effective leadership and organization due the effects of warfare, or peaceful tribal dispersion to several reservations, and because their traditional social structures were undermined by government policies, Indian agents, missionaries, and reservation schools. There came a time for each tribe, in modern life, when the hold of their native spirituality had disintegrated to such an extent, or even collapsed, that it no longer was valid for many people. Christianity, or a mixture of Christian and native religious beliefs and practices, replaced it.

And yet, to a remarkable degree, a number of Native American religions survive today across the nation. In the 1960s and 1970s, it became evident that significant numbers of traditionalists and their spiritual teachers still remained in many tribes, keeping alive much of the beliefs and practices of their ancestors. Of course, a considerable amount of it had experienced some change or taken on accommodating forms and ideas over the years, but in the Pacific Northwest—among both Puget Sound tribes and the Plateau peoples—Indian and tribal *pride* had revived, fed in large measure by spiritual beliefs, practices, and ties to their traditional homelands that had never died.

Many young Indians of the late 1960s sparked the revival, looking to tribal traditionalists to teach them what they knew or remembered. By the 1970s, many elders, who were also Christians, joined this new interest in their own traditional religions, and the strength of the revival was seen in modern litigation. Native peoples with land and water claims now often fervently spurned financial settlements that would absolve their connections to traditional spiritual places.

In New York State, a Seneca woman rebuffed congressional remuneration for reservation land wanted by the Army Corps of Engineers for a reservoir. "The White man views land for its money value," she said. "We Indians have a spiritual tie with the earth."[16] In New Mexico, the Taos Indians, already mentioned, for years refused any money for their sacred Blue Lake area. In South Dakota, the Sioux in the 1980s refused to accept a monetary settlement for the Black Hills, the seat of their traditional religion, which was lost after the Plains wars of the 1870s. And in the Pacific Northwest, retaining land, fish, and water rights have been more important to many of the tribes than cash offerings. Native American spiritualism and the attachment to their homelands are now stronger and more vital than the public generally recognizes, and is growing stronger and more meaningful all the time.

Notes

1. See especially such Indian human rights cases as *Bender v. Wolff, Crane v. Erickson, Little Raven v. Crisp, Peck v. Meachum, Sequoyah v. Tennessee Valley Authority, Bear Ribs v. Taylor, Frease v. Griffith, Left Hand Bull v. Carlson, Ross v. Scurr, Marshno v. McManus,* and *Badoni v. Higginson,* as well as cases involving a Kootenai River dam in Montana, a Jemez, New Mexico, geothermal power plant, a Point Conception, California, liquefied natural gas terminal, and the return of a Zuñi sacred war god statue, all described in Native American Rights Fund, *Annual Reports* (Boulder, Colorado, 1977–1981).

2. Subcommittee on Indian Affairs of the Senate Committee on Interior and Insular Affairs, Hearings on H.R. 3306, S. 1624, and 1625, 90th Cong., 2d sess., September 19–20, 1968, pp. 203–4, 220. Also see, Dean M. Kelley, "The Impairment of the Religious Liberty of the Taos Pueblo Indians by the United States Government," *A Journal of Church and State* 9 (Spring 1967):1962.

3. George Gibbs, *Indian Tribes of Washington Territory* (Fairfield, Washington: Ye Galleon Press, 1978), 12.

4. Federal Agencies Task Force, *American Indian Religious Freedom Act Report (P.L. 95-341)* (Washington, D.C., August, 1979), Appendix C.

5. The cases denying Indian religious freedom claims were *Sequoyah v. TVA* and *Badoni v. Higginson.*

6. There is an extensive anthropological literature on Indian religions—three accessible summaries regarding the Pacific Northwest can be found in Ruth Underhill, *Indians of the Pacific Northwest* (Washington, D.C.: Bureau of Indian Affairs, 1944); Philip Drucker, *Indians of the Northwest Coast* (New York: American Museum of Natural History, 1963); and Hermann Haeberlin and Erna Gunther, *The Indians of Puget Sound* (Seattle: University of Washington Press, 1930). Other information is included in such general works as James G. Swan, *The Northwest Coast* (New York, 1857), and in more recent detailed studies, such as James A. Teit, "The Salishan Tribes of the Western Plateaus," *45th Annual Report* (Washington, D.C.: Bureau of American Ethnology, 1930); Leslie Spier, *The Prophet Dance of the Northwest and Its Derivates*, General Studies in Anthropology 1 (Menasha, Wisconsin: George Banta, 1935); Marion W. Smith, *The Puyallup-Nisqually* (New York: Columbia University Press, 1940); Click Relander, *Drummers and Dreamers* (Caldwell, Idaho: Caxton Press, 1956); Deward E. Walker, *Indians of Idaho* (Moscow: University of Idaho Press, 1978); *Conflict and Schism in Nez Perce Acculturation* (Pullman: Washington State University Press, 1968); and Theodore Stern, *The Klamath Tribe* (Seattle: University of Washington Press, 1966).

7. "Journal of Alfred Seton," Sleepy Holly Restoration, Tarrytown, New York; unpublished manuscript, p. 175.

8. Underhill, *Indians of the Pacific Northwest*, 16–17.

9. Gibbs, *Indian Tribes of Washington Territory*, 9.

10. Clifford M. Drury, *Chief Lawyer* (Glendale, California: Arthur H. Clark, 1979), 268.

11. Alvin M. Josephy Jr., *The Nez Perce Indians and the Opening of the Northwest* (New Haven, Connecticut: Yale University Press, 1965), 325–26. Minutes of the council are in the L.V. McWhorter Manuscript Collection, at Manuscripts, Archives, and Special Collections, Washington State University, Terrell-Holland Library, Pullman, Washington. See also, Col. Lawrence Kip, *Journal* [1855 Indian Council at Walla Walla] (1897), 19–22.

12. Josephy, *Nez Perce Indians*, 326.

13. James Mooney, "The Ghost Dance Religion," *14th Annual Report* (Washington D.C.: Bureau of Ethnology, Smithsonian Institution, 1896), 721.

14. Oliver O. Howard, *Nez Perce Joseph* (Boston, 1881), 64.

15. "Chief Joseph's Own Story," *North American Review* (April 1879).

16. Alvin M. Josephy, *Now That the Buffalo's Gone* (New York: Knopf, 1982), 129.

VII
The Mind of the Founders: An Assessment of the Washington Constitution of 1889

James M. Dolliver

W ASHINGTON WAS ADMITTED *to the Union in 1889, together with the other Omnibus Bill states of North Dakota, South Dakota, and Montana. Following in 1890 came Idaho and Wyoming. The constitutions of these states had much in common—they were relatively long documents, they enumerated several forms of public dishonesty and corruption, and their writers most often were well-educated young males of substantial means from various walks of life.*

This last similarity was readily apparent in the 75 delegates who assembled at Olympia on July 4, 1889, to draft the Washington Constitution. In addition, however, one of Washington's founding fathers previously had served as speaker of the Michigan house of representatives and as governor of Arizona Territory, and another delegate had been a powerful political leader in Alabama during the Reconstruction period.

Although the Washington delegates relied on the state constitutions of Oregon, California, and Wisconsin as models, they wrote a Declaration of Rights that invites comparison with the Bill of Rights of the U.S. Constitution. Moreover, the "paramount duty" clause of the Washington Constitution was wholly unique for the field of public education. An assessment of the framers' underlying premises in 1889 and of the viability of those premises today—particularly concerning individual rights and public education—will illuminate the history of those concerns and help define some of our current issues.

It has been said that Alexis de Tocqueville's *Democracy in America* is the most quoted and least read book in America. If this is true for de Tocqueville, it probably also is true that constitutions generally, whether of the United States or of the individual states, are the most cited and least read documents in

American society. Constitutions generally are little regarded as works for literary pursuit. Most of the citizenry, except for the likes of lawyers, judges, and perhaps professors, have never read them through. These documents are important, however, because they enable us to convert abstract political theory into concrete governmental reality.

In order to understand the Constitution of the State of Washington, we have to take a brief side excursion and think about the U.S. Constitution. Although the two documents have some differences, in many regards they are quite similar. In large measure, the presuppositions that went into framing the federal Constitution also went into the framing of the Washington Constitution. In this regard, those who prepared the U.S. Constitution followed three overriding principles.

First was a belief that self-government could secure what the Declaration of Independence called the "unalienable rights" of "life, liberty, and the pursuit of happiness." Or, as Lincoln put it in the Gettysburg Address, that a "nation conceived, in Liberty, and dedicated to the proposition that all men are created equal…can long endure." This was an outrageous notion for the times. Those who framed the American Constitution were students of history and government. They knew there never had been a society and government in which democracy had functioned over a long period of time in a large area. Previous democracies simply had not been able to long preserve "life, liberty, and the pursuit of happiness"; nor had it brought to ultimate fruition the notion that all persons "are created equal." The framers also knew why democracy did not prevail; it had fallen either into despotism or demagoguery.

But they had the audacity to say that they could make it work—not simply in a small, homogeneous state, which Rousseau suggested was the only place it could succeed, or in a New England town meeting, or ancient Athens, or in an Italian city state. Rather, they said, it could work in a vast, sparsely occupied, but relatively heterogeneous geographical expanse.

Second, the federal framers never doubted Locke's maxim that "the people shall judge." The question that bothered them was not *whether* the people should judge; that was taken as a given. The dilemma they faced was this: *how* should the people judge? Not only did they take the audacious step of saying that democracy—self-government—was the way to preserve the liberty and ideals expressed in the Declaration of Independence, they also believed in what by any standard was a hardheaded and clear-eyed understanding of human nature. They neither looked back to a legendary Eden, nor did they look forward to an equally mythic utopia. They took people as they were. Two passages from *The Federalist* give an indication of how the framers looked at this elusive thing called human nature.

In the celebrated Number 10 of *The Federalist,* James Madison defined factions by saying he meant "a number of citizens, whether amounting to a majority or a minority of the whole, who are united and actuated by some common impulse of passion, or of interest, adverse to the rights of other citizens or to the permanent and aggregate interests of the community."

And in Number 55, Madison stated:

> As there is a degree of depravity in mankind which requires a certain degree of circumspection and distrust, so there are other qualities in human nature which justify a certain portion of esteem and confidence. Republican government presupposes the existence of these qualities in a higher degree than any other form. Were the pictures which have been drawn by the political jealousy of some among us faithful likenesses of the human character, the inference would be that there is not sufficient virtue among men for self-government; and that nothing less than the chains of despotism can restrain them from destroying and devouring one another.

Not only did the framers try to do something that had never been done successfully, they also proposed that it could be done without adopting a utopian concept of human nature. How were they going to do all this?

That gets us to the **third** principle. They thought it could be done because they had, in the words of Alexander Hamilton in Number 9 of *The Federalist,* discovered great improvements in what he called the new "science of politics." The framers said, yes, they understood that democracy or self-government, when it had succeeded for even a limited period of time, had worked in a very small area, and they also conceded the limitations of human nature. But they believed, inherent in the constitutional document itself, that there were governmental provisions allowing democracy to flourish in the United States and that would take care of, accommodate, and lessen the dangers of factious human nature with which all of mankind is possessed.

The federal framers succeeded by establishing a government founded on the idea of republicanism and federalism. Furthermore, they did it in a written document. We tend sometimes to forget that part of the framers' genius was putting their ideas in writing. They did not rely on the customs of the past, ongoing legislation, or one or two ancient documents, as did the British. They wanted to have a living, vital document called the Constitution, which in itself would accommodate the kind of country in which they lived and the kind of people that inhabited it. Thus Hamilton indicated four things he thought important—(1) the allocation and distribution of power,

(2) legislative checks and balances, (3) an independent judiciary, and (4) an elected representative self-government.

The Constitution also set forth those areas forbidden to government involvement (e.g., Article 1, Sections 9 and 10) in which the powers of both Congress and the states are strictly and carefully restricted. In constitutional principle, the framers had provided for a limited granting of power for a limited government; the framers wanted to protect individual rights. The Bill of Rights was added not long afterward. Regarding minority and individual protections, the Constitution stands as the eloquent centerpiece to the effort that every generation in America must continually face—to resolve tensions between majority rule as juxtaposed to individual/minority rights and equality.

Finally, the Constitution, by providing for regular elections and amending procedures, allowed for orderly change. Put another way, the Constitution provided for the legitimacy of successor governments. We tend to pay little attention to that process after two centuries of using it on a regular basis. The legitimacy of the succeeding government—and the fact that it is recognized as legitimate—is one of the marvels and glories of the American constitutional system, which is maintained by regular free elections. Equally important is a procedure for making amendments to the Constitution.

Even this brief discussion of the U.S. Constitution is enough to indicate that the framers of Washington's Constitution had some of the same basic underlying ideas when they convened at Olympia in the summer of 1889. Some facts and figures will help provide an understanding of regional events up to that time. Washington had been a territory since 1853. In the 1870s, Walla Walla had hosted a constitutional convention with 15 delegates in attendance. They were men of modest means and experience, representing a territory that then had only about 70,000 residents, with just two cities boasting populations approaching 4,000—Walla Walla and Seattle. The people of the territory did adopt the constitution written at Walla Walla, although by a small vote. Scholars have since indicated, with some justification, that the whole exercise was simply an attempt, when Washington finally became a state, to include the Idaho Panhandle. The Walla Walla constitution, however, did not even get out of the congressional committees in Washington, D.C., and the quest for statehood stalled.

A decade later, however, several things had happened making the granting of statehood inevitable. First, the transcontinental Northern Pacific Railroad was completed across Washington to tidewater at the "City of Destiny"—Tacoma.

This effectively tied the eastern and western parts of Washington together commercially. By that time, too, the territory had 300,000 people and was in the midst of an economic boom. Perhaps most important, in the 1888 national election the Republican Party had swept the field in the U.S. congressional races and also gained the presidency by a narrow electoral vote. During most of the 1880s, Democrats had opposed the addition of new states in America's northern tier because of a well-grounded fear that those states would vote Republican. As long as the Democrats either held the presidency or one of the houses of Congress, there would be no new states in the Northwest. But now with full Republican control, six states entered the Union—Washington, South Dakota, North Dakota, and Montana in 1889; and Idaho and Wyoming in 1890. Under this Republican rule, a Democrat of the times supposedly said that new states "did not come in singly but in bunches."

Thus, admission was finally guaranteed, with the only question being in regard to when Washington would write a constitution and vote on it. All was simply a matter of timing and formalities. On February 22, 1889, Grover Cleveland, the lame duck Democratic president bowing to the inevitable, signed the enabling act, or Omnibus Bill. On July 4, the constitutional convention convened in Olympia. Seven weeks later on August 22, it adjourned after completing its duty. On October 1, Washington voters ratified the constitution, and, on November 11, 1889, Washington gained admission as the 42nd state in the Union.

The 75 delegates who wrote the Washington Constitution were an interesting lot. The split along party lines showed 43 Republicans, 29 Democrats, and 3 independents. Delegate John R. Kinnear later claimed: "It was a non-partisan convention and politics at no time dominated or appeared in the discussions."[1] While partisan politics may have been muffled, the record actually disproves this statement as a whole. Democrats did, however, head a number of committees—e.g., the Committee for the Preamble and Declaration of Rights.

The delegates, in contrast to those who had met at the Walla Walla convention, were generally prosperous, as well as politically knowledgeable and effective. Most earlier had lived in other states, where some had gained prior experience in government and politics. Some had served on courts and participated in a variety of other high-ranking government activities. Their average age was 45. For good or ill, one-third of them were lawyers.

What was the political climate like in 1889? What were the concerns of the people in regard to the new constitution? There were five primary areas of greatest public interest. They wished to prevent (1) personal abuse by public office holders, (2) the private use of public funds, and (3) concentrations of power, whether inside or outside of government. They also demanded (4) the preservation of individual liberties and (5) provisions for public education.

Newspapers of the time, on both editorial and front pages, frequently printed articles focusing on key issues, such as restricting and regulating large corporations (particularly the railroads), and woman suffrage and prohibition—all of which were considered by the constitutional convention. In fact, especially heated controversy arose over woman suffrage. In response, the convention's gentlemen did what delegates or legislators on occasion do—they referred the decision to the people. Washington's all-male voting citizenry, however, eventually turned down both suffrage and prohibition. (Women had to wait until 1910 for the right to vote, and statewide prohibition was finally approved by initiative in 1914.) At the time of the convention, newspapers also were giving a great deal of attention to the ownership of valuable industrial-area tidelands, and the municipal condemnation of private land—the delegates also addressed these latter two matters.

On January 28, 1889, journalist S.R. Frazier wrote to territorial Governor Eugene Semple asking a pair of questions:

> 1. What existing, or prospective, interests in Washington deserve special constitutional protection?
> 2. What should be the character and extent of such special constitutional provisions?

Governor Semple wrote back:

> Replying to your letter of Jan. 28th in regard to protecting certain interests by Constitutional provision—I must say that in my opinion the fewer special features contained in an organic Law [the state constitution] the better. Such a document should have an ample bill of rights so as to secure the largest personal liberty consistent with proper administration of the government and should be so framed as to give the Legislature full power over all corporations and full power over the question of taxation. Novel features should be avoided as much as possible in a Constitution leaving experiments to the Law making power which is more quickly responsive to the will of the people.[2]

How did the delegates respond to the points raised by Governor Semple, as well as other issues? First, there is the question of the long-term allocation of power. Today, little attention is paid to this aspect of constitutions and far more time is devoted to bills of rights. While bills of rights are essential, I believe that the most important thing constitutions do is to allocate power—flowing from the people to the government. The assignments of power in the Washington Constitution are quite comprehensive and, in some ways, quite detailed.

The constitution established the principle of one person-one vote, and any fair reading shows quite conclusively a directive for the bicameral legislature to apportion legislative districts based on census data. Unfortunately, that was not done for most of our history—not until the state came under a federal court order in 1965. In practice, then, originally Washington did not practice one person-one vote in legislative apportionment.

In looking at other issues, Article 2, Section 28, Subsections 1 to 18 had a host of limitations regarding special private legislation—obviously, the constitution was meant to get at some particular problems that existed during the territorial period. A few examples will give the flavor of these concerns and how the framers handled them. The legislature was prohibited from enacting any private or special laws in the following cases:

> 6. For granting corporate powers or privileges…
> 9. From giving effect to invalid deeds, wills or other instruments [there apparently were some lawyers in Olympia in those days taking care of their clients]…
> 14. Remitting fines, penalties or forfeitures…
> 17. For limitation of civil or criminal actions.

Article 2 also included provisions against logrolling (tradeoffs of support between legislators) that have worked fairly well over the years. To prevent logrolling, clarity in legislating is demanded. For instance, Section 19 provides that there shall be only one subject in a bill—today, the 9-member state supreme court is called upon constantly to define what that means. In addition, the subject of a bill shall be in the title itself. Section 38 forbids any amendment or change in a bill that is not within the scope and object of the bill. As a result, presiding officers and the lieutenant governor are constantly ruling on whether an amendment to a bill is within a bill's scope and object.

There are some very specific provisions on bribery and corrupt solicitation (Article 2, Section 30). Although the federal Constitution has no similar measures, Washington Territory previously had experienced some problems of this kind.

Article 2, Section 33 deals with the unhappy subject of "alien land" ownership. In 1885–1886, a wave of anti-Chinese agitation had swept across the West, with outbreaks occurring in both Seattle and Tacoma. At least one school of thought holds that the alien land provision was an anti-Asian piece of constitutional tinkering. I am convinced it was not. In the convention debate on this issue, those who supported the alien land provision were instead focusing on the fact that 21 million acres in the United States already were owned by foreign syndicates—European, British, and others—and thus foreign ownership was a growing concern. Those on the other side of the issue said that the new state should not inhibit foreign capital needed for development. In any event, it later became clear that this unfortunate provision was used as an exclusionary device against Japanese who owned land in Washington. (Finally, after a number of attempts, the alien land provision was stricken from the constitution in 1966.)

In dealing with the executive branch of government, the framers had a singular aversion to any concentrations of power—from this antipathy, we get our fractionated executive. The constitution designated eight separately elected statewide executive officials—governor, lieutenant governor, state treasurer, secretary of state, attorney general, state auditor, commissioner of public lands, and superintendent of public instruction (in 1907, the state legislature created a ninth—the insurance commissioner). Each operates independently, and each has control over the administration of substantial appropriations. In fact, the governor controls the allocation of only about one-third of the monies appropriated by the legislature. Also, a provision mandated that no salary increases could be received during the term of any executive (a restriction that was repealed in 1968). The convention considered giving the governor the power to set an agenda when the legislature was called into special session, but this was not done and governors ever since have regretted it.

The most interesting characteristic of the state's judiciary is its unified court system. Washington did not fall into the trap of some eastern states by creating a variety of courts—e.g., common pleas, oyer and terminer, probate, and surrogate courts. Washington has one court of general jurisdiction, the superior court. In the constitutional convention, however, there was an attempt to amend Article 4, Section 3 relative to the election of supreme court judges by allowing a restrictive voting procedure. The whole idea, stated quite candidly on the floor by the Democratic minority, rested on the assumption that without the proposed amendment the people would elect only Republicans. When the matter came up for a decision, the convention rejected it on a straight party-line vote, making the sanguine comments of delegate John R. Kinnear about the lack of partisanship seem a bit disingenuous.

Another provision, Article 4, Section 8, restricted absenteeism among judges:

Any judicial officer who shall absent himself from the state for more than sixty consecutive days shall be deemed to have forfeited his office: *Provided,* That in cases of extreme necessity the governor may extend the leave of absence such time as the necessity therefor shall exist.

In short, it allowed for the riddance of any judge guilty of excessive absences.

Article 12 dealt with business regulation—as already indicated, the framers were leery of corporate power, while also realizing that corporations were essential to Washington's growth and prosperity. The dilemma lay in providing enough regulation to control corporations, but not so much as to discourage out-of-state investors. Washington then depended in large measure on outside investment in manufacturing, transportation, natural resources extraction, real estate, and other businesses. Where to draw the line was, and continues today, to be the question. A century ago, the framers did not know the answer, but they did the best they could. Article 12 seems to have worked reasonably well, afterward being amended only three times. Included are a number of specific protective provisions against watered stocks, trusts, and monopolies. A variety of special privileges for the legislature included legislative extension of existing franchises.

The foregoing list suggests only some of the actions framers took to make sure that no person or governmental or other body gained excessive power. One other office is something of a curiosity, at least in the tenure of its occupant. What about the concentrations of power in the judicial system? More specifically, what about the chief justice? In its complexity, the constitutional stipulation concerning that official resembles tide tables, eclipses of the sun, and phases of the moon. It works like this: every two years three of the justices are scheduled to run for reelection two years hence. Of that group, the senior justice elected to a full term and who has least recently had the post becomes the chief justice. Although carrying a distinguished title and onerous responsibilities, it is really a highly ephemeral office.

Some specific provisions in the constitution addressed local problems, often to the amusement of modern-day Washingtonians. Article 2, Section 24 originally stated that the legislature could not authorize a lottery or grant a divorce. Of course, the lottery restriction has disappeared, but the legislature still cannot grant an individual divorce. A peculiar set of historical circumstances helps explain this restraint. The second territorial governor, Fayette McMullen, came to Washington with two thoughts in mind—to secure a divorce, and then get out of the territory as quickly as possible and return to Virginia where he planned to marry the wealthiest woman in the commonwealth. He accomplished both.[3] Convention delegates were familiar with the shameful story and wished to make certain that nothing like this happened again.

Article 1, Section 24 is another example of a response to some other specific local circumstances of late territorial times:

> The right of the individual citizen to bear arms in defense of himself, or the state, shall not be impaired, but nothing in this section shall be construed as authorizing individuals or corporations to organize, maintain or employ an armed body of men.

Students of constitutional law will recognize that this guarantee of the right to bear arms is substantially different from a similar provision in the U.S. Constitution.[4] Because of the existing federal stipulation, this state assurance may seem trivial. Again, however, there is a historic derivation. In 1888 at Cle Elum and Roslyn, the railroad bosses owning the mines faced a workers' strike and brought in armed strikebreakers. Without debate, at least as shown by the convention journal, the delegates apparently reacted adversely to a corporation's importation of a privately organized and employed "armed body of men." In effect, private armies or private militias are prohibited in Washington.

The above provisions are fairly straightforward. Difficulties arise, however, when the state supreme court is called upon to interpret the meaning of the more arcane and ambiguous parts of the constitution. The power of the federal judicial branch to interpret the U.S. Constitution was recognized by many prominent Americans from the beginning. In Number 78 of *The Federalist,* Hamilton concisely set out the notion of judicial review. Then, in the great case of *Marbury v. Madison* (1803), Chief Justice John Marshall stated decisively that the U.S. Supreme Court had the power of judicial review—i.e., the right to review legislative acts and to declare unconstitutional those in conflict with the Constitution. The states, too, had adopted this same kind of court view in their own domains.

Then, what is it that courts do? Essentially, when courts interpret parts of a constitution they take the "empty vessel" of the words in the document and try to pour meaning into them. A reading of the U.S. Constitution and the Washington Constitution will readily provide an understanding of this point. The words read well and there is some meaning in them. But what do the words represent when they come face-to-face with a specific situation? Judges are constantly called upon to declare the meaning of a constitution in this context. How do they go about doing it? When courts become embroiled in controversy, as they do from time to time, it is usually because of public disagreement with an interpretation.

Constitutional interpretation is no different from interpreting any other kind of document. Ultimately, four steps are taken, although the search for a solution can end with success at any of the points.

First, courts look at the text itself. What are the words? What is their meaning? While this analysis is good as a beginning, it usually is not the final answer. The meanings of words can change over time—sometimes very quickly in just a few years; other times, over several decades or longer. Words that may have been appropriate in 1889 to explain a set of circumstances do not necessarily have the same definitions a century later.

Second, after a court has reviewed the text, it tries to discern the intent of the constitution's framers. What did they have in mind? What were their intentions when they put the words on paper? In fact, a great controversy now exists over whether or not contemporary judges should look back and try to discover the framers' intent. While there are honorable people on both sides of the dispute, those who believe that the historical viewpoint is important, I think, have by far the better case. It seems altogether logical that a judge should at least attempt to discover the original writers' viewpoint.

The notes of James Madison and other delegates who prepared the U.S. Constitution remain available today, but this is not the case regarding Washington's constitutional framers. In Olympia, two shorthand reporters—the best in the territory, so the record indicates—came to the convention to take down every word, and they did, in fact, compile a complete record. The convention then adjourned, but without paying the reporters, who consequently gathered their notes and went home. The state never offered payment, and the convention notes apparently were never transcribed.

One set of notes seems to have been lost in the transfer from one office to another. As for the other set, there are two conflicting stories. One version has the documents simply being tossed into a furnace by one of the shorthand reporters—a rather prosaic ending. A perhaps more believable account claims that the notes remained stored in the attic of a frame house in Tacoma until sometime in the 1930s, when the residence burned down. In any event, there is no detailed official record of the Washington constitutional convention, so reliance must be put on the bare-bones official journal, unofficial contemporary accounts, newspaper articles, recollections, and reminiscences. Interestingly enough, these sources together are better than might be expected; they provide a fairly adequate record for today's judges.

Third, courts look at the gloss that has been placed upon the words, both in earlier Washington Supreme Court decisions, and by courts in other state jurisdictions that have similar or identical provisions in their constitutions.

Fourth—and this is the difficult part—judges must try to apply the constitution to contemporary times. What did the constitution mean in 1889? This is important. But it is equally important to decide what the words mean a century later when applied to particular modem problems and situations that, quite literally, often were never imagined by those who wrote the document in 1889. The challenge, then, is to convey the constitution from 1889 to the present day.

Some examples of this process will illustrate how the crucial function of constitutional interpretation is carried out by today's Washington State Supreme Court. In effect, what happens when old principles are applied to new facts? We can start with Article 8, Section 5, dealing with the lending of state credit, which reads in its entirety:

> The credit of the state shall not, in any manner be given or loaned to, or in aid of, any individual, association, company or corporation.

This short provision sounds straightforward and unambiguous, and back in 1889 it probably was. For example, the state could not lend public money to a railroad, which was a major public concern at the time; everyone understood precisely what the framers were talking about. But a century later, circumstances had taken on a somewhat different cast. By 1985, the state had established the Washington Higher Education Facilities Authority, which was allowed to enter the financial market and sell bonds. The proceeds from the bonds were then lent to various private colleges and universities for the construction of campus buildings.

During the intervening century since 1889, the state had developed different needs. Consequently, to meet those new demands, it had adopted a different kind of financing to take advantage of a different tax system. The genius of the Washington Higher Education Facilities Authority started soon after the state borrowed money. First, whoever bought the bonds did not have to pay income tax on the interest. Second, the paying off of the bonds was done at a lower interest rate. Thus, there was a substantial fiscal advantage to both the borrower and lender. In addition, the State of Washington was not liable for default because these were not general obligation bonds, but rather nonrecourse revenue bonds. This meant that in the event of default there was no recourse against the state by the lender; the bonds were funded by revenues paid by the individual colleges and universities.

In the case of *Higher Education Facilities Authority v. Gardner* (1985), Governor Booth Gardner had refused to sign off on bond documents, resulting in an application for a writ of mandamus, which would order him to do so. The Washington State Supreme Court had struggled for about 15 years with the question of the lending of state credit (i.e., regarding Article 8, Section 5). In this instance, the court finally did clarify what the constitution meant, by deciding that the non-recourse revenue bonds of this nature were not banned by the constitutional provision. The court, then, took old principles, applied them to new facts, and remained, I think, entirely consistent with the intent of those who framed the constitution.

The second example is one that may be more familiar—it is Article 9, Section 1, which contains the celebrated statement:

> It is the paramount duty of the state to make ample provision for the education of all children residing within its borders, without distinction or preference on account of race, color, caste, or sex.

What do these marvelous words mean? Nobody ever had to say. For about 80 years, it was one of those great sentences in the constitution that went uninterpreted. The situation was unique, because not a single other state constitution has language identical to this provision. Yet, the meaning of the words was a mystery because no one had ever actually explored the depths of the "paramount duty" provision. Finally, in the 1950s and 1960s, old doctrine and new facts intertwined.

Beginning in about 1957 and running well into the late 1960s and early 1970s, the legislature proved unwilling to appropriate the kind of monies considered necessary to fully maintain and operate the public schools. Consequently, public schools had resorted to special levies presented to voters. Such a revenue source may be appropriate for enrichment programs, and might be acceptable for 5 or 10 percent coverage of maintenance and operation costs. But, by the late 1960s and the early 1970s, reliance on levies was reaching 35 or 40 percent of maintenance and operation costs. The Washington Constitution requires a 40 percent voter turnout and a 60 percent voter approval rate on special levies. With these rather stringent constitutional requirements regarding voting—and with perhaps 40 percent of a school district's maintenance and operation budget riding on the outcome—the schools and students became engaged in something of a periodic financial crap shoot, and not the "orderly" financial management of public schools.

In the mid-1970s, a Seattle school district brought action that resulted in the celebrated case of *Seattle School District No. 1 v. State* (1978). The state supreme court decided that the State of Washington must accept the paramount duty and obligation to make "ample provision for the education of all children" within its boundaries. This responsibility, the court held, does not rest on the local school districts, to be met by special levies, but rather on the state, which has an obligation to provide and fund basic education. In a lawsuit a few years later, the court added a definition of basic education.

Was the court true to the thoughts of the framers here? The court's vote of 6 to 3 on the Seattle school district case would suggest considerable sentiment on both sides of the issue. Yet, taking into account, the school funding problems of the 1960s and early 1970s, along with the absolute preeminence that the constitution's writers gave to public education, particularly in using the words "paramount duty," the action taken by the court seems altogether appropriate and consonant with the intent of the framers.

Next we can consider the Declaration of Rights, a part of the state constitution that for years drew little attention, except for an article dealing with the freedom of religion. This article received special attention when the courts discovered that its meaning was so strictly construed as to prohibit the hiring of chaplains at various state institutions, such as prisons and facilities for the blind. An amendment (Article 1, Section 11) proved necessary to allow the appointment of these chaplains. Otherwise, the Declaration of Rights essentially lay fallow for many years.

The constitutional convention heard little argument about this part, except for two sections. One was on the "taking clause"—i.e., the matter of eminent domain, which filled several pages of discussion in the journal. The other regarded the Preamble to the constitution, where the issue became whether or not to include a reference to a deity. The original version, reported from the committee to the convention, did not do so: "We, the people of the State of Washington, to secure the blessings of liberty, ensure domestic tranquility and preserve our rights, do ordain this constitution."

This language is similar to the Preamble to the U.S. Constitution, but was defeated in Olympia on the floor, 45 to 22. An alternative—"We, the people of the State of Washington, grateful to the Supreme Ruler of the Universe for our liberties, do ordain this constitution"—was adopted overwhelmingly, 55 to 19, and is still in the constitution.

Other parts of the Declaration of Rights are identical to those in the U.S. Constitution, while elsewhere the language differs somewhat from the federal Bill of Rights. The full impact of the differences is not readily apparent.

Article 1, Section 22 provides for the constitutional *right of appeal* in all criminal prosecutions. About half the state constitutions have a similar provision, but it is not contained in the federal Bill of Rights. Another area in which a substantial amount of controversy has arisen in recent years is Article 1, Section 5 (freedom of speech), which says: "Every person may freely speak, write and publish on all subjects, being responsible for the abuse of that right."

Another subject of spirited discussion concerns Article 1, Section 7, which is the state's version of the federal Fourth Amendment, although the language is completely different. It reads: "No person shall be disturbed in his private affairs, or his home invaded, without authority of law."

Each of these provisions, with the exception of the right of appeal, has been the source of lively debate before the Washington State Supreme Court in recent years. In fact, state courts nationwide have revived their interest in their own constitutions. Some observers have said that this resurgence is the result of "liberals" and "moderates" on the state supreme courts who think the U.S. Supreme Court was becoming more "conservative" and who wanted to prevent such conservatism from occurring in their states. This is a highly questionable analysis. Rather, something more profound is happening.

To set the stage, relatively few cases arose during the past century involving the Declaration of Rights of the Washington State Constitution, particularly in comparison with the great number of cases concerning the federal Bill of Rights. Furthermore, those cases that did arise were primarily noted for not having any real need of analysis of the Washington Constitution's language, thus interpretation and new precedent was minimal. Before 1960, it seemed, there was hardly any reason to look at the state's Declaration of Rights.

Since 1960, however, the first eight amendments of the federal Bill of Rights have been incorporated into the state picture—i.e., made to apply to the states as well as the federal government. It should also be noted that members of the U.S. Supreme Court now were encouraging state courts to give more attention to their own constitutions.

Furthermore, when state supreme court justices take the oath of office, they swear to uphold the Constitution of the United States and the constitution and laws of the State of Washington. To honor such a pledge, it was becoming absolutely necessary for the justices to gain the fullest understanding of the Washington Constitution, and that is what they have been doing.

In a celebrated case from the Washington State University campus, *State v. Chrisman* (1980) the issue was the privacy of a student's dormitory room where a police officer had found a banned drug. The Washington Supreme Court, excluding certain evidence, reversed the conviction of the defendant, basing its action on an understanding of the federal Fourth Amendment, which prohibits unreasonable searches and seizures. The case went to the U.S. Supreme Court, which disagreed with this interpretation of the Fourth Amendment and reversed the state decision. On remand, or reconsignment, from the U.S. Supreme Court, the state supreme court reconsidered the case and again reversed the conviction, this time relying on the state constitution's protection of privacy (Article 1, Section 7) to exclude the evidence. The Washington court found the state's Declaration of Rights gave greater protection to the individual than did the federal Bill of Rights. Because the U.S. Supreme Court may not review the interpretation by a state court of its state constitution, the decision stood.

A final observation on the interpretation of the Declaration of Rights concerns the fundamental premises of the framers when they wrote the document. The difficulties involved here may be illustrated by the case of *Alderwood Associates v. Washington Environmental Council* (1981)—4 of the 9 justices were on the plurality, 1 had a separate opinion, but in concurrence with the result of the plurality, and 4 dissented. The issue was whether the Washington Environmental Council could collect signatures at the Alderwood Mall north of Seattle when the private owners of the shopping center did not want them to do so. As a matter of fact, the owners got an order enjoining the collection of the signatures.

The division in the court reflected the difficulty of understanding the fundamental premises of the framers. Did the framers mean that the Declaration of Rights should protect individuals against the government, which is the standard doctrine, or did they mean that it should protect persons not only against the government, but also against private citizens as well? In other words, are individuals shielded not only against the City of Seattle, King County, or the State of Washington in free speech matters, but also against the Alderwood Mall or other private citizens who may infringe upon their rights of free speech? This is an extremely important issue and has stimulated intense discussion in the legal community.

To discover the framers' intent here involves more than a textual analysis or study on a section-by-section or word-by-word basis. What one has to discover is the underlying and fundamental premise—i.e., against whom was this safeguard to be applied: the individual, as well as the state? Most courts that have acted on the issue in recent years have taken the view that the purpose of a declaration of rights is to protect the individual against the state, not one individual against another. It is my belief that this was the fundamental premise of the Washington framers. In the *Alderwood* case, however, 4 justices backed the protection of individuals against individuals, while the remaining 5 justices found that the protections of the Declaration of Rights applied only to the acts of government. That issue was not dispositive of the case, however, as a different combination of 5 justices ended up agreeing (based on differing rationales) that the environmentalists could collect signatures at the mall. Even though the decision held that the environmentalists had the right to collect signatures, the division on the court suggests that in Washington the larger issue as to the application of the Declaration of Rights is far from settled.[5]

Today, Washingtonians stand in the lengthening shadow of those individuals who gathered at Olympia in the summer of 1889 to write the constitution for a new state. The framers did their job well. The constitution they formed in 1889 is, in its essentials, just as valid and just as vibrant today as it was a century ago.

The responsibility facing modem Washingtonians, then, is in grasping the vision that the delegates had for the 42nd state.

Suggestions for Further Reading

Beckett, Paul L. *From Wilderness to Enabling Act: The Evolution of a State of Washington.* Pullman: Washington State University Press, 1968.

Clayton, Cornell W., Lance T. LeLoup, and Nicholas P. Lovrich, eds., Foreword by David Ammons. *Washington State Government and Politics.* Pullman: Washington State University Press, 2004.

"Drafting Washington's State Constitution: A Newspaperman Offers His Comments on the Olympia Convention of 1889." *Pacific Northwest Quarterly* 45 (January 1957):22–24.

Knapp, Lebbeus J. "The Origin of the Constitution of the State of Washington." *Washington Historical Quarterly* 4 (October 1913):227–87.

Mires, Austin. "Remarks on the Constitution of the State of Washington." *Washington Historical Quarterly* 22 (October 1931): 276–88.

Nice, David, John Pierce, and Charles Sheldon, eds. *Government and Politics in the Evergreen State.* Pullman: Washington State University Press, 1992.

Rosenow, Beverly P., ed. *The Journal of the Washington State Constitutional Convention, 1889.* Seattle: Book Publishing Co., 1962.

Sheldon, Charles H. *A Century of Judging: A Political History of the Washington Supreme Court.* Seattle: University of Washington Press, 1987.

_____. *The Washington High Bench: A Biographical History of the State Supreme Court, 1889–1991*. Pullman: Washington State University Press, 1992.

Notes

1. John R. Kinnear, "Notes on the Constitutional Convention," *Washington Historical Quarterly* 4 (October 1913):277.
2. S.R. Frazier to Eugene Semple, January 28, 1889, and Semple to Frazier, January 30, 1889, Washington State Archives, Olympia.
3. For a somewhat different version of this story, see Gordon Newell, *Rogues, Buffoons, and Statesmen* (Seattle: Hangman Press-Superior Publishing, 1975), 33–34.
4. Bill of Rights, Article II: "A well regulated Militia, being necessary to the security of a free State, the right of the people to keep and bear Arms shall not be infringed."
5. This issue appears to have been settled in *Southcenter Joint Venture v. National Democratic Policy Committee,* 113 Wn.2d 413, 430, 790 P.2d 1282 (1989): "Accordingly, we hold that the free speech provision of our state constitution protects an individual only against actions of the State; it does not protect against actions of other private individuals."

VIII
Growing Up American in
the Pacific Northwest

Gordon Hirabayashi

*D*URING WORLD WAR II *some 112,000 persons of Japanese descent, about 70,000 of whom were American citizens, were removed from their homes along the Pacific Coast and placed in detention camps. Gordon Hirabayashi, while a senior at the University of Washington in 1942, was arrested and convicted for resisting the curfew and violating a military internment order. He was imprisoned for a year.*

His early landmark case, Hirabayashi v. United States *in 1943, became the first challenge of the wartime relocation program to reach the Supreme Court. Although the ruling was unfavorable, one justice commented that the curfew order bore "a melancholy resemblance to the treatment [then being] accorded members of the Jewish race in Germany and other parts of Europe."*

During the 1980s, Hirabayashi's petition for a rehearing based on coram nobis, *a little-known recourse for those whose trials were flawed by "fundamental error" or "manifest injustice," resulted in a judicial review. In 1987, the Ninth U.S. Circuit Court of Appeals reversed his wartime convictions; the federal attorneys chose not to take the case to the Supreme Court. His judicial efforts were featured on the television news show* 60 Minutes, *and in a PBS documentary,* A Personal Matter: Gordon Hirabayashi v. the United States.

For Washingtonians, especially after statehood in 1889, growing up meant growing up American. It meant the acquisition of American values as expressed in the Declaration of Independence; it also meant learning to subscribe to and uphold the Constitution, including the Bill of Rights and other amendments. But how does a Washingtonian who is a member of a visible minority group handle the concepts of democracy on one hand and the experiences of racism on the other? For such an individual, growing up American is a formidable challenge. The obstacles of defeatism, bitterness, and succumbing to a second-class status are constantly present.

What, then, are the options for an American citizen confronted with the dilemma of either obeying a U.S. Army general's proclamation or upholding the Constitution? This essay, based on considered reminiscence and subsequent reflection, explores how one Washingtonian of Japanese descent coped with the World War II relocation program.

The morning of Sunday, December 7, 1941, was quiet and unusually pleasant in Seattle. At midday, many of those attending the University Friends Meeting (Quakers) had drifted outside to visit and enjoy the day. Then, one of our members who had stayed close to the radio that morning hurriedly approached the rest of us and broke the shocking news: Japan had bombed Pearl Harbor; we were at war!

Coping with the Wartime Crisis

On the one hand, news of war alone was startling. It was unreal and unbelievable. On the other hand, the tragedy of a war between my country of birth, the United States, and my country of heritage, Japan, was the worst possible scenario I could imagine. With racism already rampant on the West Coast, particularly toward those of Asian descent, how would we confront additional hostility and hysteria? All of my parent's generation were *Issei* immigrants (legally) ineligible for naturalization; war with Japan automatically transformed them, at least technically, into "enemy aliens." It would not be until 1952 that they could become American citizens.

On February 19, 1942, two and a half months after the Pearl Harbor attack and the declaration of war on Japan, President Franklin D. Roosevelt, acting under his emergency war powers, issued Executive Order 9066. That decree delegated broad powers to the secretary of war, and to the military commanders under him, to protect the national security, including removal of individuals from military areas. Entire groups of people might be transferred based on "reasonable classification." For several months, a clandestine power struggle had raged between the War and Justice departments over the various gray areas of authority in the execution of national security measures. Executive Order 9066 signaled victory for the War Department.

At the time of America's entrance into World War II, the federal government established the peculiar category of *non-alien,* as in "all persons of Japanese ancestry, both alien and non-alien." A citizen, according to the dictionary, is "a member of a state; a person, native or naturalized, who owes allegiance to a state, and is entitled to protection from it." An alien is someone who is not a citizen. What, then, was a non-alien? Why did the government not straightforwardly say "both aliens and some citizens"? Yet the government soon posted an official proclamation on post office bulletin boards and telephone poles announcing the forthcoming exclusion of certain classes of persons from designated areas. It began with: NOTICE: TO ALL PERSONS OF JAPANESE ANCESTRY, BOTH ALIEN AND NON-ALIEN. I felt forsaken as a citizen to be included in this strange kind of categorization. It appeared that the federal government was more interested in suspending citizens' rights than in protecting constitutional guarantees regardless of race, creed, religion, or national origin.

Another proclamation, issued March 24, 1942, restricted the movement of certain individuals and was generally referred to as the curfew order. In the West Coast command area, General John L. DeWitt's curfew confined all enemy aliens (German, Italian, and Japanese nationals), *plus non-aliens of Japanese ancestry*, to their residences between 8:00 p.m. and 6:00 a.m. and restricted travel to a radius of five miles from their homes. It was devastating to be singled out as somehow sinister because of ancestry. Nevertheless, in accordance with my upbringing, it was my initial intent to obey the orders. I was living in an international dormitory, Eagleson Hall, adjoining the University of Washington campus. My dozen dorm mates all became my volunteer timekeepers. "Gordon, it's five minutes to eight," one would say. I would pick up my books and rush back from the library or the coffee shop. After several days of this routine, the question came to me while I was hurrying home: "Why am I rushing back and my dorm mates are not? Am I not an American citizen the same as they?" The answer was obvious to me, so I turned around and went back to the library. Thereafter, I ignored the curfew. I never was arrested, probably because the curfew seemed as strange to the police as it was to citizens in general, especially in the University District.

Many personal crises and momentous decisions lay ahead. Fortunately at the time, I was unaware of that future. There was no time for a favorite pastime—procrastination. Neither was there the leisure to ascertain the right course of action after the usual reflective consideration. I had to make decisions immediately. Distinctions between realistic actions and idealistic ones became clouded without the customary criteria available. Accurate information was hard to come by. Frequently, in such circumstances, those in my situation are forced to follow their ideals, their principles, as the best way to be realistic.

Shortly after I decided to ignore the curfew came the forced removal proclamation, euphemistically calling for "evacuation" from the western half of Washington and Oregon, all of California, and the southern half of Arizona. Evacuation is a humanitarian term usually meaning to remove a population for its safety, in the face of earthquake, fire, flood, or danger of military attack. In this case, it was clearly a tactic employed by the government to sugarcoat an oppressive action. Nazi Germany also resorted to similar euphemisms. I had felt that the rumored federal exclusion and detention orders, when they appeared, would actually apply only to enemy aliens, not to citizens or so-called "non-aliens." I had these hopes dashed when I learned that the decrees did indeed mean "all persons of Japanese ancestry, both alien and non-alien." Significantly, enemy aliens of German and Italian ancestry were not included.

In the meantime where was the Constitution? On the West Coast in 1942, the military situation did not warrant imposing martial law, as had been invoked in Hawaii immediately after the Pearl Harbor attack. Thus, the government did not suspend constitutional rights in a wholesale manner and the courts, as well as most other civilian institutions, remained in operation. Today, it seems unbelievable that the United States was capable of the racism and gross disregard of the Constitution that were about to occur.

At the end of winter term in March 1942, I dropped out of the university. It was clear to me that I would not be around long enough to complete the spring session. I then volunteered for the newly established Seattle Branch of the American Friends Service Committee (Quakers). My assignment involved helping those Japanese American families whose fathers had been detained immediately after Pearl Harbor. The mothers were busy closing up the houses, arranging for storage, and preparing young children to carry their things on the trek to internment camps. In early April 1942, while helping these families get to the pick-up station for the bus ride to the Puyallup fairgrounds, I assumed that in a few weeks I would be joining them.

A few days later, I confronted another thought: if I could not accept the curfew, how could I acquiesce in this wholesale uprooting and forced confinement behind barbed wire? As with the curfew issue, I knew that I could not submit to exclusion. It was not just a refusal, a negative action; rather it was my earnest intent as an American citizen to uphold the Constitution, the most positive action available to a citizen. Even though the exclusionary orders bore the imprimatur of the Western Defense Command on behalf of the U.S. government, I knew I must refuse what I considered to be a gross violation of the Constitution. It was important, even obligatory, in order for me to maintain my standing as an American.

Strange as this position seemed to many at the time, I was attempting to behave as a responsible citizen, as other Americans around me were doing with different forms of patriotism. So, like the other Americans who were not covered by the proclamations, I ignored the curfew.

Although I had dropped out of the university, I arranged to remain in the dormitory near the campus and continue my job of tending the furnace and sweeping the floors. Such temporary arrangements were not unusual then, as many students were awaiting calls to military service or were getting ready to leave for work in defense plants. My parents, who, before leaving Japan, had converted from Buddhism to a non-institutionalized form of Christianity called *Mukyokai,* were still living in the White River valley south of Seattle. My mother ran a roadside produce store near Auburn and my father worked on a nearby farm. They were expecting to be uprooted sometime in May. They did not know where they would be moved, but thought that I would come home in time to join them for the exodus. I had to explain what was happening to me, and tell them that I would not be joining them. Because of travel restrictions and the demands on my time by the Quaker service work, I had to telephone home to give my parents this unpleasant news.

When my mother heard my reasons, she complimented me for straight thinking and the courage to make such a decision. She agreed with the soundness of my position and said that she and my father wholeheartedly supported my stand. "But," she concluded, "we are all in a very special situation. If our family gets separated, we may never get back together again. Please," she pleaded, "put your principles aside on this occasion, come home, and move with us. We don't know where we are going or for how long, and heaven knows what will happen to you if you confront the government. Please come home."

As much as possible, I tried to assure her that with my father and my two high-school-age brothers on hand, the family would be able to meet the crisis. As for myself, I told her, I had friends and a support group behind me. Undoubtedly, I would be arrested, but she need not worry, that I would be treated like the hero in *The Count of Monte Cristo,* a novel she had read recently. Finally my mother broke down and pleaded with me to come home to keep the family together. If the government could uproot a whole group on the basis of ancestry, she worried, it could easily move our family around to different places, making it difficult for us ever to find each other again. My mother's tears and apprehension were the hardest things I had to face in the entire crisis. But I had to refuse her pleas. After I hung up, a considerable time elapsed before the tears on my cheeks and in my heart dried. Because of strong family ties, I felt guilty for a long time.

Shortly after my parents moved from a temporary camp in Pinedale, near Fresno, California, to the more permanent Tule Lake camp in northern

California, two women who had earlier been uprooted from the Los Angeles area trudged the dusty road from the opposite end of the compound looking for my mother. When they finally located her, the two women said they had heard that the mother of the fellow in jail fighting for their rights was housed in that block. They had come to greet her and to say "Thank you!" In recounting this episode, my mother wrote about what a great lift she had received from that visit. When I read her letter, the weight of family guilt suddenly disappeared. I knew then that nothing I could have said or done by being with her could have given her greater satisfaction.

My legal battle was having its ups and downs. A day or so after I made my decision to challenge the federal proclamations, Mary Farquharson, state senator from the University District and a YMCA and YWCA supporter, came to see me at Eagleson Hall. She had heard that I was going to challenge the forced removal proclamation. When I confirmed the rumor, the senator stated her full and unconditional support for my position and asked if I was planning to take legal action. So far, I explained, I had my hands full just making my personal stand. While I was aware that a test case was possible, I had not given it much thought. She told me she was part of a local action group seriously concerned about the erosion of citizens' rights in the wake of war hysteria, including the injustice to Japanese Americans. If I did not already have plans for a legal battle, Senator Farquharson said, her group wanted to assume that responsibility. It would provide them with a foothold to stem a threatened wartime assault on civil liberties, and at the same time give them an opportunity to deal with a specific case.

A strategy emerged. The Seattle group, composed of civil liberties advocates, Quakers, members of peace organizations, and professors, business people, and ministers in the University District, would take the initial steps. Then the national American Civil Liberties Union (ACLU) would take over. Senator Farquharson had received assurances of support from Roger Baldwin, executive director of the national ACLU. Unfortunately, Baldwin later had to tell Farquharson that the national ACLU board, in a split vote, refused to back him on my case. The main reason, we subsequently learned, was that several of the ACLU board members were faithful adherents of the New Deal reform program and felt compelled to stand by President Roosevelt in the war effort as well.

The heretofore informal local group, in order to manage the rapidly emerging issues, then organized itself as the Gordon Hirabayashi Defense Committee, with businessman Ray Roberts as chair and treasurer, and Senator Farquharson as general secretary. Arthur Barnett, my personal legal advisor and a fellow Quaker, was a member of this local body and endorsed the new plans. As legal liaison, Barnett had the responsibility to find an attorney qualified to handle the complicated constitutional issues. He first secured the services of a capable young lawyer from one of the most prestigious firms in Seattle. When the news of my arraignment appeared in the papers, identifying the lawyer, the Teamsters Union approached the head of the firm and threatened to withdraw its business if the attorney persisted in defending "that Jap." He regretfully left my case. Barnett already had confided to me that finding and keeping an attorney during that period of war hysteria would be difficult. Now he had to secure another lawyer. Fortunately, we acquired an experienced constitutional expert, Frank Walters, who guided my case to the Supreme Court.

Meanwhile, the day after the government forced all other Japanese Americans to leave Seattle, I remained in the now-forbidden city, defying the military order that had required "all persons of Japanese ancestry" to register for evacuation. Not wishing to implicate the University YMCA in "harboring a criminal" because of its care for me, I went with my legal advisor, Arthur Barnett, to the FBI to turn myself in.

While hearing my statement, the FBI agent stopped and asked: "If you feel that strongly about the exclusion order, what did you do about the curfew?"

In return I asked him if he had been out after eight o'clock the previous evening.

He answered yes.

I then responded, "Like you and other Americans, so was I."

He quickly came back with: "Then you have broken the curfew regulation as well as the exclusion order." As a result, I also was charged with ignoring the curfew.

Later, I was taken to meet the Army captain in charge of the uprooting process in the Northwest. During a lengthy conversation, I learned that registration and forced removal in both southern and northern California were a 100 percent success, and that he was determined for the Northwest to be the same. I tried to be cooperative by suggesting that he could order a couple of his men to take me forcibly by automobile to the Puyallup assembly camp, throw me out at the administration building, and quickly drive away. He would then, like California, have his 100 percent record. For an instant he seemed to consider this option, but he soon shook his head, saying: "Can't do it. That would be illegal." I was appalled. Here he was deeply involved in the uprooting and detention behind barbed wire of 112,000 persons without a hearing, purely because of their ancestry, and he could not bring himself to throw in one more because I refused to register for the exclusion and removal proclamation.

After about six weeks in jail, my fellow inmates insisted that I become "mayor" of the "tank." The federal government had rented part of the King County jail as a holding place for those charged in federal cases; the tank had a capacity of 40 persons—half of the space being a large bullpen and the other half containing ten cells with four bunks each. Before I was taken into custody, Barnett warned me that I should be careful in jail because, although my companions might be lawbreakers, they could also feel patriotic and take offense at my stand. Accordingly, the inmates' proposal came as a surprise. The role of mayor involved administering affairs inside the tank, representing their grievances to officials, and keeping the peace. Over my protest that I hardly approved of the existing "kangaroo court" system in the tank, the other prisoners rammed through my election, saying that they would go along with any changes I wanted to make. I agreed to try it for a week—which stretched into five months.

One evening shortly before my October trial in Seattle, the night officer escorted a new "inmate" into the tank. The officer stopped by my cell and asked where the new arrival should be quartered. I joked with him about disturbing us by bringing prisoners in during our sleeping hours. Then I looked at the fellow beside the guard and saw who he was. "It's Dad!" I exclaimed, and arranged to have him placed in my cell. My mother had already been put in the women's tank. Unknown to me, the government had subpoenaed both of my parents as witnesses from the Tule Lake concentration camp in California, presumably to establish the fact that they were from Japan and that I was their son and therefore of Japanese ancestry, making me subject to the curfew and exclusion proclamations.

It was really preposterous. I had never denied my origins but had steadfastly maintained that ancestry did not constitute a crime or a tendency to commit one. Moreover, as an American, I argued that my citizenship was guaranteed by the Constitution regardless of race, creed, color, or national origin. I felt it grossly callous of the government to subpoena my parents as witnesses, and then put them in jail for 10 days. Of course, even a harmless, God-fearing couple of Japanese descent could not obtain a hotel room or other public accommodations at that time. My legal team told me later that they had tried to get the government's permission to lodge my parents privately. When the officials balked, my lawyers then proposed that the owners of the designated home be deputized, and thus my parents would be technically in custody. The officials also refused this suggestion.

But there was a silver lining. I had five wonderful days of visiting with my father before the trial, and another five days afterwards. My mother spent the 10 days being treated like a queen by her fellow inmates, who were street walkers, shoplifters, embezzlers, and the like. On the day of the trial she was late making an appearance because six women prisoners decided to give her a royal beauty treatment, including hair styling, a facial, and a manicure.

Until this visit, my parents had worried about my physical condition. No more! While they noted that the tank was bug-infested and the food greasy, they also learned that the inmates were warm, friendly people. Moreover, I was the mayor of my tank. Nothing I wrote in letters alleviated their concerns about my well-being nearly as much as their trip to Seattle under federal subpoena.

After I had languished in jail for five months, my trial finally came on October 20, 1942. I was charged with both curfew and exclusion order violations. My lawyer argued effectively on constitutional grounds, emphasizing that I had never been accused of posing a danger for espionage or sabotage, the two ostensible reasons for the exclusion proclamation. In the end, however, the presiding judge gave these instructions to the jury (this is a paraphrase since no record of the judge's words appears in the transcript): "You can forget all the talk about the Constitution by the defense. What is relevant here is the public proclamation issued by the Western Defense Command. You are to determine this: is the defendant a person of Japanese ancestry? If so, has he complied with the military curfew and exclusion orders, which are valid and enforceable laws? If he has not, you are instructed to bring in a verdict of guilty."

In actuality that was the conclusion of my "trial"; the obedient jury was out only 10 minutes before returning with a guilty verdict. In spite of the discouraging adverse lower court decisions that found me guilty on both counts, I remained optimistic. I believed that when my case finally reached the U.S. Supreme Court, I would have my day. After all, I reasoned, upholding the Constitution is the *raison d'etre* of that high tribunal. When my appeal reached the Supreme Court, however, I discovered to my dismay that it, too, had gone to war. The highest court in the land ruled unanimously against me on the curfew violation, delaying the exclusion issue for later consideration. In the face of this rejection, I at first questioned the effectiveness of the Constitution. What good was a Constitution if its grand provisions were suspended in time of crisis? That was exactly when individual citizens, especially underdogs, most counted on its basic guarantees.

Fortunately, I did not give up on the Constitution. Perhaps it was something like the lesson expressed in an East African Basuto proverb: "Do not abandon your old values unless there is something of value to replace them." Regardless of the Supreme Court setback, I could not forsake the most fundamental principles upon which I had always based being an American. Instead, I slowly began to revise my perspective under the new circumstances. Until now I had regarded the members of the Supreme Court as a group above ordinary human weaknesses. In my emerging understanding, they became instead a group of nine people endowed with all the noble and ignoble qualities of other human groups. Furthermore, in the 1940s, the court was all male and all white. Most importantly, I began to distinguish between the Constitution and those entrusted to uphold it. The Constitution is not very useful if authorities suspend it each time we run into a crisis.

Growing up in a Hostile Society

At this point I would like to go back to the personal, social, and political climate in the State of Washington as I grew up, and the special kind of bicultural base from which I entered this society and learned to cope with it. I grew up in a rural farm community south of Seattle between Kent and Auburn. My parents were Japanese immigrants. I did not learn to speak English until I began elementary school. Growing up in the pre-World War II period not only exposed me to the hardships of the Great Depression, but also to two kinds of duality—first, the cross-cultural norms of a Japanese ancestry *vis-a-vis* American ways and values, and secondly, the inconsistency of American (also "Occidental" or "Western") ideals versus the practice of them in Washington.

In brief, on the first aspect, Japanese life is group-centered; downgrading the relative importance of the individual. As a result, there is a strong sense of social etiquette (in Japanese, *ōn*); a feeling of duty to the group to which one belongs—family, clan, firm, nation (*giri*); as well as a sense of sympathy and compassion for others (*ninjo*). Certain behavioral characteristics become associated with these concepts, such as an emphasis on self-effacement and a tendency toward understatement. In Japan, self-effacement is balanced by others in the group who counteract the understatements, and generally these patterns are socially equalized.

In Western society, traditional cultural values for Japanese Americans do not always function automatically. The age-old custom of grandparents softening the austere discipline of the parents was frequently missing because the grandparents were absent. Also, the sympathetic support of others in the community, normally expected, often was not present in the new setting.

As an example, Japanese tourists, businessmen, and other visitors to America have frequently reported being hungry after rather lavish dinners held in their honor. The American hostesses had usually stopped encouraging second helpings when the guests modestly said they were full. In Japanese social balancing, however, it is necessary for the dinner guest to start refusing seconds when only half full, knowing that the hostess will continue to bring additional servings until the fourth or even fifth refusal. In other words, Japanese social customs are often misunderstood outside the context in which they normally operate.

Growing up in a Japanese home created serious problems for me at school. Because Japanese students tend to be quiet in classroom discussions (*otonashii* and *enryo*), the teacher would often encourage me by saying: "Speak up, Gordon. What do *you* think?" The restraint of the Japanese value system lay heavily on my shoulders, telling me not to blurt out something nonsensical that would bring shame to me and my family. So I frequently sat silent. However, I was anything but a wallflower socially, taking part in extracurricular activities and the Boy Scouts in which I was a Life Scout and a senior patrol leader.

At school I learned about and subscribed wholeheartedly to American ideals, such as the doctrine in the Declaration of Independence "that all men are created equal; that they are endowed by their Creator with certain unalienable rights; that among these, are life, liberty, and the pursuit of happiness." Before long I realized, however, that these lofty principles fell far short in the practical world where employment inequities and social discrimination existed. Members of minority groups had little hope for becoming school teachers, engineers, or civil servants. Restaurants and hotels refused to cater to them, and public swimming pools and private clubs permitted minorities only through service entrances. This was the social climate in which I grew up during the 1920s and 1930s.

Over and above the hunger and unemployment of the Great Depression in the 1930s, an overt national double standard on equality and racism complicated things for minority groups. Human rights laws virtually did not exist then. For example, the exclusions of minorities from owning housing in the better residential areas were often backed by private contracts and therefore were legally enforceable. In addition to zoning provisions, restrictive covenants on real estate often specified that resale must be to a "white gentile," or terms to that effect. Not until after World War II were such covenants ruled unconstitutional.

In 1940 while attending the Presidents' School, a leadership training program jointly sponsored by the YMCA and YWCA at Columbia University in New York City, I became more aware of the special conditions existing in Washington. About 25 of us from universities across the country, mostly working students, organized our own extracurricular activities, using the subway for transportation to free museums and inexpensive eating places. In New York, I was surprised to discover, the *only* condition that determined my participation in these social events was whether I could afford them. Back home I always had to consider whether I would be refused admission at the door for racial reasons. During the time in New York, therefore, I experienced a new dimension of freedom and equality.

By contrast, a year later and just before the war, I went to the Downtown YMCA in Seattle to apply for a job. This position had ideal hours for a working student of 4 p.m. to 10 p.m. I was told about it by the University of Washington YMCA director, who had been asked by the Downtown YMCA to recommend a suitable student applicant. When I appeared for the scheduled interview, I had to wait an hour. Most of this time I spent reading the "Y" bulletin board, filled with news, pictures, and statements about the organization's world brotherhood programs. Strangely enough, however, I suddenly got the idea that I was not the kind of student employee the Downtown YMCA wanted.

When the associate director finally invited me into his office, he appeared ill at ease and spent some time getting around to saying that the job was not for me—nothing personal, you understand. Since he had served the "Y" overseas in China, he must have sorely dreaded the interview. I sensed his plight, but felt a responsibility to have him give me an explanation, although I did not want to be discourteous. Finally, he said that since the Downtown YMCA must raise funds to run its world brotherhood programs, it could not risk alienating potential contributors by placing a non-white attendant at the front desk. When I expressed difficulty in understanding the inconsistency of violating the spirit of world brotherhood in order to raise money for world brotherhood, he turned red and could not speak for a while. After we had discussed the matter for about 20 minutes, I left his office with the satisfaction that I had made my point.

Following World War II, human rights legislation (such as fair employment and open accommodations acts) reduced many of the more blatant forms of discrimination, but disappointments continued. When I was released from prison for the final time in 1945, I explored the idea of utilizing some of the baking skills that I had learned behind bars. A bakery in the University

District expressed interest in hiring me, but I had to be a union member first. Reportedly, the union had never allowed a minority person to join its ranks. On the basis that I lacked certified work experience, the union would not accept me, and without this membership the employer could not hire me. So I returned to the university to complete my final undergraduate year.

After earning my Bachelor of Arts degree, my professors encouraged me to enter the graduate program in sociology and offered a teaching assistantship. The next year I was recommended for a renewal with a "promotion" to teaching associate, which meant I would be involved in classroom instruction. At this point, the university president questioned the appointment of a person with a prison record to a position where he would be teaching students. The sociology chair defended the job offer, stating that, although the federal government had pressed its case against me during wartime, the department was satisfied that I had cleared my record in court and in prison. Since the department had carefully reviewed my academic credentials and teaching potential, and had approved my appointment unanimously, the chair saw no reason to change his recommendation. Grumbling that he thoroughly disapproved of the candidate's wartime stance, the president signed my contract. I finished my Ph.D. in sociology at the University of Washington in 1952.

Growing up Japanese American in Washington caused those who encountered discrimination to develop a kind of antenna to detect and avoid unpleasant incidents. For most Japanese Americans, the ultimate objective was survival, not confrontation. A Japanese proverb describes it well: *Deru kugi wa utareru*—"the nail that sticks out is the one that gets hit." Therefore, to avoid trouble, one should become inconspicuous, and, above all, avoid confrontation. Common wisdom dictated that there was no way minority persons could win in the long run, so they should not do anything that would draw attention to them and their activities. Some Japanese Americans carried this philosophy to its ultimate conclusion during World War II. They acquiesced in, or actually supported, the abrogation of their rights as citizens in the name of patriotism, loyalty, and the war effort.

Raising constitutional and moral questions during World War II, as I had done, was not the norm. Had Japanese American leaders known of my situation while they were still in Seattle, they probably would have confronted me, saying: "You are not even dry behind the ears. How can you take such a step that will create difficulties for the whole group? How do you know there won't be a backlash? How do you know you are right and the rest of us are wrong?" I would have had difficulty answering their questions. But I would have had questions for them also. How could they defend America and the Constitution by acceding to a decision made by military authorities to suspend constitutional guarantees, especially when there had been no suspension of the Constitution when martial law was declared? In the end, I would not have changed the views of the Japanese American leaders. And they would not have changed my mind.

Justice and Vindication after 44 Years

The U.S. Supreme Court decision in my wartime court action is often referred to as the "Hirabayashi Curfew Case" because of the circumstances of my original conviction. In Seattle federal district court, the judge gave me two sentences of 90 days each, to be served concurrently, for the counts of violating the curfew and ignoring the exclusion order. The Supreme Court, deciding that it needed to uphold only one of the concurrent sentences—since my imprisonment was the same for both counts—elected to review only the lesser curfew violation. At the oral hearing, however, most of the questions and answers dealt with the exclusion order, and only briefly at the end was the curfew issue argued "for the same basic principles."

In 1942, at my sentencing in federal district court, neither the judge, the prosecution, nor my defense attorney had seemed fully aware of the implications of the concurrent sentences. Originally I had been sentenced to 30 days on count I (ignoring the exclusion order) and 30 days on count II (curfew violation), to be served consecutively, for a total of 60 days. When the judge asked if the prisoner had anything to say, I told my attorney to inquire if the judge could add 15 days to each of the counts so that the total would be 90 days. The reason for this seemingly strange request was that a "jailhouse lawyer" had advised me that I would have to get at least 90 days if I wanted to serve my time outdoors, for instance, in a road camp. Otherwise, my jailhouse informant said, the Bureau of Prisons would not take the trouble to move me from jail to a road camp. The judge, in good humor, said he had no objection to raising the time by 15 days on each count; in fact, he suggested simplifying the matter by making it 90 days on each count, to be served concurrently. We all agreed to that. None of us realized then that the Supreme Court would use the two concurrent sentences as an excuse to dwell on the curfew violation and avoid ruling on the constitutionality of the exclusion program.

As for my own fate, when the Supreme Court ruled against me on the curfew count in June 1943, I faced a 90-day sentence. The U.S. attorney in Spokane, who had jurisdiction over my imprisonment, decided that I should serve the time in the federal tank of the Spokane County jail. He pointed out that the nearest federal prison camp on the West Coast was located in the restricted military zone, and that the next nearest one was in the vicinity of Tucson, Arizona, some 1,600 miles away. And, he added that he did not have travel funds to send me that far. In response, I argued that I had purposefully asked for an additional 30 days on my sentence because I wanted to be in a prison camp with outdoor work. Although sympathetic to my plea, the U.S. attorney replied, in effect: "Too bad. I can't help you." In desperation, I thought of alternatives. Finally, we worked out a plan for me to go to Tucson on my own. The U.S. attorney even wrote a "To Whom It May Concern" letter explaining the circumstances of my trip in case I ran into trouble.

Since I hardly wanted to pay my own way to prison, I decided to hitchhike to Arizona. Following the intermountain highway from Spokane through Boise and Salt Lake City, it took me two weeks to reach Las Vegas, where I gave up on thumbing rides from the infrequent cars traveling during that gas-rationing era. I took a bus from there to Tucson. When I reported to the U.S. marshal's office at the end of my journey, the officials said they had no notice of my incarceration, and that I should turn around and go home. I would have welcomed these instructions, but I knew it would be only a matter of time until the federal bureaucracy uncovered my papers, and I would have to return to Tucson. Moreover, I certainly did not fancy hitchhiking back to Spokane, not to mention the ordeal of a dreadfully slow round trip.

So, I suggested that the Tucson U.S. marshal's office telephone or telegraph the U.S. attorney in Spokane, the federal judge in Seattle, and the Federal Bureau of Prisons in Washington, D.C., to clarify my status. The cooperative staff agreed to do so, and also suggested that while waiting for the replies, I should attend an air-conditioned movie to escape the Arizona heat. When I returned to the office at 7 p.m. that evening, a car waited to take me to the Tucson prison camp in the Santa Catalina Mountains, where I would work on a road-building project. The U.S. marshal's staff not only had received multiple confirmations of my incarceration, but also had found their own copy of the orders deep in their file basket.

On my hitchhiking trip to Tucson, I had visited for a few days with my parents in Weiser, Idaho, where they were working on a sugar beet farm. I also spent a day in Salt Lake City at the wartime headquarters of *The Pacific Citizen,* the news organ of the Japanese American Citizens League. The only time I had to use the "To Whom It May Concern" letter was with a central Utah sheriff, who had kindly given me a ride. When he asked how far I was going, I replied that I was headed for the Tucson prison camp to serve a sentence. The sheriff bolted upright, nearly drove us off the road, and skidded the car to a stop. As the dust and gravel settled, I quickly told him not to worry because I had a letter authorizing the trip, and showed it to him. Although somewhat puzzled by my unusual mode of travel to prison, he finally decided to let it continue without taking me into custody, and gave me a ride as far as he was going.

The whole experience would have been more unusual, even enjoyable in one sense, if I had known at the time that Tucson was in a forbidden military zone too. It was at the Tucson camp that I started learning the baking trade. Unfortunately, 90 days was too short to get the full training. In fact, I gained my release just as I was learning the art of baking a cake. Later, as a conscientious objector, I served a year in the McNeil Island federal prison on a draft evasion conviction. I considered fighting that case through the appeals process, because I felt it also involved discrimination on the basis of ancestry, but by this time I was tired of courts and judges.

I never relinquished the hope that some day, in some way, the court decisions would be corrected. My wartime case, and those of Fred Korematsu and Minoru Yasui, remained dormant for more than 40 years. Normally, after a Supreme Court verdict, the case is presumed to be permanently closed. During the early 1980s, however, Aiko Herzig-Yoshinaga, a senior archival researcher for the Commission on Wartime Relocation and Internment of Civilians (CWRIC), discovered an original draft of the document written by General John L. DeWitt, *Final Report: Japanese Evacuation from the West Coast, 1942,* which was used to justify Japanese American removal and relocation. Although this copy had supposedly been shredded four decades earlier, it had somehow escaped and was lying un-filed on the desk of an archival clerk. Herzig-Yoshinaga noticed that the original draft differed from the official version of the *Final Report* used in my federal court hearings in 1942–1943, particularly where the original stated it would be impossible to separate the Japanese American sheep from the goats (the loyal from the disloyal) *no matter how much time was available for the process.* In contrast, the official version used in my case declared that the lack of time because of the wartime emergency made mass exclusion the only alternative (the "military necessity" thesis). The wayward original was to play a significant role in both the court hearings of the 1980s and the Japanese American redress movement.

About this same time Peter Irons, a legal historian and political science professor, was investigating the conduct of the lawyers on both sides of the Japanese American wartime cases. Irons found in the government's files correspondence from Edward Ennis, a Justice Department lawyer who had prepared the Supreme Court brief in my case, written to Solicitor General Charles Fahy. In it, Ennis alerted Fahy to the existence of a Naval Intelligence report contradicting the U.S. Army's claim of widespread disloyalty among Japanese Americans, and urging individual loyalty hearings instead of mass internment. Furthermore, Ennis informed Fahy that the Justice Department "had a duty to advise the Court" about the existence of this report, and that "any other course of conduct might approximate the suppression of evidence." Fahy apparently ignored the warning, and withheld from the Supreme Court these findings regarding racial bias in the mass internment.

In January 1983, after conferring with Peter Irons about the newly discovered federal records, Fred Korematsu, Minoru Yasui, and I, through our attorneys, jointly announced plans to petition for a writ of error, *coram nobis*, in the respective federal district courts where our wartime convictions were issued. *Coram nobis* is not a right for a hearing. Rather, it means that in the event of misconduct and suppression of evidence affecting a court's decisions, petitions requesting a new hearing may be filed. With the archival evidence from the government's own files, the courts in all three cases agreed to hear our petitions, Korematsu's in San Francisco, Yasui's in Portland, and mine in Seattle.

My case, the last of the three to get a hearing, involved a change in the Justice Department's court strategy from the earlier Korematsu and Yasui actions, which essentially vindicated the Japanese Americans. The federal attorneys now vigorously fought for dismissal, not so much on substantive issues involving the government's misconduct, but on technicalities, such as *laches*. They maintained that the time allowed for a petition had expired—i.e., I should have requested the rehearing 40 years earlier. On the basis of a second technicality, the Justice Department stated that since I was now a successful university professor, I obviously did not suffer from the wartime convictions, and therefore did not qualify for a *coram nobis* petition. In 1986, Judge Donald Voorhees of the federal district court ruled that since it was not reasonable for me to have access to the relevant documents until the 1980s, the time allowed for a petition should be restricted to that period. As to whether or not I was suffering as a professor, the U.S. Ninth Circuit Court of Appeals found in my favor and stated in its ruling of September 24, 1987: "A United States citizen who is convicted of a crime on account of race is lastingly aggrieved."

In my first *coram nobis* court action in 1984, the federal district judge declared there should be evidentiary hearings—i.e., something like a trial with witnesses and cross-examinations. This session occurred a year later in June 1985, and involved seven full days, whereas my wartime trial had lasted less than one day. The ringing decision rendered in February 1986 overturned my major conviction on violating the exclusion order. The judge, however, allowed the minor curfew conviction to stand. My attorneys appealed the curfew ruling, believing it should have been overturned along with the exclusion order reversal. In turn, the Justice Department lawyers cross-appealed the reversal of the exclusion order conviction.

In September 1987, the Ninth Circuit Court of Appeals ruled in my favor—"the judgment of the District Court as to the exclusion conviction is affirmed. The judgment as to the curfew conviction is reversed and the matter is remanded with instructions to grant Hirabayashi's petition to vacate both convictions." In addition, the unanimous opinion declared that "General DeWitt was a racist" and that his orders were "based upon racism rather than military necessity."

To my dismay, the federal government chose not to appeal this decision, and my case is apparently closed with the victory at the circuit court of appeals level. Unfortunately, however, the wartime rulings at the Supreme Court level in the Hirabayashi, Korematsu, and Yasui convictions remained unchanged, creating a strange paradox, especially since constitutional authorities consider the so-called relocation cases as the most flagrant "wholesale violation" of civil liberties in American history, and a blight on the high court's record.

The Hazards of Growing Up American

Growing up American in Washington in the early part of the 20th century involved hazards. It was still a time of western development with a semi-frontier atmosphere. Longstanding residents fended for themselves against latecomers. Their methods of self-protection frequently emerged as strategies of scapegoating against identifiable weaker groups, such as visible minorities. Most notably, a virulent brand of anti-Asian racism became a feature of West Coast society, including Washington. I grew up in that atmosphere where confrontation with racism was inescapable.

In addition, during my formative years, America experienced one of the most traumatic and eventful 15-year periods of its history—the Great Depression of the 1930s followed by the most extensive total war ever seen. To make matters worse, a large part of the 1920s leading up to the Great Depression also had been a time of hardship and struggle for my family and others.

The Depression affected every aspect of American life as no other national catastrophe before or since. We saw "Hooverville" shanty towns; large numbers of jobless and hopeless people, many jumping on railroad freight cars going east, west, north, and south looking for work; long lines of people at soup kitchens and in breadlines; and the federal government's attempts to counteract these hardships with such programs as the Works Progress Administration (WPA) and the Civilian Conservation Corps (CCC). Like the Depression, World War II sent a shock wave through American society; everything seemed to be affected—churches, jobs, education, family life. All those who grew up during those 15 years, 1930–1945, carry scars that mark their attitudes and behavior in ways younger generations find difficult to understand.

The Great Depression hardships and the stresses of the war inevitably shaped my life. Moreover, I could hardly escape frequent encounters with the West Coast strain of racism. Perhaps it seems unlikely that the spirit of democracy could take root in such an atmosphere. On the other hand, the historical record shows that the democratic impulse often surges most noticeably under conditions of tribulation and oppression. It was so in my personal experience. I could not give up on the hope of democratic ideals that I had learned growing up. They gave me a perspective and a set of goals that guided my life and intellectual development, despite the temporary setbacks and the lack of understanding on the part of others.

Every cloud has a silver lining, and one must choose whether to focus on the dark cloud or on the brighter side. In my own life, as suggested in these pages, some positive forces always arose to keep me going. Although the commanding general of the Western Defense Command wanted to remove all persons of Japanese ancestry from specified areas on the West Coast, a Washington state senator and her group of civil rights activists fought for the rights of Japanese Americans, even while being defiled in public as "Jap lovers" and traitors. Even though a labor organization would not admit me into the Baker's union, I had the satisfaction of knowing that a bakery in the University District really wanted to hire me, and this episode led me to finish my undergraduate degree. The university president might want to fire me as a teaching associate because of my prison record, but the sociology chair fought for my appointment and won. When the Downtown YMCA official turned me down for a job, the director of the University YMCA where I was a member became more devastated and upset than I was.

Democracy is obviously a group effort, but it requires the commitment of individuals. In fact, during struggles for justice and fair play, individual action must be joined by group support, or equality before the law will cease to exist. My case and the cases of others in the redress movement seeking acknowledgment of wrongdoing and compensation for wartime exclusion injustices have become national issues. During World War II, some Americans who were not of Japanese ancestry fought for our cause, not only out of sympathy for innocent victims held behind barbed wire, but also for the sake of all American citizens and their basic constitutional rights.

When the courts considered my *coram nobis* petition in the 1980s, many individuals and groups, incensed by the wartime injustices, joined in the battle—the general public with moral and financial support; the young *pro bono* lawyers in Seattle, some twenty-five to thirty of them between 1982 and 1987, who contributed time and legal expertise worth about $400,000; the media, which gave the events thorough coverage; the Committee to Reverse the Wartime Japanese American Cases, which was formed to conduct a publicity and fund-raising campaign; and many others concerned about the well-being of our democratic system. It is also gratifying that those seeking redress for the injustices of World War II saw Congress pass the Civil Liberties Act of 1988, in which the federal government apologized and agreed to pay $20,000 to each surviving Japanese American interned during the war.

Long ago I realized that the Constitution had not failed me. Instead, those responsible for upholding the Constitution had failed in their jobs. The Constitution is a magnificent document, which has inspired millions around the world, but it is just a scrap of paper if the American people fail to uphold it. We should always remember Thomas Jefferson's admonition that "every government degenerates when trusted to the rulers of the people alone. The people themselves are its only safe depositories."

Selected References

Chuman, Frank F. *The Bamboo People: The Law and Japanese-Americans.* Del Mar, California: Publishers, Inc., 1976.

Commission on Wartime Relocation and Internment of Civilians. *Personal Justice Denied: Report of the Commission on Wartime Relocation and Internment of Civilians.* Washington, D.C., 1982.

Daniels, Roger. *Asian America: Chinese and Japanese in the United States since 1850.* Seattle: University of Washington Press, 1988.

_____. *The Decision to Relocate the Japanese Americans.* Philadelphia: Lippincott, 1975.

_____, Sandra C. Taylor, and Harry H.L. Kitano, eds. *Japanese Americans: From Relocation to Redress.* Salt Lake City: University of Utah Press, 1986.

Fine, Sidney. "Mr. Justice Murphy and the Hirabayashi Case." *Pacific Historical Review* 33 (1964):195–209.

Fisher, Anne Reeploeg. *Exile of a Race,* 3rd ed. Kent, Washington: F and T Publishers, 1987.

Hirabayashi, Gordon. "Am I an American?" In Peter Irons, ed., *The Courage of Their Convictions: Sixteen Americans Who Fought Their Way to the Supreme Court.* New York: Penguin Books, 1990.

_____. *Good Times, Bad Times: Idealism Is Realism.* Argenta, B.C.: Argenta Friends Press, 1985.

Hohri, William M. *Repairing America: An Account of the Movement for Japanese-American Redress.* Pullman: Washington State University Press, 1988.

Irons, Peter. *Justice at War.* New York: Oxford University Press, 1983.

_____, ed. *Justice Delayed: The Record of the Japanese American Internment Cases.* Middletown, Connecticut: Wesleyan University Press, 1989.

_____. "Return of the 'Yellow Peril.'" *The Nation,* October 19, 1985, front cover and pp. 376–79.

Miyamoto, S. Frank. *Social Solidarity among the Japanese in Seattle,* 3rd ed. Seattle: University of Washington Press, 1984.

Weglyn, Michi. *Years of Infamy: The Untold Story of America's Concentration Camps.* New York: William Morrow, 1976.

Wilson, Robert A., and Bill Hosokawa. *East to America: A History of the Japanese in the United States.* New York: William Morrow, 1980.

Selected Legal References

Hirabayashi v. United States, 320 U.S. 81 (1943).
Hirabayashi v. United States, 627 Federal Supp. 1445 (Western District Washington, 1986).
Hirabayashi v. United States, 828 Federal 2nd 571 (9th Circuit, 1987).
Korematsu v. United States, 323 U.S. 214 (1944).
Yasui v. United States, 320 U.S. 115 (1943).

IX

"There was No Better Place to Go"— The Transformation Thesis Revisited: African-American Migration to the Pacific Northwest, 1940–1950

Quintard Taylor

A NUMBER OF HISTORIANS, including most notably Gerald Nash and Carlos Schwantes, have argued "the transformation thesis"—namely, that World War II brought overwhelming, permanent change to the West that inevitably ended the region's position as an economic "colony" of eastern capital and established it for the first time as a "pacesetter" for much of the rest of the nation. Recently, however, a smaller group of historians have challenged the idea of sweeping transformation as ending "regional" colonialism, and of the West becoming a molder of national social and cultural trends. The second group, which includes among others Roger Lotchin, Albert Broussard, and Stuart McElderry, all argue that continuity rather than change was the watchword for the World War II decade. Indeed Lotchin, the leading "transformation" critic, claims the wartime changes were "remarkably ephemeral."[1]

This essay examines these conflicting visions of the West and World War II through the joint prism of African-American and Pacific Northwest history. I am not so much interested in determining which historians are correct; rather, I wish to use this debate to get a more accurate assessment of African-American life in the Pacific Northwest, and gauge the impact of the presence of black Pacific Northwesterners on the rest of the region's inhabitants.

One point is beyond dispute. African-Americans came to the Pacific Northwest during the 1940s in unprecedented numbers. Drawn by the prospect of employment as defense workers or by assignments as military personnel, the African-American population of Washington, Oregon, and Idaho grew from 10,584 to 43,270 between 1940 and 1950.

The most dramatic change took place in the largest coastal cities. Between 1940 and 1950, Seattle's black population grew 306 percent, from 3,789 to

15,410. The comparable figures for Tacoma were 650 in 1940 and 3,205 in 1950, a 393 percent increase, while African-American Portland grew from 1,931 in 1940 to 9,495 in 1950, a 392 percent increase. Portland's figures are misleading because the city actually had 22,000 African-Americans in 1945 before the population declined to just fewer than 9,500 by the end of the decade. Other cities, especially in Washington, had spectacular increases. Bremerton's black population grew from 77 to 743 in the war decade, an 865 percent increase. Pasco's black populace expanded from 27 to 980, a 3,529 percent increase, and Vancouver, which had just 10 African-Americans in 1940, saw its black population explode to 879 by 1950, an 8,690 percent increase.[2]

African-American population increase in selected urban areas, 1940 to 1950.			
City	1940	1950	% increase
Seattle	3,789	15,410	306%
Tacoma	650	3,205	393%
Portland	1,931	9,495	392%
Bremerton	77	743	865%
Pasco	27	980	3,529%
Vancouver	10	879	8,690%

The migration of over 30,000 African-Americans primarily to the Pacific Northwest's largest cities, Seattle, Portland, and Tacoma, in the 1940s represented a profound change that made these cities—for good and ill—increasingly similar to the rest of urban America. This migration intensified a concentration of African-Americans in the region's largest population centers—by 1950, 74 percent of Washington's blacks lived in the Seattle and Tacoma metropolitan districts, while 95 percent of Oregon's blacks resided in one city, Portland. In her study of the East Bay communities in California, Marilynn Johnson concluded that the World War II era migration made cities such as Oakland, Berkeley, and Richmond "younger, more southern, more female, and noticeably more black" than ever before.[3] That conclusion has equal salience for Pacific Northwest cities.

The African-American concentration in Seattle, Tacoma, and Portland also intensified what can be called the proletarianization of the black work force. After decades of laboring in menial positions on the periphery of the economy, black workers gained access to employment in wartime shipyards and aircraft factories, enhancing both their earning potential and their social prestige. Robert C. Weaver, a black World War II-era government economist, concluded that the war generated "more industrial and occupational diversification for Negroes than had occurred in the seventy-five preceding years."[4] However, this industrialization of the African-American work force was far more erratic than most historians have noted. Black access to defense production employment came with setbacks, as occurred immediately after World War II when many African-American workers were quickly dismissed during post-war economic retrenchment. Yet, exposure to defense plant employment, no matter how brief, persuaded many to vow never again to be relegated to the kitchen or the porter's station.

African-American employment history from 1940 to 1950, however, illustrates the difficulty in fulfilling that vow. To cite just one example, as late as 1940 only 10 percent of Portland's black men and 3 percent of the city's black women were engaged in industrial work. Conversely 73 percent of the men and 86 percent of the women were domestic servants—chauffeurs, butlers, maids, porters. By 1945, according to one source, 95 percent of black migrants in Portland were engaged in shipyard work for the three Kaiser shipyards (as compared with 77 percent of the white migrants). When the war ended, African-American labor seemed destined to return to its traditional pre-war patterns of employment; 5,500 black shipyard workers lost their jobs between July and November 1945, with many having no choice but to return to menial work. By 1950, 18 percent of the men and 8 percent of the women were engaged in manufacturing work, while 40 percent of the men and 75 percent of the women were again in domestic service.[5]

Seattle's black workers fared slightly better, at least in part because of a greater number of industrial facilities in the Washington city, and because of the higher numbers of pre-war factory workers. In 1940, 17 percent of the men and 4 percent of the women were factory operatives, while 52 percent of the men and 83 percent of the women were in domestic service. Wartime employment opportunity, of course, quickly changed those figures. In 1940, there were only a dozen black shipyard workers in Seattle, yet by 1945, 4,078 worked in that occupation. In 1940 there were no black aircraft workers; by 1945, 1,233 worked principally at Boeing. Strikingly, black women led the way in this new employment, an economic development with enormous implications that would be felt far beyond the World War II years.

In May 1942, Boeing hired its first black aircraft production worker—
Dorothy West Williams. By July 1943, 329 blacks worked at Boeing, 86
percent of them women. As in the Portland shipyards, many of these jobs
did not survive the end of the war. By 1950, 27 percent of the men and 12
percent of the women were engaged in manufacturing work, mainly at Boeing, while 29 percent of the men had returned to domestic service along with
68 percent of the women.

**Percentages of Portland's African-American labor force in industrial
work and domestic service, 1940 and 1950.**

	1940	1950
Men:		
Industrial work	10%	18%
Domestic service	73%	40%
Women:		
Industrial work	3%	8%
Domestic service	86%	75%

**Percentages of Seattle's African-American labor force in industrial work
and domestic service, 1940 and 1950.**

	1940	1950
Men:		
Industrial work	17%	27%
Domestic service	52%	29%
Women:		
Industrial work	4%	12%
Domestic service	83%	68%

What does this mean? Roger Lotchin and others would probably conclude
that World War II gains were temporary, and certainly for black women the
argument is persuasive. Hitler may have "gotten black women out of the
white folks' kitchen," as one female aircraft worker said in 1943, but, when

he was gone, many of them dropped the welder's torch and again picked up the broom.[6]

But one could also argue that certainly not all of the workers became menial servants again. The wages earned during the war and the status derived from holding jobs comparable to those of white workers for the first time, or from wearing the uniform of the United States military, would translate into greater demands and bolder action on a number of fronts, including civil rights. Even if they no longer held defense jobs, their brief but crucial wartime experience convinced many African-American women and men that they could, and eventually would, return to more lucrative factory employment.

African-American success in the World War II industrial workplace could be measured not only by access to the shipyards and factories, but also by black workers' collective challenge of discriminatory policies and practices imposed by both management and organized labor. By 1942, African-American workers discovered that their pre-war exclusion from shipyards and aircraft factories was soon replaced by anti-black discrimination within them. Consequently, they launched a concerted campaign to end that discrimination, which generated consequences felt far beyond the Pacific Northwest. Throughout the war years, African-American workers at Boeing challenged the "whites only" clause of the International Association of Machinists (IAM) constitution. The Machinists union allowed the entry of black workers into Boeing only as a "temporary concession" to wartime labor shortages. Knowing that their post-war access to Boeing jobs could disappear again if the IAM chose to enforce the ban, black Boeing employees joined sympathetic white and Asian employees to campaign for the clause's removal from the union's constitution. By 1948, a racially integrated delegation from the Pacific Northwest persuaded the union at its national convention in Grand Rapids, Michigan, to remove its nearly century-old ban.[7]

African-American shipyard workers in Portland challenged the discriminatory practices of the International Boilermakers Union that relegated them to segregated "auxiliary" locals. Portland's black workers created the Shipyard Negro Organization for Victory (SNOV) and drew upon the support of a local black newspaper, the *Portland Observer*, the NAACP, and the Fair Employment Practices Committee (FEPC), which in November 1943 held hearings in the city on Boilermaker discrimination. The FEPC ordered the Boilermakers to disband their auxiliary local. Unfortunately the victory came in the spring of 1945, just months before the shipyards would be dismantled and virtually all workers, black and white, were dismissed. Nonetheless, the post-war Boilermakers union opened its ranks to African-American shipyard workers throughout the nation, in large measure because of the efforts of black workers in Portland.[8]

The African-American migration also permanently altered race relations in Seattle, Portland, and Tacoma, as the newcomers demanded the social freedom and political rights denied them in their former Southern homes. But it also made black-white relations the focal point of far more discussion and anxiety than ever before. "WE CATER TO WHITE TRADE ONLY" signs appeared in movie theaters and restaurants in Seattle and Portland, and also in Yakima, Walla Walla, and Pendleton. Interracial tension in the Portland and Seattle shipyards almost led to riots in 1943 and 1944. Moreover, literally hundreds of minor racial disturbances involving random, senseless attacks perpetuated by blacks and whites throughout the Pacific Northwest exacerbated regional racial tension. The sense of urgency among public officials was best articulated by Seattle Mayor William F. Devin in a July 1944 speech at the University of Washington where he announced:

> The problem of racial tensions is…going to affect us not only during the War, but also after the War, and it is our duty to face the problem together. If we do not do that, we shall not exist very long as a civilized city or as a nation.[9]

All of this is not to say that the Pacific Northwest first experienced "race" and racial conflict in the 1940s. Anyone familiar with the history of this region cannot ignore the century-long contestation between native peoples and European-Americans, and the numerous attempts in the late-19th and early-20th centuries to marginalize Asians. But what seems striking is how quickly in the 1940s the focus of interracial anxiety and conflict shifted to black-white relations. A 1946 survey of race conditions in Spokane conducted by the Sociology Department at Washington State University found that despite the long history of regional anti-Asian sentiment, and the recently concluded war with Japan, anti-black prejudice was significantly stronger than anti-Japanese-American sentiment.[10]

But regional race relations were not simply a question of just blacks versus whites. Increasingly, African-Americans and Asian-Americans began to eye each other cautiously, alternating between potential alliance and palpable antipathy. The best example of this development can be seen in post-war black-Japanese relations. By 1945, when it became evident that the Japanese evacuees would return to the West Coast, the greeting they would receive remained in doubt. Thousands of African-American migrants to Seattle had moved into the previously Japanese neighborhood along Jackson Street and seemed unwilling to share it with evacuation returnees.

Many of the African-American newcomers harbored little sympathy for the former residents. John Okada's novel, *No-No Boy*, about evacuation returnee IchiroYamada, captures this sentiment. When returning from an Idaho internment camp in 1945, Okada's protagonist, Yamada, found his old Jackson Street neighborhood filled with recently arrived Southern blacks, who failed to recognize him either as an "oppressed minority" or a person displaced from his former neighborhood. When scorned and ridiculed by the newcomers, Okada described it as "persecution in the drawl of the persecuted."[11]

Despite the tension that Okada described, some concerned Asian-American and African-American citizens attempted to establish the first institutional link between the two communities through the Jackson Street Community Council (JSCC). Formed in 1946 to support neighborhood businesses and voluntary social service agencies, the JSCC quickly became, however inadvertently, a model for inter-ethnic cooperation. Its officers rotated among its Japanese-American, Filipino-American, Chinese-American, and African-American membership, as did its "Man of the Year" selection.

Moreover, in an early attempt at cultural pluralism and ethnic sensitivity, the council in 1952 selected four queens, Foon Woo, Rosita DeLeon, Adelia Avery, and Sumi Mitsui, to represent the Chinese-American, Filipino-American, African-American, and Japanese-American communities, respectively. Avery was ultimately selected as Miss International Center, entitling her to represent the JSCC in all public functions. The tension between African-Americans and Asian-Americans never disappeared, but the JSCC allowed a forum for public discourse over political conflicts and cultural differences. Similar organizations did not exist in most other West Coast cities, including Portland, during the immediate post-war period.[12]

The increasing influence of African-Americans in the region's politics also was a consequence of World War II migration. Before World War II, two African-Americans, William Owen Bush (1890) and John H. Ryan (1922), were elected to the Washington legislature. Both men represented overwhelmingly white districts and, given their light-skinned complexions, many of their constituents did not realize their racial ancestry. In 1950, however, Charles Stokes, representing the 37th Legislative District in central Seattle, became the first African-American to sit in the legislature while representing a heavily black district. Stokes, a Republican attorney, was in fact one of the recent migrants, having arrived from Topeka, Kansas, in 1944. Stokes' election marked the beginning of almost continuous African-American representation for the district. He also served as a model for future black office holding in the region until the late 1980s. Most successful African-American politicians would come from significantly, if not predominately, black districts.

The elevation of African-Americans to office in Oregon would lag behind Washington by two decades. In 1972, William McCoy became the first black member of the state legislature. However, the pattern in Oregon would be much the same as north of the Columbia River—African-Americans were elected in significantly black districts.[13]

Meanwhile, white politicians, such as Oregon legislators Richard Neuberger and Mark O. Hatfield, were aware of African-American votes and embraced political agendas that promoted civil rights. In 1949, Neuberger, a Democratic state senator from Portland, and Hatfield, a Portland area Republican representative, co-sponsored Oregon's Fair Employment Practices Act. Four years later, Hatfield was co-sponsor of the state's first civil rights act. Neuberger and Hatfield (both of whom eventually served as U.S. Senators from Oregon) were part of a small but growing group of Oregon and Washington politicians who publicly cultivated support among African-American voters.[14]

This support for black civil rights stemmed not only from political expediency, but also a growing concern about racial injustice. The response of Oregon Republicans to racial discrimination directed against one of their delegates at the 1949 National Young Republicans Convention in Salt Lake City is one illustration of the changing attitudes. Charles Maxey, a wartime migrant, Portland barber, and NAACP activist, who was selected as a delegate to the convention, found upon reaching Salt Lake City that he was not allowed to stay in the hotel hosting the convention. After making temporary housing accommodations with a local African-American family, Maxey declared he would introduce a resolution condemning his exclusion. The entire state delegation supported his request, modifying it to allow the specific resolution to be introduced by Clay Myers, Vice-Chair of the College Republicans for the state of Oregon. The resolution specifically prohibited the Young Republicans from holding any future conventions in public accommodations that discriminated against blacks. After intense and often emotional debate, the resolution was adopted by the full convention.[15]

The rapid growth of the African-American population in the Pacific Northwest strengthened regional civil rights organizations, allowing them for the first time to successfully pursue an effective agenda. In the decade following World War II, a number of organizations dedicated to pressing for rights for people of color, or at least ending the most egregious forms of discrimination, emerged in the region's largest cities. Three racially integrated Pacific Northwest organizations—the Oregon Committee for Equal Rights (formed in1950) and the Committee on Inter-racial Principles and Practices, both headquartered in Portland, and the Seattle-based Christian Friends for

Racial Equality—were examples of this growing trend toward interracial cooperation. By 1945, too, an Urban League chapter had been formed in Portland, joining the fifteen-year-old chapter in Seattle.

The most striking example of growing public concern about civil rights, however, was the expansion of multiracial NAACP branches in the region. The Seattle NAACP, for example, increased its membership from 85 in 1941, to 1,550 by 1945. Portland's NAACP organization, one of the first west of the Mississippi River, had doubled from 500 members to 1,000 by the end of the war. Before World War II, these branches were the only ones in the region, but, by 1950, NAACP branches were added in Tacoma, Spokane, the Tri-Cities (Richland, Kennewick, and Pasco), Bremerton, Walla Walla, and Vancouver. Moreover, representatives from all of the region's branches met annually to discuss civil rights questions affecting blacks throughout the Pacific Northwest.[16]

One way to gauge the success of an organization's civil rights agenda is by observing its ability to influence public policy. In this regard, the NAACP branches in Washington and Oregon were remarkably effective. Both had forged broadly based political coalitions, including progressive labor unions, sympathetic churches, fraternal organizations, as well as the Urban League. Such coalitions constituted a veritable civil rights establishment that for the first time in the region's history could mobilize financial, legal, and political resources to support civil rights legislation. These coalitions in Oregon and Washington obtained passage of Fair Employment Practices Laws (FEP), allowing these two Pacific Northwest states to join the ranks of only eight states with such laws before 1950. Moreover, the Oregon Committee for Equal Rights was able in 1953, in the wake of the FEP legislation, to gain passage of the state's first civil rights statute, a measure that banned discrimination in public accommodations.

These organizational strategies and tactics served as a model for subsequent efforts in following decades. Though there is no question that racial attitudes changed far more slowly in the 1940s than many people of color would have liked, it is seriously misleading to assume, as have some of the critics of the "transformation school," that post-war blacks reverted to the pattern of pre-war obsequiousness in the face of bigotry and discrimination.[17]

On the other hand, those who posit the wartime "transformation" thesis almost always assume it to mean an improvement in the lives of the region's African-Americans. In many ways they are correct, as the examples above attest. However, transformation also resulted in a decline in some aspects of the quality of life. Nowhere is this more evident than in housing. Severe overcrowding, endemic to all of the cities in the region, became especially acute in the black community and accelerated the physical deterioration of predominantly African-American neighborhoods.

African-American newcomers faced a chronic wartime housing shortage that—although a problem shared by white and Asian populations—was exacerbated by a long history of discrimination in residential housing. In Seattle by 1945, over 10,000 blacks occupied virtually the same buildings that housed 3,700 African-Americans five years earlier. Most black newcomers in Tacoma were channeled into the Hilltop District, which provided a spectacular view of Puget Sound and little else.

Conditions in Portland were worse than in Washington. Half of the 22,000 wartime migrants remained in the city, and the other half took up residence in Vanport, the nation's largest wartime housing project. Whether they lived in Portland proper or Vanport, black residents were racially segregated. In 1945, a Portland Urban League official publicly articulated a long-standing belief among African-Americans concerning the linkage between segregated housing and societal well-being. He declared: "A Man who must crowd his wife and children into an unsafe and unsanitary home…becomes an unstable citizen."[18]

We should be clear about the cause of the deteriorating housing situation. Restrictive covenants, the centerpiece of residential housing discrimination, had a long history in Seattle, Tacoma, and Portland before World War II, ensuring that it was virtually impossible for African-Americans to live outside certain prescribed districts. During World War II, such covenants served as invisible walls, concentrating the rapidly growing African-American population into single neighborhoods. In Portland, for example, the neighborhood was Albina—a narrow corridor stretching north from downtown toward the Columbia River. In Albina, zoning laws were set aside during World War II as homes were transformed into apartments, and businesses were built in front yards or occupied converted garages. In spite of these loosened restrictions in Albina, many newcomers continued to have to sleep wherever they could find space, including in churches, movie theaters, automobiles, and on pool hall tables.[19]

Not all migrants perceived this as a concern; after all, many of the newcomers came from the South where such housing conditions were common. Other workers, who focused on making money quickly and vacating Portland (or Seattle or Tacoma) at the end of the war, cared little about the lasting consequences for neighborhoods. Such apathy caused the *Portland Observer* to lament in a 1945 editorial:

The Negro people are passively witnessing the development of a first-rate ghetto with all the potential for squalor, poverty, juvenile delinquency and crime. It is obvious that the herding of Negroes into the [Albina] district portends economic and social problems of far reaching significance for this city.[20]

In Seattle and Tacoma, public housing lessened the burden on migrants. Seattle's public housing director, Jesse Epstein, refused to allow the kind of racially segregated occupation that had evolved in other cities throughout the region. Said Epstein: "We have an opportunity to prove that Negroes and whites can live side by side in harmony…but it's going to require skill and patience to make it work."[21] In Seattle, to a large extent, it did work as African-American and white residents lived side-by-side in Yesler Terrace and other local housing projects.

Portland officials, however, supported by the Chamber of Commerce and other civic groups, discouraged the construction of public housing precisely because they feared that migrants might stay in the region if it were available. In effect, Portland's housing "shortage" was an instrument of public policy. Stuart McElderry has shown that in addition to the usual hostility to "residential integration" in white neighborhoods by private citizens and real estate or mortgage lending groups, the Housing Authority of Portland (HAP), a government agency appointed specifically to address the wartime housing shortage, actually blocked the construction of badly needed public housing in northeast Portland. HAP even opposed the building of Vanport, although pressure from the Kaiser Company and the federal government eventually garnered HAP's reluctant endorsement. Yet, when the war ended, the agency recommended to the Federal Housing Authority (FHA) the demolition of 484 public housing units in three projects to make room for post-war industrial expansion. Fortunately for many migrant black families having limited access to private housing, the FHA refused to eliminate these units.[22]

Portland's housing crisis was never resolved. No doubt, African-Americans (as well as other migrants) who slept in cars, churches, theaters, and taverns never knew that this situation was generated by more than "wartime lumber shortages." When one looks at the region as a whole, it becomes apparent that the modern "ghettos" are the result of private and public actions beginning long before World War II, but the long-term consequences first became apparent during the large-scale wartime migration.

The varied impacts of World War II can be seen most graphically in the differing histories of the immediate post-war African-American communities in Seattle and Portland. Unlike most American cities, where economies were buoyed by wartime production followed by post-war economic slumps, Seattle remained prosperous. Seattle's leading employer, Boeing, now received Cold War-instigated military contracts and saw a steady growth in commercial airline orders throughout the late 1940s. Consequently, the city's African-American population grew by 5,000 between 1945 and 1950, as defense industries continued to recruit black workers. The outlook for blacks in Seattle was so encouraging that the *Chicago Defender*, the nation's largest African-American newspaper, urged in 1951 that people leave the Midwest and East for Puget Sound.[23]

By contrast, Portland's blacks, the vast majority of whom were Kaiser shipyard employees in 1945, had to find new occupations when the yards closed that year. A fortunate minority gained other industrial employment. Others were absorbed into the service industries of the city, and a good number (though not the majority) returned to menial employment. However, what is most striking about Portland's post-war black community is its shrinking size. Between 1945 and 1947, an estimated 11,000 African-Americans, about 50 percent of the 1945 population, simply left the city. Poor job prospects in Portland sent them north to Seattle, south to California, and in some instances back to the South.

Yet the flight of thousands of blacks from Portland was not simply due to the closure of the shipyards. As already explained, the intentional housing shortage prompted by city policies had much to do with their departure. After interviewing city leaders in 1950, a Portland *Oregonian* reporter wrote: "City officials are still guided by the wishful thought that most of the Negroes will go back home, leaving the city untouched by racial 'problems.'" The reporter's view was shared by Julius A. Thomas, a Portland Urban League official, who noted in 1947 that many Pacific Coast blacks considered Portland "just like any southern town…the most prejudiced city in the West."[24]

The contrasting examples of Portland and Seattle in the 1940s suggest that historians need to continue to carefully examine the growing body of documentary evidence on African-American life in the region. The data from those times well illustrates an increased level of civil rights political activity in the large cities and its growing influence on public policy at the state level. Moreover, blacks gained access to numerous industrial jobs that were closed to them before World War II. Admittedly, some of the spectacular wartime gains were lost in the late 1940s, but the pre-war pattern of reliance on doing menial employment would never completely return. Or, as one post-war observer noted, "the white worker…may still come to the table first and take the best seat, but now the Negro sits there too."[25]

But it is equally true that certain prejudicial public attitudes toward the African-American newcomers, as well as some local government and business policies, often resulted in greater residential and public school segregation. Thus, the Pacific Northwest proved not nearly as liberal regarding racial issues as many residents—black and white—had previously believed. Ultimately, that realization prompted African-Americans to generate a protracted civil rights movement in the 1960s.

A rationale for that activity can be surmised in a statement by Larry Richardson, who, in a 1975 Washington State University dissertation, asserted that African-Americans migrated to this region with the belief that it offered racial equality as well as employment opportunity. Richardson contends that when the migrants realized the Pacific Northwest did not fulfill these promises, the newcomers joined with established black residents in challenging discrimination. That challenge was inevitable, Richardson asserts, because African-Americans "who had migrated West to improve their lot came to realize that it was the end of the line both socially and geographically. There was no better place to go."[26]

Notes

1. Quoted in Roger W. Lotchin, "The Historians' War or the Home Front's War? Some Thoughts for Western Historians," *Western Historical Quarterly* 26, no. 2 (Summer 1995):195. For the best articulation of the transformation thesis, see Gerald D. Nash, *The American West Transformed: The Impact of the Second World War* (Bloomington: Indiana University Press, 1986), and *World War II and the West: Reshaping the Economy* (Lincoln: University of Nebraska Press, 1990). See also Carlos Schwantes, "The Pacific Northwest in World War II," *Journal of the West* 25, no. 3 (July 1986):4–18. On the critique of the transformation thesis, see Roger W. Lotchin, "California Cities and the Hurricane of Change: World War II in the San Francisco, Los Angeles, and San Diego Metropolitan Areas," *Pacific Historical Review* 63, no. 3 (August 1994):393–420, and "The Historians' War or the Home Front's War?" 185–96; Albert S. Broussard, *Black San Francisco: The Struggle for Racial Equality in the West, 1900–1954* (Lawrence: University Press of Kansas, 1993); and Stuart McElderry, "Boundaries and Limits: Housing Segregation and Civil Rights Activism in Portland, Oregon, 1930–1962" [a *Pacific Historical Review* article forthcoming at the time of this Pettyjohn presentation]. Paul Rhode specifically counters the economic arguments of Nash in "The Nash Thesis Revisited: An Economic Historian's View," *Pacific Historical Review* 63, no. 3 (August 1994):363–92.

2. On the 1940 and 1950 population figures, see U.S. Bureau of the Census, *Sixteenth Census of the United States 1940, Population*, vol. II, *Characteristics of the Population* (Washington,

D.C.: Government Printing Office, 1943), parts 6, 7, tables 31, A-36, C-36; and U.S. Bureau of the Census, *Census of Population 1950*, vol. II, *Characteristics of the Population* (Washington, D.C.: Government Printing Office, 1952), parts 37, 47, table 34.

3. See Marilynn S. Johnson, *The Second Gold Rush: Oakland and the East Bay in World War II* (Berkeley: University of California Press, 1993), 58.

4. Quoted in Ronald Takaki, *A Different Mirror: A History of Multicultural America* (Boston: Little, Brown, 1993), 398. For a discussion of the proletarianization process among black urban workers, see Joe W. Trotter, *Black Milwaukee: The Making of an Industrial Proletariat, 1915–45* (Urbana: University of Illinois Press, 1985), chaps. 2, 7.

5. See, U.S. Bureau of the Census, *Sixteenth Census of the United States 1940, Population*, vol. III, *The Labor Force* (Washington, D.C.: Government Printing Office, 1943), part 4, table 13; and U.S. Bureau of the Census, *Census of Population 1950*, vol. II, *Characteristics of the Population* (Washington, D.C.: Government Printing Office, 1952), part 37, table 34.

6. The "kitchen" quote appears in Sherna Berger Gluck, *Rosie the Riveter Revisited: Women, the War, and Social Change* (Boston: Twayne, 1987), 42. For the statistics on the Seattle black work force, see U.S. Bureau of the Census, *Sixteenth Census of the United States 1940, Population*, vol. III, *The Labor Force* (Washington, D.C.: Government Printing Office, 1943), part 5, table 13; U.S. Bureau of the Census, *Census of Population 1950*, vol. II, *Characteristics of the Population* (Washington, D.C.: Government Printing Office, 1952), part 47, table 34; and Quintard Taylor, *The Forging of a Black Community: Seattle's Central District, from 1870 through the Civil Rights Era* (Seattle: University of Washington Press, 1994), 161.

7. For a detailed discussion of the role of black Boeing workers in the integration of the International Association of Machinists, see John McCann, *Blood in the Water: A History of District Lodge 751 of the International Association of Machinists and Aerospace Workers* (Seattle: IAM&AW, 1989), 47–49; and Taylor, *The Forging of a Black Community*, 164–65.

8. On the campaign in Portland, see Alonzo Smith and Quintard Taylor, "Racial Discrimination in the Workplace: A Study of Two West Coast Cities during the 1940s," *Journal of Ethnic Studies* 8, no. 1 (Spring 1980):35–54.

9. Quoted in Taylor, *The Forging of a Black Community*, 167–68.

10. See Tolbert Hall Kennedy, "Racial Survey of the Intermountain Northwest," *Research Studies of the State College of Washington* 14, no. 3 (September 1946):166, 237–42.

11. See John Okada, *No-No Boy* (Seattle: University of Washington Press, 1978), 5.

12. See Taylor, *The Forging of a Black Community*, 174–75.

13. On black officeholders in Washington, see Quintard Taylor, "A History of Blacks in the Pacific Northwest, 1788–1970," Ph.D. dissertation, University of Minnesota, 1977, pp. 187–88, and *The Forging of a Black Community*, 176. On William McCoy's election, see the Portland *Oregonian*, November 8, 1972, p. 4M, D.

14. See Rudy N. Pearson, "African Americans in Portland, Oregon, 1940–1950: Work and Living Conditions—A Social History," Ph.D. dissertation, Washington State University, 1996, pp. 177–80, 184; and Taylor, "A History of Blacks in the Pacific Northwest," 235.

15. For a full account of this episode, see James Strassmaier, "1949—Oregon Young Republicans Strike Blow for Civil Rights: An Interview with Charles Britton Maxey," *Oregon History* 38, no. 4 (Winter 1994–95):12–15.

16. See McElderry, "Boundaries and Limits," 16–17; and Taylor, *The Forging of a Black Community*, 170–71.

17. On anti-discrimination laws in Oregon and Washington, see Taylor, "A History of Blacks in the Pacific Northwest," 233–34, 244.

18. Quoted in the Portland *Oregonian*, June 24, 1945, p. 2.

19. See Quintard Taylor, "The Great Migration: The Afro-American Communities of Seattle and Portland during the 1940s," *Arizona and the West* 23, no. 2 (Summer 1981):113–14, 117, 122–23; and McElderry, "Boundaries and Limits," 14.

20. Quoted in the *Portland Observer*, July 20, 1945, p. 4.

21. Quoted in Taylor, *The Forging of a Black Community*, 169.

22. For a discussion of the HAP policy on wartime and post-war housing, see McElderry, "Boundaries and Limits," 13–21.

23. See Taylor, *The Forging of a Black Community*, 175.

24. See Portland *Oregonian*, June 17, 1945, p. 8, and April 23, 1947, p. 10. The estimated 11,000 person post-war population decline is reported in the *Oregonian*, June 16, 1947, p. 8. Although Portland lost more people than most West Coast cities, its experience is not unique, nor is the attitude of its public officials. Oakland, Richmond, and other shipbuilding centers had staggering unemployment rates. In Vallejo, for example, half of the black population of 4,000 was unemployed in 1947, and it seems Richmond and Vallejo officials made every effort to drive black migrants away. See Cy W. Record, "Willie Stokes at the Golden Gate," *Crisis* 56, no. 6 (June 1949):175–79; and Shirley Ann Moore, "The Black Community in Richmond, California, 1910–1963," Ph.D. dissertation, University of California, Berkeley, 1989, pp. 160–62.

25. Quoted in Katherine Archibald, *Wartime Shipyard: A Study in Cultural Disunity* (Berkeley: University of California Press, 1947), 99.

26. Quoted in Larry S. Richardson, "Civil Rights in Seattle: A Rhetorical Analysis of a Social Movement," Ph.D. dissertation, Washington State University, 1975, p. 32.

X

Mexican American Street Gangs, Migration, and Violence in the Yakima Valley [1]

E. Mark Moreno

THE YAKIMA VALLEY of south-central Washington historically has been a major center of agricultural activity. Since the first relatively large communities of Mexican Americans arrived after World War II, both the overall valley population and the number of its Latinos have grown significantly. After 1947, thousands of World War II-era contract Mexican *bracero* workers left the Pacific Northwest, but migrants from Texas came to fill the labor gap in the Yakima Valley's expanding agricultural economy.

This latter group formed Mexican American communities in the lower valley towns of Sunnyside, Toppenish, Wapato, Grandview, and other places. A state labor supervisor noted the "increase in the numbers of Texas Mexicans available for sugar beet work…It is thought these workers probably displaced the number of contracted workers previously used."[2] In 1951, a priest arrived in the Yakima diocese to specifically serve Mexican Americans, and more than 500 children of this group were baptized in one night during the next year.[3]

By 1980, Yakima County had about 172,500 people, of which 25,455 were "of Spanish origin," as they were called in census terminology.[4] Today, the Yakima Valley continues to experience rapid growth in population. Between 1990 and 2000, the county's Latino numbers (which includes immigrants and those born in the United States) increased from approximately 45,000 to 89,000. As of 2005, Latinos constituted 39 percent, or well over one third, of the Yakima County population of 230,000.[5] Significantly, the escalation of gang violence since 1990 has paralleled the county's population growth. This is the first comprehensive study of Mexican American street gangs in the Yakima Valley.

Over most of the past six decades, as Mexican Americans and Mexican immigrants have furnished a majority of the Yakima Valley's laborers, virtually no violence involving Mexican American street gangs was reported in local news stories. Local residents believe that before the 1990s, violence with firearms was almost unknown in the valley. Such outbreaks began occurring, however, during the 1990s, and have continued in the following years.

In early summer 2001, the Mexican American community in Yakima, the county seat, was roiled by related back-to-back killings. Nineteen-year-old Victor Serrano was killed by a gunshot wound to the chest in central Yakima, following an exchange of threats. Ten days later, Antone "Tony" Masovero was shot twice in the head as he sat in a car, not far from the first murder scene. The victims were members of rival groups rooted in California.[6] Serrano's gang was affiliated with the *Sureño* (Southern) faction, based in Southern California, and Masovero's with the *Norteño* (Northern) faction, located principally in northern and central California. The gangs developed in the Yakima Valley after several California members migrated to the area about 1990.

Though gangs in the Yakima Valley might seem to be a relatively new phenomenon, interviews with six former or inactive valley gang members, as well as 15 other residents of the Mexican American community, indicate that Latino gangs have existed there since the 1960s. Violence with firearms was extremely rare, however, until the arrival of the California gang members in the 1990s. These interviews also reveal that there are many reasons why Mexican Americans in the Yakima Valley join gangs but that racism is among the most important.

Many young Mexican Americans, according to the interviews, perceive a racial and class divide between themselves and whites. Young Mexican Americans in Yakima County, which still has primarily an agricultural economy, are often children or grandchildren of farm workers, while whites are often growers, suppliers, or professionals. In addition, they feel they discern racism within the schools, where Mexican American and white students seldom mix and teachers are believed to be hostile to Latino students. Such perceptions often lead to gang membership.

The Yakima Valley attracted thousands of Mexican American migrant workers from Texas after World War II, shortly after the Bracero Program was discontinued in the Pacific Northwest.[7] Among these workers were *pachucos*. This term was understood in different ways in different regions around the country, but it generally refers to members of a Mexican American street culture who wore clothing that set them apart from others in their demographic group and from white Americans. Pachucos were political to the extent that they made a conscious but "inarticulate rejection of the straight world and its organization."[8]

Pachuco culture in the United States stretches back at least eight decades, probably originating in El Paso, Texas; though, recorded information on early pachucos in El Paso is scant. As Eduardo Obregón Pagán noted, they apparently were not the kind to "leave behind written records of their life and world; nor were they the kind to wax nostalgic in later years and talk about their experiences to their children, let alone outsiders from another cultural world."[9] Pachucos in El Paso used the *calo'* argot, which was derived from a dialect spoken by Spanish gypsies (brought to the New World after the conquest of Mesoamerica in the 16th century) and influenced by Mexican indigenous languages.[10]

The most famous pachucos were the young men and women targeted by servicemen during the 1943 zoot suit riots in Los Angeles.[11] Although much has been documented and written on that period in Southern California, interviews reveal that in the postwar years the term pachuco also was applied to individuals in the Yakima Valley who adopted a certain style of dress, particular mannerisms, and the calo' argot. Thus, it was not a cultural phenomenon confined specifically to zoot-suiters of wartime Los Angeles, nor was it narrowly urban in nature. Yet in the Yakima Valley, pachucos did not register on the public radar, as a thorough review of Yakima newspaper articles from the 1950s through the 1970s demonstrates. For instance, the *Yakima Herald-Republic* does not mention the presence of pachucos or ethnic Mexican American street gangs during this period, although the term pachuco had become nationally known after the zoot suit riots.[12]

Ignacio Martinez, 71 years old when interviewed in June 2004, made the Yakima Valley his home in 1964. After World War II, while still living in San Antonio, Texas, he had adopted the pachuco style of dressing. He wore *derechos*, dress shoes that were narrow in the front and flat at the tip, and the zoot suit style of pants, which had narrow cuffs so that the baggy pant-leg could droop over the ankle. Martinez and others he considered pachucos wore short-sleeved shirts, which they left unbuttoned, over T-shirts. Zoot suits were worn in Texas, he said, but they were prohibitively expensive; khakis and T-shirts replaced zoot suits for the pachuco of little means.[13]

Amalia "Mali" Ramirez, a lifelong resident of Sunnyside, in the lower Yakima Valley, recalled seeing men dressed in pachuco style when she was a young girl in the mid-1950s. Once, she observed a knife fight between two men she understood to be pachucos, at a migrant labor camp near Moses Lake, in central Washington: "They wore the 'wife-beater shirts' [sleeveless undershirts] and the *tirantes*, suspenders." She added that they both had a *crucita*, a small cross, tattooed on their foreheads and "could manipulate those blades like nobody's business." (Eduardo Obregón Pagán observed that pachucos in El Paso also wore cross tattoos on their foreheads "in a manner reminiscent of the practice on Ash Wednesday.")[14]

Blanche Razo, who migrated to the Yakima Valley from Texas in 1944 at age six, remembered a small group of female relatives and friends in Wapato that called itself Las Cinco Pachucas in the late 1950s. Some wore "radiant cross" tattoos (of a cross with four lines radiating from it) on their hands, spoke calo', and wore their hair in high pompadours held in place with knitting needles.[15]

Marijuana smoking and the consumption of other drugs were among the customs of the old pachuco lifestyle in El Paso, at least among some individuals. This is demonstrated by the existence of calo' slang words for marijuana (such as *mota* and *yeska*) and a joint (such as *leño*). The Spanish word for peanut, *cacahuete*, was used as a term for barbiturate pills.[16] Recorded pachuco songs of the post-World War II era in the Southwest celebrated violence and drug usage, similar to "gangsta" rap by modern African American and Latino artists:

> My last words to my father
> Were that they bury me not in Califa,
> But that I be buried in Arizona
> With three sacks of marijuana.
> With an outside visa
> And a shot in the arm,
> I don't want any morphine now—
> But just a good weed.[17]

Califa is calo' slang for California.

Some pachucos, as they moved along migrant routes to find work, may have been connected to drug underworlds of the West. The precise nature of their travels remains a topic that has not been thoroughly studied. Pachucos have been described as "young men, usually seasonal laborers, unemployed, and highly mobile individuals."[18] Their world also entailed violence, as demonstrated by the knife fight described by Amalia Ramirez.

Interviews reveal that some Yakima Valley pachucos were involved in the drug trade. Monica Guillen of Sunnyside recalls that her mother, a self-described pachuca, "trafficked" in drugs. She lived in the lower Yakima Valley, home to the first settled communities of Mexican Americans in Yakima

County.[19] Guillen's mother and stepfather traveled frequently from the lower valley to Mexico and back during the 1960s and 1970s.[20]

As a child, other students derided Monica's mother in grade school for her dark skin, calling her "nigger." It was this kind of treatment in school that eventually led her to embrace pachuco culture, and marry a man of similar inclinations, Guillen said.[21] Her mother became "the wildest out of her siblings. Packin' her pistols…my mom was hard core." Guillen's stepfather dressed in what she considered pachuco style. He and his friends "always dressed really nice, you know the plaid shirts with the T-shirts underneath, the Dickies, nice and pleated…and the Stacies."[22] (Dickies is the brand name of a type of work pants, and Stacies is short for Stacy Adams, a brand name of leather dress shoes.)

Both the mother and stepfather associated with a lower valley circle of friends around Los Suses, a couple whose nicknames were similar—Suse and Suzie. El Suse and his friends dressed in the pachuco style and dyed their black hair, which they combed into a pompadour, with hydrogen peroxide to give it an orangish color. The women tattooed their faces with small dots that resembled beauty marks. As was common among pachucas of earlier years, they plucked their eyebrows and redrew them with eyebrow pencil.[23] Monica, who has an advanced college degree, today works as an education professional and is married with two children. Her mother died of natural causes in February 2004.

Though Los Suses and their friends did not call themselves a gang, groups of Mexican Americans in local high schools did identify themselves as such during the late 1960s and 1970s. They gave themselves names such as The Stokelys (apparently named after a local agricultural interest), Los Perros (The Dogs), Los Rojos (The Reds), Las Huiscles (meaning unknown), and Las Osas (The Bears). The last two gangs consisted of young women.[24] Although little information on these groups is available, it appears that clothing styles, dancing, and fistfights were their central interests.[25]

In the 1970s, young people modified the pachuco look and began referring to themselves as *cholos*, a term that is still used today. Though cholo apparel did not necessarily denote gang membership, its wearers often had an adversarial view of the world, with loyalty toward their neighborhoods expressed in acts of violence against young men of other neighborhoods.[26] Cholo culture developed in the barrios of Los Angeles, and grew in popularity as the industrial base declined in western urban areas, joblessness increased among Mexican Americans, and Chicano political activism declined among young people.[27] During this period, cholo culture supplanted mainstream Mexican American culture in the Southwest and Pacific Northwest.

A manifestation of cholo was the lowrider, a car with the frame lowered to ride close to the ground. Mexican American men spent weekends doing alterations on older American-made automobiles, outfitting them with hydraulic pumps that made a car body "jump." *Low Rider*, then a crudely produced magazine that featured these cars, was founded in San Jose, California, in 1977. Youths waited anxiously each month for the latest issue. The magazine displayed photos of Chicanas and Chicanos across the Southwest wearing khaki pants, black leather shoes or rubber-soled "winos," and plaid shirts buttoned at the top, called "flannels" today in the Yakima Valley. Contributing writers submitted fiction on barrio life, and street historians wrote about lowrider history.[28]

The magazine inspired young people in the lower Yakima Valley to adopt the cholo lifestyle. Jose Sevilla grew up in Toppenish, just south of the city of Yakima. In junior high school, Sevilla began wearing cholo clothes as Mexican American young people in the lower valley adopted this style in the 1970s. "Everything just started blossoming. I got a hold of a *Low Rider* magazine. I think [the magazine] had a lot of influence on the Latin people, on the Mexicanos here. Because they wanted to be like the people in California." And, the clothing was affordable for most Mexican Americans in the Yakima Valley.[29]

Yakima Valley cholos in those days did not form "neighborhood" gangs, as modern gangs do.[30] Rather, town allegiance motivated inter-group violence. Jose and his Toppenish friends fought with youths from other towns in the lower valley area, such as Sunnyside and Wapato. Disagreements and personal vendettas escalated to where young men from one town would drive to another town, looking for individuals to "jump." Weapons such as knives, chains, and clubs were used, but gunfire was rare, even if some carried firearms.

One night, Sevilla was caught "slipping," or walking alone without the protection of friends.

> I was walking through a not-so-lighted area in town and there was this group of guys that we didn't get along with that were in town—and they caught me slippin' by myself and they actually "put the boots" to me really well and they cut me with a razor. They were from Sunnyside.[31]

Though he acknowledged *Low Rider's* influence, Sevilla identified the primary reason why he and his friends adopting cholo clothes and mannerisms was because of pachuco family heritage and ethnic identity. He did not name socioeconomic inequality or racism as reasons.

We would look back on my dad's photo albums from when he was growing up, my *tíos* [uncles] all of them, they were all in front of '64 Chevy Impalas, you know? All dressed in khakis and white T-shirts leaning up against the front of the car...We pretty much thought, "That's us."[32]

Sevilla, and others in the Yakima Valley, believe that the influence of migrants from California led to local youths adopting the Sureño and Norteño symbols, which were unknown when Sevilla was a self-described cholo. "A lot of families [moved] their families over here to get away from all the violence of gangs. But I think all they did was just introduce the way of gang life in California to the Mexican kids here in Washington."[33]

The current north-south regional gang affiliation among Latinos in the West has roots in the California prison gang wars of the 1960s and 1970s. In the late 1950s, a group of Mexican American inmates at Deuel Vocational Institute in Tracy organized a gang called the Mexican Mafia. The group's members were natives of East Los Angeles. A rival prison group, La Nuestra Familia, formed in the mid-1960s. Its members came predominantly from San Jose, Salinas, and Fresno—all agricultural centers north of Los Angeles.[34] This rivalry resulted in countless murders and injuries, as the two gangs fought over drug territories and for control of other criminal enterprises in California cities. It has since taken on regional characteristics, with the Mexican Mafia identified with Sureño gangs and the Nuestra Familia with Norteño gangs.[35]

By the early 1980s, gangs in California's barrios had begun using "numbers" to represent territory that they had claimed. These numbers appeared in graffiti and in body tattoos. Sureños adopted the number 13 (written in Arabic or Roman numerals), which at first represented Southern California, including Los Angeles and its environs, San Diego, and Orange County. The symbol now represents Mexico and El Salvador as well.[36]

Norteño gang members used the number 14 (also written in Arabic or Roman numerals), which represents northern and central California, including San Jose, Salinas, and the San Joaquin Valley. The symbols can also be written as *X3* and *X4*. The two factions adopted colors as well—the Sureños blue and Norteños, red—and wear clothing and write graffiti in those colors. Graffiti denoting the factions can be found at many public spaces in the Yakima Valley.

Some studies conducted in the 1990s argued that gang migration had little impact on membership and recruitment, because gangs new to an area would not recruit large numbers of locals.[37] However, four of the Yakima Valley interviewees indicated that the gangs to which they belonged had been started by migrants. Other informants did not mention migration, but they belonged to gangs with names such as Florencia 13, Playboys, and Tiny Boy Sureño, which are similar or identical to the names of Southern California street gangs.[38]

In 1999, an informal survey showed that at least 58 girls and young women in Yakima belonged to all-girl Norteño or Sureño gangs. And a former member reports that gang members from Fresno, in the San Joaquin Valley, started a gang called La Raza XIV in impoverished southeast Yakima, an area nicknamed "the Wasteland" by its residents in the early 1990s. It is not known why these gang members chose the Yakima Valley as their new home.[39] Nevertheless, the migration of the Norteño and Sureño elements to the Yakima Valley in the 1990s has had a profound impact on the area, increasing the level of gang involvement and of gang-related violent crime.[40]

Gang membership has grown as well in other western rural areas, such as in southern New Mexico, where a survey of 400 high school juniors and seniors indicated that one in four claimed membership in a gang.[41] Another study in Nevada showed that roughly 20 percent of 169 students in a random sample identified themselves as gang members. The authors cited economic and ethnic changes caused by rapid growth as reasons for gang involvement in rural areas.[42]

Eloy Aldama, a former La Raza XIV member, describes life as a Yakima Valley gang member. When Aldama's family moved to the Wasteland in the early 1990s, they lived only two doors down from the house of several La Raza XIV gang members. "They had the XIV tag [tattoo] on their chest…and then the 14 right here," Aldama said, pointing to his arm. (Gangs in Fresno, where La Raza XIV's founders are from, claim F-14 as their geographic symbol and are hostile to Southern California gang members and other northern factions.)[43]

At nine years of age, Aldama was offered membership in the gang. "They were always bangin' and stuff…just writing on walls, and I was like, 'Well, that's cool,' you know? 'They're breaking laws, why don't we break laws with them?'"

He was initiated through a beating, a common ritual among Chicano gangs. "When I was nine, they were like, 'You wanna get in?' I was like, 'Yeah!' So…they started beating up on me." Four gang members, all in their late teens, took part in the beating. Afterward they told him, "We're like family. We'll back you up in anything." Aldama added, "Whatever they told you, you believed."[44]

Group activities centered around selling drugs, acquiring weapons, and preparing for attacks either from or against a gang called Varrio Sureños Locos, whose territory was nearby. Any member with influence, such as Aldama, could acquire drugs to sell, or get firearms, just by asking. (Police patrol cars were a rare sight in the Wasteland, according to Aldama.) His gang membership took a toll on his already difficult family life. His mother, an immigrant from Mexico, was struggling to raise nine children on her own by doing a variety of jobs, including agricultural and warehouse work; the family slept on the floor to avoid being hit in a drive-by shooting. Fortunately, at age 15 he was "rushed out" of La Raza by another ritual beating, and quit the gang. As of June 2004, Aldama had been admitted to a university in eastern Washington.[45]

To understand why people such as Aldama join gangs, it is useful to examine previous research on gang membership. In his study of Southern California gangs, James Diego Vigil argued that gang membership results from "multiple marginality"—i.e., alienation from mainstream society and institutions because of poverty, lack of positive self-identities, and troubled home lives. This leads to "choloization," whereby youth in impoverished neighborhoods are socialized not by families or community institutions, but by gang members. Most of Vigil's subjects came from single-parent or unstable family homes.[46]

In extensive work conducted in the 1970s and 1980s, Joan Moore found that gang members in some Los Angeles barrios believed their gang membership was an expression of Chicano pride. Social conditions of the Mexican American community and the legacy of the zoot suit riots led these gang members to view white authority and culture with hostility.[47]

These earlier studies are of somewhat limited use in the Yakima Valley, however, because the Mexican American community has been much more fluid than in the urban areas studied by Vigil and Moore. Four Yakima Valley subjects had changed addresses several times before reaching adulthood, so it is difficult to compare their cases with the longtime residents of settled barrios. Only one person interviewed—Aldama—could be described as impoverished, in an unstable family environment, and in a neighborhood of long-term residents. His case was the only one that fit the complete "choloization" model.

Most of the valley's Mexican American communities have not undergone "barrioization," the long-term process of neighborhood segregation and isolation described by Albert Camarillo, for example.[48] In addition, both Moore and Vigil emphasize the generational nature of gang membership in Southern

California. But in the Yakima Valley, violent gangs were a new phenomenon of the 1990s, rather than the result of generations of gang members living in the same neighborhoods.

Nevertheless, Yakima Valley's Mexican Americans and those in established barrios often cite similar reasons for joining gangs. Expressions of Chicano pride appear to be factors in gang formation and membership, as demonstrated by gang names such as Brown Pride Locos and La Raza XIV. And Mexican American gang members in the valley often believe whites in the community are prejudiced against them. (Vigil and Moore found that perceived racism resulted in the rejection of mainstream American culture by Chicano gang members.)

The valley's Donny Zamudio was one of those citing identification with Chicano culture as a reason for joining a gang. Zamudio explained that he joined because he did not identify with the Euro-American students at his school, which was located in an affluent part of the city. Zamudio himself grew up in a two-parent family and lived in a comfortable two-story home, surrounded by open spaces. But he preferred the company of gang member cousins in neighboring Toppenish and immersed himself in local gang lore.[49] Jose Sevilla joined a gang because he identified with his father, who dressed in khakis and shiny black shoes in classic Chicano street style. Sevilla said that he and others were also influenced by pictures of California barrio life published in *Low Rider* magazine.[50]

Gang symbolism and camaraderie, set against a backdrop of limited social opportunities within an agricultural economy, also often attracted Yakima Valley Mexican Americans to the gangs. Eloy Aldama proudly sported red bandannas on his head and each shoulder, a red belt, and red shoelaces.[51]

One Mexican American girl, whom I will call Whisper, joined a predominantly African American gang based in west Yakima because she was attracted by its rules, rituals, and regulations. Her older sister, a Sureña, introduced her to several Latino gang members, but Whisper eventually decided to join the West Side Hustlers because Mexican American gang members "shot into people's houses."[52]

West Side's gang codes appealed to Whisper. The members were involved primarily in drug dealing, but they themselves were not allowed to use drugs other than marijuana and alcohol. Violence against rival gangs was to be resorted to only when necessary. After asking several times to be "rushed in," she was administered the ritual in 1997, at the age of 15.

> They just wanted me to stop fighting, they just wanted to see how long I would go, but I kept getting up after I'd fall down. They're like, "Stay down!

Stay down!" So it was probably about three minutes, but if you had three minutes with these big ass guys on you, it seems like a long time (laughs)! Ah, man! I was black and blue. Afterwards, they picked me up. And they all hugged me. They gave me my flag and that was it.[53]

The flag was a white bandanna; the gang's colors were white and black.[54]

Other female gang members' reasons for joining may have been related to their gender roles as Chicanas—some seem to have joined as a form of empowerment. Traditionally, Chicanas are expected to take care of a family's physical needs—to cook, keep house, and run errands, for example. Within traditional Chicano culture, women are not supposed to be aggressive, and physical acts of violence or protection are left to men. "I don't trust guys," said one young woman, a member of a Norteña gang called Varrios Rojas Carnalas. "Guys are dogs. Girls are tired of being pushed around by them and they can't use us girls no more."[55] When Whisper was asked, however, she refuted any idea that her gang involvement was related to gender and empowerment.

The roles of economics and racism should not be discounted in the case of gang involvement in the Yakima Valley. Although none of the people interviewed cited poverty as a factor leading to gang membership, it was clear that Aldama grew up as a socially and economically disadvantaged youth. In 1990, as gang members arrived from California, census figures indicated significant levels of poverty and underemployment among those of Mexican origin. Only an estimated 13,603 out of 24,526 of such people over age 16 worked in some capacity. Most earned under $25,000; some 1,200 families earned less than $10,000. About 1,000 families lived below the federal poverty level.[56]

Among all persons interviewed, there was a general perception of racism in the community, at times discussed in vague terms. Many young Mexican Americans in the Yakima Valley have parents who work as laborers in low-paying agricultural jobs, often without medical benefits. There are few stable, well-paying employment opportunities, outside or within the agricultural sector. These youths face an uncertain future. In addition, a type of class stratification has arisen, in which Mexican Americans view whites as racially prejudiced against them. Whites in the community, local Mexican Americans believe, are more likely to hold elective office, own local farms, and be professionals. A similar phenomenon has been noted in the San Joaquin Valley of California, which also has an economy based on agriculture and a high level of gang activity. And like the Yakima Valley, the San Joaquin Valley has large numbers of young people, limited job opportunities, and ethnic and class hierarchies unique to agricultural economies.[57]

Perceptions of racism and class division manifest themselves in local schools, where white families more often can afford to pay for their children's involvement in athletics and other activities, and where the two groups maintain limited contact with each other. Some of those interviewed mentioned experiencing racism at local schools.

"Some of the teachers are like, 'Man, Hispanics are dumb,' and all this other crap," Aldama said. "I mean, we could never do anything about it, 'cause the superintendent ain't gonna believe us."

One teacher remarked that her initial reaction to a Spanish language immersion program for teachers was, "Oh, here we go—another Mexican thing." She eventually supported the program, but this comment came from a kindergarten teacher of a district with 54 percent Latino enrollment. A teacher at a high school in which Latinos constituted 47 percent of the student body said that there were only three Latino faculty members.[58]

Donny Zamudio said he joined a gang as a self-defense mechanism against perceived racial hostility in his high school: "There were a lot of Mexicans that didn't get into gangs and stuff. They were always getting in trouble because they'd get picked on and got in fights."

In a study of Chicano students in Yakima schools, one young man said he eventually joined a Norteño gang because of feelings of alienation. "I remember going into class filled with *gabachos* and taught by *gabachos*," he said. "It was a very humbling experience for me. I was always made to feel as if I did not belong."[59] *Gabachos* is a common caló term for whites and is not considered derogatory.

Other interviewees saw school as nothing more than a place where gangs recruit new members. "You're into your studies and your schoolwork, mostly. But gang members are all around and then you first meet them. That's how it all starts," said one, a former Sureño gang member.[60]

Whether informants viewed the schools as places of racism or places for gang recruitment, their observations support Vigil's assertion that social institutions fail to provide positive self-identities to young Chicanos.[61] Although most of my informants did not directly cite poverty, racism, or economics in their decision to join gangs, it is clear that many young Mexican Americans in the Yakima Valley perceive a sense of bias against them, especially in the education system. Further research can perhaps flesh out the links between gangs, racism, and socioeconomic factors.

A common thread in this study is gang migration. In the 1950s, pachuco culture arrived in the Yakima Valley with migrant workers, and *Low Rider* magazine later influenced a generation of young Chicanos who adopted the cholo style. But it was gang migration that brought California-style gang symbolism, colors, and "rushing in," along with escalating degrees of violence. Once settled, the gangs become entrenched in local communities.

"There is an internal reasoning to the Chicano gang subculture and because of its sense of camaraderie it is able to attract and socialize many youths," Vigil observed.[62] The criminologist Albert K. Cohen noted that a gang, once established, "may achieve a life which outlasts that of the individual who perpetrated its creation, but only so long as it continues to serve the needs of those who succeed its creators."[63] This is rapidly becoming true in the Yakima Valley.

Notes

1. A version of this article originally appeared under the same title in the *Pacific Northwest Quarterly* 97, no. 3 (Summer 2006):131-38.
2. Erasmo Gamboa, "Under the Thumb of Agriculture: Bracero and Mexican American Workers in the Pacific Northwest, 1940–1950," Ph.D. dissertation, University of Washington, 1984, 321. See also, Josue Estrada, "Texas Mexican Diaspora to Washington State: Recruitment, Migration, and Community, 1940–1960," Master's thesis, Washington State University, 2007.
3. Gamboa, "Under the Thumb of Agriculture," 382.
4. U.S. Census Bureau, *1980 Census of Population and Housing, Yakima, Washington* (Washington, D.C., 1983), 1, 10.
5. U.S. Census Bureau, *1990 Census of Population...Washington*, 2 vols. (Washington, D.C., 1993), 1:18; Yakima County, Washington, State and County Quickfacts, U.S. Census Bureau: quickfacts.census.gov web site.
6. *Yakima Herald-Republic*, June 3, 2001, 1B.
7. See Erasmo Gamboa, *Mexican Labor and World War II: Braceros in the Pacific Northwest, 1942–1947* (Seattle: University of Washington Press, 2000).
8. Stuart Cosgrove, "The Zoot Suit and Style Warfare," *History Workshop Journal* 18 (Autumn 1984):89.
9. Eduardo Obregón Pagán, *Murder at the Sleepy Lagoon: Zoot Suits, Race, and Riot in Wartime L.A.* (Chapel Hill: University of North Carolina Press, 2003), 37.
10. Mauricio Mazón, *The Zoot-Suit Riots: The Psychology of Symbolic Annihilation* (Austin: University of Texas Press, 1984), 2–4.
11. Beatrice Griffith, *American Me* (Boston: Houghton Mifflin, 1948), 45–46, 55–56; Pagán, *Murder at the Sleepy Lagoon*, 36–39.
12. Gamboa, *Mexican Labor and World War II*, 114.
13. Ignacio Martinez, interview by author, June 16, 2004, Parker, Washington.

14. Amalia "Mali" Ramirez, interview by author, June 16, 2004, Sunnyside, Washington; Pagán, *Murder at the Sleepy Lagoon*, 38.

15. Blanche Razo, interview by author, July 1, 2004, Toppenish, Washington.

16. Lurline Coltharp, *The Tongue of the Tirilones: A Linguistic Study of a Criminal Argot* (Tuscaloosa: University of Alabama Press, 1965), 129, 213, 226, 282.

17. George C. Barker, *Pachuco: An American-Spanish Argot and Its Social Functions in Tucson, Arizona* (Tucson: University of Arizona Press, 1970), 35–38.

18. Douglas Henry Daniels, "Los Angeles Zoot: Race 'Riot,' the Pachuco, and Black Music Culture," *Journal of Negro History* 82 (Spring 1997):210 (quotation); Pagán, *Murder at the Sleepy Lagoon* 38.

19. Monica Guillen, interview by author, June 26, 2004, Sunnyside, Washington; Gamboa, "Under the Thumb of Agriculture," 321–82.

20. Guillen interview.

21. Ibid. See also, Catherine S. Ramirez, "Crimes of Fashion: The Pachuca and Chicana Style Politics," in *Meridians: Feminism, Race, Transnationalism* 2, no. 2 (2002):2, 15–17.

22. Guillen interview.

23. Ibid.

24. Jesse Villanueva interview, July 2, 2004, unincorporated area, Yakima County.

25. Alicia Villanueva, interview by author, June 4, 2004, unincorporated area, Yakima County.

26. James Diego Vigil, "Cholos and Gangs: Culture Change and Street Youth in Los Angeles," in *Gangs in America*, C. Ronald Huff, ed., (Newbury Park, California: Sage, 1990), 116–17.

27. Ernesto Chávez, *"Mi Raza Primero!" (My People First!): Nationalism, Identity, and Insurgency in the Chicano Movement in Los Angeles, 1966–1978* (Berkeley: University of California Press, 2002), 117–20.

28. See "history book," Low Rider; lowridermagazine.com/historybook web site. Pagán, in *Murder at the Sleepy Lagoon*, makes use of pachuco photographs culled from old *Low Rider* issues.

29. Jose Sevilla (assumed name), interview by author, June 14, 2004, Yakima, Washington.

30. For more on cholo street gangs, see Jack Katz, *Seductions of Crime: Moral and Sensual Attractions in Doing Evil* (New York: Basic Books, 1988), 90–93; and Marjorie S. Zatz, "Los Cholos: Legal Processing of Chicano Gang Members," *Social Problems* 33 (October 1985):13–30.

31. Sevilla interview.

32. Ibid.

33. Ibid.

34. *Los Angeles Times*, November 11, 1992, 2B, September 28, 1993, 1B; John Irwin, *Prisons in Turmoil* (Boston, 1980), 190; Jimmy Fuentes (assumed name), telephone interview by author, June 25, 1993 (Fuentes was an inmate at the Corcoran State Prison in California).

35. John Donovan, *An Introduction to Street Gangs in California* (Sacramento, California: S.N., 1988), 17–18; Gabriel C. Morales, *Varrio Warfare: Violence in the Latino Community* (Seattle: Tecolote, 2000), 32–38.

36. Ibid.; Donovan, *An Introduction to Street Gangs*, 17.

37. See, for example, Cheryl A. Maxson, Kristi J. Woods, and Malcolm W. Klein, "Street Gang Migration: How Big a Threat?" *National Institute of Justice Journal* (February 1996):26–31.

38. Donny Zamudio (assumed name), interview by author, May 23, 2004, Pullman, Washington; Eloy Aldama (assumed name), interview by author, June 25, 2004, Yakima,

Washington; Art Arredondo (assumed name), interview by author, June 18, 2004, unincorporated area, Yakima County; Sevilla interview.

39. *Yakima Herald-Republic*, February 28, 1996; Aldama interview.

40. For a study indicating that gang migration does affect gang membership and recruitment, see Scott H. Decker and Barrik Van Winkle, *Life in the Gang: Family, Friends, and Violence* (Cambridge, England: Cambridge University Press, 1996), 85–92.

41. G. Larry Mays, Kathy Fuller, and L. Thomas Winfree, "Gangs and Gang Activity in Southern New Mexico: A Descriptive Look at a Growing Rural Problem," *Journal of Crime and Justice* 17, no. 1 (1994):25–44.

42. William P. Evans, Carla Fitzgerald, Dan Weigel, and Sarah Chvilicek, "Are Rural Gangs Similar to Their Urban Peers? Implications for Rural Communities," *Youth and Society* 30 (March 1990):277.

43. Aldama interview; Morales, *Varrio Warfare*, 45.

44. Aldama interview.

45. Ibid.

46. James Diego Vigil, *Barrio Gangs: Street Life and Identity in Southern California* (Austin: University of Texas Press, 1988), 9–11, 35, 39, 172–73.

47. Joan W. Moore, et al., *Homeboys: Gangs, Drugs, and Prison in the Barrios of Los Angeles* (Philadelphia: Temple University Press, 1978); Joan W. Moore, *Going Down to the Barrio: Homeboys and Homegirls in Change* (Philadelphia: Temple University Press, 1991).

48. Albert Camarillo, *Chicanos in a Changing Society: From Mexican Pueblos to American Barrios in Santa Barbara and Southern California, 1848–1930* (Cambridge, Massachusetts: Harvard University Press, 1979).

49. Zamudio interview.

50. Sevilla interview.

51. Aldama interview.

52. Whisper (assumed nickname), interview by author, July 2, 2004, Yakima, Washington.

53. Ibid.

54. Ibid.

55. *Yakima Herald-Republic*, February 18, 1997, 1A. A gang with a similar name, North Side Carnalas and claiming 33 members, was noted in a 1999 informal survey. A Sureña gang reported 25 members.

56. U.S. Census Bureau, *1990 Census of Population*, 1:389, 394.

57. See Ramón D. Chacon, "A Case Study of Ghettoization and Segregation: West Fresno's Black and Chicano Community during the 1970s," *SCCR Working Paper Series*, No. 12, Stanford Center for Chicano Research, Stanford University, California; Tomás Mendez, "A Descriptive Statistical Study of Gang Members," paper presented at the Second Annual California McNair Symposium, Berkeley, California, 1994 (abstract available at mcnair. berkeley.edu/94CASymposium web site, s.v. "Tomas Mendez").

58. Aldama interview (1st and 2nd quotations); *Yakima Herald-Republic*, July 3, 2004, 1C, 6C (last quotation).

59. Zamudio interview (1st quotation); Marcos Pizarro, *Chicanas and Chicanos in School: Racial Profiling, Identity Battles, and Empowerment* (Austin: University of Texas Press, 2005), 230.

60. "Spanky," interview by author, May 7, 2001, Yakima, Washington.

61. Vigil, *Barrio Gangs*, 68.

62. Ibid., 37.

63. Albert K. Cohen, in *Delinquent Boys: The Culture of the Gang* (Glencoe, Illinois: Free Press, 1955), 65.

XI

Rethinking the Region: Gender, Race, and Class in Pacific Northwest History[1]

Susan Armitage

SINCE THE DRAMATIC DEBUT of the New Western history in 1987, writing about the U.S. West has changed markedly. In response to the new view of the West—in Patricia Limerick's phrase, as a "meeting ground of peoples"—environmental, racial/ethnic, and gendered studies have proliferated.[2] But while academic scholarship on the West as a whole has changed, sub-regional textbooks, such as those for the Pacific Northwest, remain largely locked in Frederick Jackson Turner's Frontier Thesis emphasis on Euro-American pioneer settlement and development.

As I puzzled over this discrepancy, especially concerning gender (my own specialty), I realized that the concepts of gender and regionalism are deeply at odds. In the pages that follow I will explain how I reached that conclusion and how, drawing on my own experience as a textbook writer, I envisage a new regional framework that can accommodate the new gendered, raced, and environmental perspectives that have become commonplace in publications about the U.S. West as a whole.

When I first started writing about women in Pacific Northwest history, almost thirty-years ago, I thought it was just a matter of filling in the blanks. If I could research the lives of women and write about their activities and concerns, then other (usually male) historians would add women's history to their narratives. I soon discovered that it was hardly that simple. First, my own general category of "woman" turned out to require substantial modification to allow for differences in race, class, location, and time. Then I began to notice the limited ways historians recognized women. When they did incorporate women in their narratives, it was usually to confirm an existing stereotype, as for example quoting from women's diaries to emphasize the sad and pitiful aspects of the Overland Trail experience, never the adventurous ones; or to use the writings of reluctant pioneer females to confirm the gender stereotype that women were conservative and retrospective while, in contrast, men were forward-looking.[3]

As time went on, more regional historians began to mention women, but only the most famous ones. For example, Carlos Schwantes' most widely-adopted college textbook of more than 500 pages lists only nine women in the index—suffragists Abigail Scott Duniway and May Arkwright Hutton, author Mary Hallock Foote, politicians Bertha Landes, Maurine Neuberger, and Dixie Lee Ray, missionaries Narcissa Whitman and Eliza Spalding, and, of course, Sacajawea. Of those, only three—Whitman, Duniway, and Hutton—get more than a brief mention.[4]

I hasten to stress the many good things about this text. Schwantes deserves major credit for a clear new conceptualization and periodization of Pacific Northwest history. Characterizing the Pacific Northwest as a geographical hinterland, Schwantes organizes his text around the stages of its gradual incorporation into the nation as a whole—economically, politically, and culturally. Clearly written, with many attractive maps and pictures, the Schwantes text is an improvement over its predecessors. It has been greeted warmly, and widely adopted for classroom use. But for all of its good points, the volume's scant attention to women and racial/ethnic groups made me begin to question my initial assumption that the Pacific Northwest regional story simply needed to be enlarged to incorporate new points of view.

My classroom experience validated my growing belief that more was at stake than simply adding new characters. As I taught Pacific Northwest history, I discovered that my students thought that the lives and concerns of women were mundane compared to the much more interesting events in men's lives. I soon sensed that the class only perked up when I returned to the customary narrative of events that they all believed was the "real" Pacific Northwest history. This attitude was so common (and, I suspect true elsewhere for regional history) that I found myself naming it "The Great Men and Little Women Syndrome." In short, great men fight wars, explore the unknown, rush for gold, and lead political movements, while little women, true to the image made famous by Louisa May Alcott, stay close to home and find their true satisfaction in domestic life. Placed side by side, men always loom larger than women

I realized that either I had to concentrate on the few famous women who were judged as successful in male-dominated arenas such as politics, or propose changes in the way we tell our regional story. The larger issue was how to craft narratives about daily lives, which are the stuff of social history, that could compete with the political-military Pacific Northwest tales that my students already knew. I will suggest such a narrative in the pages that follow.

First, though, some definitions are in order. Gender is a relatively new term encompassing much more than the undifferentiated "woman" with which U.S. women's history began in the 1970s. Today the term "gender" or "gender system" is used to denote the many complex beliefs and activities that determine the relationships between the sexes at any given historical moment. In contrast to myself and other historians initially focusing on women, modern scholars in gender studies are not much concerned with the simple recovery of the women's experience and its addition to recorded history. Gender historians assert something much more fundamental, which is that gender is a key analytic tool, as important as class and race, and always interlocked with them. These are not stand-alone concepts. There is not just race, nor just gender, nor just class, but a historically exact mixture, and what it adds up to is an understanding of the power relationships in a society as a whole. Not incidentally, this entails a new way of writing history.[5]

Regionalism is a much older term than gender. Historians tell us that Americans thought in regional or sectional terms before they thought in national ones. Region was, and perhaps for some people still is, a primary way in which individuals describe their "home place." Regionalism assumes that some aspects of a particular place shape the experience of everyone living there, of both sexes and all races and social classes. These commonalities, most frequently rooted in the physical terrain and natural resources, supposedly mark one region as distinct from another. Thus, for example, both geography and history make the Pacific Northwest a different region from the South.

But in every region of the country there are problems with boundaries. According to Joel Garreau's *The Nine Nations of North America*, the Pacific Northwest is defined by the coastal strip he calls "Ecotopia," after Ernest Callenbach's popular environmental novel of 1975. In another example, the editors of the *Atlas of the New West* consider this damp coastal strip as so different from the rest of the arid West that they refuse to include it in their volume. Moreover, in environmental terms, the physical geography of the region runs north-south, not east-west, and the present-day boundary with Canada at the 49th parallel is one of the more artificial dividing lines in North America.[6]

Geography aside, today the commonly accepted borders of the Pacific Northwest are political—the states of Washington, Oregon, and Idaho, and perhaps a little bit of western Montana. Thus defined, this region consists of a narrow coastal urbanized strip where a majority of the population lives, and a much larger trans-mountain and much drier hinterland, lesser populated and traditionally devoted largely to agriculture, mining, and lumbering. Garreau rather meanly calls this interior area "The Empty Quarter"; a recent guide-book more kindly dubs it "The Great Outdoors." As this contrast indicates, the Pacific Northwest has enough internal physical differences to beg the question of regional homogeneity.

Even when it is possible to agree on regional boundaries, further problems arise with the term. Historians owe the particular usage of the word *regional-ism* to Frederick Jackson Turner. Following his lead, subsequent historians used the concept both confidently and sloppily, assuming that some thing or things in the region bound people together in ways that superseded cultural and racial boundaries. This assumption of general regional commonalities, while recognizing differences *between* regions, ignored conflicts and dif-ferences *within* regions. In effect, then, regional historians wrote only the history of the dominant cultural group and not that of subordinate ones, generally ignoring class, race, gender, and other differences. This is what I mean by asserting that the two terms, gender and region, are incompatible. Gender (and race and class) distinguish differences *within* a geographical space, however its boundaries are defined, while regionalism looks outward to contrast one region with another.

What seems to be happening, however, is that definitions of region and regionalism are quietly changing. Today's New Western history, to a greater extent than often realized, is based on a new definition of region. Donald Wor-ster, an early formulator of the New Western history, has this description:

> The history of the region is first and foremost one of an evolving human ecology. A region emerges as people try to make a living from a particular part of the earth, as they adapt themselves to its limits and possibilities. What the regional historian should first want to know is how a people or peoples acquired a place and, then, how they perceived and tried to make use of it.

Similarly, Patricia Limerick puts a somewhat less environmental and slightly more cultural twist on the same basic notion:

> Western history has been an ongoing competition for legitimacy—for the right to claim for oneself and sometimes for one's group the status of legiti-mate beneficiary of Western resources. The intersection of ethnic diversity with property allocation unifies Western history.

In effect, both Worster and Limerick[7] propose a formulation of regional-ism that is firmly rooted in social history—i.e., in the history of ordinary people, not the dominant elite. Worster, for example, asserts that the regional historian should look at the peoples of a given region and "identify the survival techniques they adopted, their patterns of work and economy, and the social relationships"—i.e., the ordinary details of their daily lives. And Limerick, in contrast to Turner, assumes that the basic regional event is conflict, not commonality. She points out that region is the ideal arena—larger than a case study, smaller than the national whole—within which to examine differences. This concept requires us to rethink the idea of region, looking at it from the inside out, emphasizing the struggle of different groups for land, legitimacy, and, as Katherine Morrissey showed in *Mental Territories: Mapping the Inland Empire*, for representation itself.[8]

This concept of region, as a place within which to explore the conflict and adaptation of diverse groups *before* reaching conclusions about commonality is still a new idea. As we rethink region, we will need to rewrite regional history. To do that, I will briefly analyze the way regional history texts are currently written and suggest ways they need to be changed.

Writing textbooks is a specialized skill, as I learned in co-authoring a multi-edition U.S. history textbook, *Out of Many*.[9] Based largely on this personal experience, my comments are meant to be generic, applying to all texts, including my own. My purpose is threefold—to identify the underlying assumptions of textbooks regarding region, to critically examine the narrative techniques that often unconsciously foster those assumptions, and to propose some alternatives.

One fundamental problem with most texts in use today is that they accept our current national context—i.e., the American nation state. They begin by seeming to suggest that the present-day boundaries of the Pacific Northwest had always existed. But in geographic terms, the regional commonalities cross borders. Geographically, the region runs north-south, not east-west, a fact that shaped the lives of the original inhabitants, the North American Indians. The Makah in what is now Washington State and the Kwakiutl of British Columbia had more in common, or sometimes in rivalry, than either did with the inland-dwelling Nez Perce. To adopt present-day boundaries commits "the archeologists' fallacy"—relegating all previous regional experience to "prehistory," by which archeologists actually mean before the written records of European-Indian contact. This automatic assumption of present-day boundaries is a tendency shared by most American history textbooks.

One of the greatest struggles I had in writing my part of *Out of Many* was when the mapmakers wanted to demark the current borders with Canada and Mexico before they actually existed. In the early 1840s, the future of the Pacific Northwest was uncertain: Would it be American? British? Or even

Russian? Textbooks always mention the uncertainty, but when the accompanying map shows the present-day boundary, the implicit message is that the result was inevitable. Such a map encourages the viewer to see the Pacific Northwest through imperial eyes and robs readers of the chance to sense the real contingency of historical events and outcomes.

The fundamental point here is that the definition of a region should come from its inhabitants, not from outside, and that the designation should be related to history and therefore changeable. Further, a text that begins with the customary boundaries immediately excludes not only the traditional border crossers such as North American Indians, whose homelands are now bisected by artificial lines, but also contemporary crossers such as Mexican and Mexican American migrant workers who are "seasonal," not "temporary," in that they return year after year. In addition, a growing number of American citizens and resident aliens are trans-national, which means that they maintain close ties with their former homelands (Mexico, China, Vietnam, for example) and regularly travel back and forth.

A second, fundamental problem is that regional textbooks are mostly centered on white male history. Most regional texts automatically focus on politics and economics. Because these remained male-dominated arenas well into the 20th century, white women and members of racial and ethnic groups are immediately relegated to the shadowy background. There are additional reasons for this bias. The Pacific Northwest has a long history of heroic tales, stretching from the 1804–1806 Lewis and Clark Expedition to the heroic "Roll on Columbia" folksong about dam-building exploits of the 1930s. Earlier historians willingly drew on this tradition. Witness Irving Stone's *Men to Match My Mountains* and Stewart Holbrook's celebration of the males he called *Wildmen, Wobblies, and Whistle Punks.* Stephen Ambrose's recent, extremely popular book about the Lewis and Clark Expedition, *Undaunted Courage,* also follows this tried-and-true format.[10]

Another reason for the persistence of white male history is that the activities of politicians and economic leaders are well documented and the lives of others are not. It is much easier to write a compelling narrative by focusing on the actions of a conspicuously notable person than it is to write about impersonal structural forces, or to use scattered, frequently uneven sources to describe the role of an unheralded group that has not been center stage in a larger drama. This certainly is one reason why "great man history"—so individualistic, so incapable of describing social depth and variety—is still being written.

New regional histories should require us to re-examine our notion of history itself. History is *not* the story of great events orchestrated by great men; in fact, it is very nearly the reverse. It is the sum total of innumerable small actions and reactions by ordinary people as they come into contact with other people, who may seem similar or very different from themselves. All of the interactions make up the events that are historically important. In this sense, *everyone* is an actor in the larger drama. Of course, the involvement of some has greater consequences, and all interactions are determined by the wider individual and group structures of race, class, and gender. This notion—that history is the sum of its structured interactions—is the basic insight of the social and cultural history approaches that now dominate the field of American history nationally. It represents something new, especially in Western history, which as a field has been deeply reluctant to move away from the heroic emphasis. Some of the newer approaches will become more apparent as I contrast them with those in most regional texts.

Most regional and national texts begin with a chapter that covers basic geography and the "First Peoples." Although this is an improvement over older treatments that described the land alone (implying that it was empty) and only mentioned native peoples at the time of contact with Europeans, the "natural history fallacy" may still occur. In this construct, native peoples become a "natural" part of the physical landscape, and because the landscape must be "tamed" or "conquered," the problem is compounded. Native people are not only denied their humanity and sovereignty, but their conquest or removal to reservations is made an inevitable part of the "taming" process.

But even when texts avoid the natural history fallacy, the anthropological trap remains. In most current regional and national texts, pre-contact native peoples have a chapter of their own, which is of a markedly different character than the rest of the text. In the Schwantes volume, "The First Pacific Northwesterners" is devoted to a survey of the early inhabitants, all of whom would have been baffled by the notion of "the Pacific Northwest" since their language, kinship ties, and trade routes often ran north-south, not east and west. They are described in measured and impersonal anthropological terms, with their "ways" described briefly, respectfully, and in aggregate. There are no individuals. It is all in the distant past. giving little sense of how these real people lived on the land and made it their own ("the first thing one would want to know," as Worster has pointed out).[11]

In the next three chapters devoted to European and American exploration and the initial stages of the fur trade, the presentation is markedly different from the previous impersonal characterization. The leading explorers are named, described in psychological detail, and made the focus of the story. That they are dependent upon constant interaction with native men and women is barely mentioned; instead, they stride with indomitable courage across the landscape. Not surprisingly, the emphasis on European forms of individual heroism makes the precontact native peoples seem remote, obligatory, and buried in a distant past.

Of course, the reason usually given for this striking difference is that the written and printed sources on European and American explorers are incomparably richer than those on American Indians , or so we are told. But there *are* other sources, namely the oral traditions of different individual tribes and groups. In Western history textbooks, one of the origin stories is often quoted, albeit more for local color than for contextual substance. In fact, the Hopi's rich and compelling narrative of journeying from the first to the fourth world has long been a favorite. There are also many collections of Northwest Indian stories and tales[12] that allow us to see the land through the eyes of native peoples. With special attention, historians can learn to use these collections systematically to write vivid descriptions of what the land meant to its first inhabitants and how they made their living. As a result, both the setting and the people come alive, revealing how real people lived in a particular place, and, as Donald Worster suggested, claimed and named it as their own.

There is another and even more compelling reason to rethink the first chapter of most textbooks. A rapidly growing cohort of Native American scholars is bringing new perspectives to the field of American Indian history, and as their scholarship grows, so does their range of vision. Ethnohistorians are looking back before contact and using combinations of anthropology, archeology, and oral tradition to probe what used to be called "prehistory." And they are claiming, as Colin Calloway asserts in *One Vast Winter Count*, that the wall between Native American history and "American" history has to come down. As Calloway declares, "The West is not a land of empty spaces with a short history; it is a vast winter count, where many people etched their histories continuously from times beyond memory." In short, Indian history is the ancient history of North America and should not be isolated from the mainstream.[13]

Closer to home, one of the most surprising and exciting aspects of the Lewis and Clark Bicentennial events in 2004-2006 was the acknowledgment, brought to audiences by representatives of Northwest tribes, of the long and rich history of native peoples in the region. Compared to a heritage of many thousands of years, the 200 years since Lewis and Clark are a blink of the eye. If regional history is about a geographic place, and the role of historians is documenting how people have lived in this space, the timeline of Pacific Northwest history must be moved backward by thousands of years. The challenge of the next generation of historians, once this long history is acknowledged, will be to adjust the regional story accordingly. Someday soon, one short introductory chapter on First Peoples in regional textbooks will no longer suffice.

In many texts, the explorers and the fur traders are followed by chapters on the Oregon Trail pioneers and early white settlement through the 1860s. The early American settlers are treated as the bringers of law, order, and, implicitly, whiteness—never as simply another immigrant group. In fairness, we must acknowledge that this is how they saw themselves. Only a brief mention is usually made of the extensive intermarriage between American and European men and native women in the fur trade as well as the early settlement period. The distinct possibility of a mixed-race society and the related notion of blended cultures was supposedly overwhelmed by the size of the white migration—i.e., by sheer weight of numbers rather than racial attitudes. By comparison in the Western chapter of the American history textbook *Out of Many*, I deliberately stressed the mixed-race character of the early Pacific Northwest frontier, so that students would realize that there were alternatives to the conscious and deliberate pattern of racialization that did actually occur.

In the popular Schwantes text, the section on early white settlement opens with an account of the deaths of missionaries Marcus and Narcissa Whitman at Waiilatpu in 1847. This violent—and atypical—episode affects the entire section, since readers will undoubtedly remember the violence, not the peaceful, if uneasy coexistence that was customary. Native peoples virtually disappear from the Schwantes narrative after the 18 pages describing the Whitman's demise and the ensuing three decades of Indian-white hostilities, and they do not reappear until the Boldt decision about fishing rights in 1974. The intervening years and events are encapsulated in a 2-page description of the four stages of Indian-white relations: (1) peaceable contacts, (2) conflict, (3) colonization, and (4) the recent and reluctant recognition of Indian rights.[14]

Every textbook writer has to summarize at times; encapsulation of admittedly more complex events is one choice. It would, however, be unacceptable for such treatment of American Indians in any new regional text that purports to fully explore inter-racial contact. Instead of encapsulation, these stages of Indian history could be presented as a basic thread running throughout the text and providing a thematic counterpoint to the dominant story of Euro-American commercial growth and development. Well-chosen examples, as part of a basic social history narrative technique, would work well. This approach has been employed by writers of some of the best-selling college-level U.S. history texts for the past fifteen years. Regional writers should follow their lead. Otherwise, American Indians remain pop-up figures, a fate shared by other races and ethnicities throughout most regional texts.

Another social history technique that regional writers need to adopt is the normalization of conflict. In most regional texts, conflicts are downplayed in several ways. One method is by fencing it off. For example, a chapter in the Schwantes text titled "Holes in the Social Fabric" contains information on 19th-century women and racial/ethnic groups that does not fit into the major theme of economic growth and development. As a result, the Seattle anti-Chinese riots of the 1880s only merit one sentence. Another more common technique is the adoption of the omniscient narrative voice. Thus railroads are built in the region apparently without human hands, and decisions about crucial matters like routes and rates are not traceable to personal decisions.

Other narrative techniques also downplay conflict—e.g., certain events are described in full detail, but their consequences are mentioned separately. In one instance, Schwantes discusses the 1900 purchase of 900,000 acres of Washington timberlands by Frederick Weyerhaeuser, who was fresh from denuding the forests of Wisconsin and Minnesota, but only in a later paragraph mentions the accompanying "ruinous competition, overproduction, and market chaos." This is classic textbook prose (and I have written my share) in which events are described, but blame is not allocated. Obviously the most important part—the effect of the economic decisions of powerful capitalists on ordinary people—is missing. In other words, the text reinforces the student mindset to think always in individualistic and personal rather than structural terms.

The reasons for changing the avoiding-conflict narrative ought to be obvious. The omniscient voice of textbooks causes events to seem inevitable and unchangeable, outside the realm of human choice. Also, the use of the omniscient voice results in a loss of the sense of individual responsibility. In textbook writing, however, assigning responsibility also imputes blame. As a result, the standard choices are to focus on well-documented figures like politicians (where someone else already has assigned blame) or to retreat into bland narrative. This is probably why students so dislike textbooks. The narrative is boring!

But this assertion begs the question of how a textbook author can successfully write about conflict. Most textbooks do not have enough space for explanation of the actual complexity and the many-sidedness of most conflicts. Some writers have solved this dilemma with a flip-flop, in which the ignored become the heroes and the major focus, while the dominant group becomes one-dimensional oppressors.[15] Historic justice may support the flip-flop, but it still seems inadequate as a narrative solution to the problem of conflict. A better solution, which is easier to name than to achieve, is to normalize conflict; that is, to treat it as the ordinary, expectable consequence of interactions between persons and groups struggling for autonomy and control. An important proviso should be added, pointing out the need for continuing attention to the changing nature of regional hegemony as the "mix" of groups and their relative successes or failures occur.

This direct approach to conflict is not the theme of most regional texts. Rather, the almost universal emphasis is on growth and maturation. Chronological metaphors like "coming of age" are common. As an example, for the later-19th century, Schwantes devotes most of his attention to describing the establishment and growth of major industries and occupations. This lends a false sense of stability to regional history, when in reality mobility and impermanence became common experiences for the majority of the population. Two groups in particular, laborers and immigrants (often the same people), were most affected by this instability.

A stronger focus on the varieties of immigration and occupations would not only recapture some of the uncertainty and difficulty in what Phoebe Judson calls "a pioneer's search for an ideal home," but would also stress commonalities among all foreign and domestic immigrants.[16] For instance, a textbook with this mantra would give as much space to the first Chinese, Scandinavian, Japanese, African American, and Chicano migrants as to the Oregon Trail pioneers. So long as these latter domestic "emigrants" hold their present privileged position, white dominance of regional history will go unchallenged. And so long as family migration and work are treated as two separate experiences, rather than as a deeply connected composite, a major aspect of regional distinctiveness will be poorly understood.[17]

Commendably, the Schwantes text devotes nearly one-half of its length to the 20th-century Pacific Northwest, with over 100 pages covering the post-World War II period. The attention to the 20th century distinguishes this textbook from earlier ones. As Schwantes notes, popular notions of the West remain rooted in 19th-century frontier mythology. As a result, he declares, "Many icons and images that derive from the history of the 19th-century American West are instantly recognizable around the world, while those pertaining to the 20th-century West are not generally recognized as being western at all."[18] In this part of the textbook, Schwantes skillfully describes and explains some of the 20th-century changes in the Pacific Northwest that help break through the 19th-century fixation. The final section, "The Pacific Northwest Comes of Age," is divided into chapters clearly explaining the demographic and economic effects of World War II, followed by chapters devoted to the postwar economy, to politics, and finally to contemporary environmental and cultural issues.

Some of the same narrative techniques used in the 19th-century chapters still appear, however, even as the region changed demographically. Although racial and ethnic groups pop up more frequently than earlier in the text, they never claim much space. Most notably, the Japanese, who are briefly mentioned as immigrants early in the 20th century, only appear again when they are rounded up and shipped off to internment camps in World War II. Even though the ordeal of internment is described sympathetically, the failure to explain in detail the extent of interwar anti-Asian sentiment makes the 1940s action seem like an aberration rather than a logical result of longstanding racist attitudes.

In fact, the common failure of mainstream textbook authors to devote space to the complete story of the Japanese immigrant experience continues to surprise me. From a narrative point of view, the story has everything—the trans-Pacific migration, the struggles of settlement, the horrors of internment, and the triumph of return and reparation. This deeply human Japanese American story could serve as the narrative thread for 20th-century Pacific Northwest history.

What can be said about the role of women in regional texts? All too frequently, the answer is "nothing." In that respect, the Schwantes text does better than most. There is fairly consistent coverage of women in politics, especially in suffrage and in their recent successes in elective office (Washington's proportion of women legislators is the highest in the nation). Famous women, in particular missionary Narcissa Whitman and suffragist May Arkwright Hutton, are profiled, and there is a page on women workers in World War II. Yet, they are tokens, granted occasional agency, but little more. Most of the many activities of women throughout Pacific Northwest history remain unmentioned. It might be argued that regional women's historians have not yet written the kind of sustained narratives that textbook authors rely on. But basically, it is because gender and race are not major categories of analysis in most regional texts. Politics, the economy, and the environment provide the main narrative structure.

Every textbook author faces the question of choices among many stories available. In his text, Carlos Schwantes has fashioned a strong and readable account from his chosen categories. He has produced a clear presentation of regional history, if by that term we mean the older definition of regionalism as a search for distinctiveness in the larger nation. The choices are the accepted ones, until the inevitable question is asked about what groups are tokenized and marginalized. But if regionalism is defined to recognize these marginalized people, in effect to look *inside* rather than *outside* the region, a new mix of elements and a new narrative style—more thematic, more contingent—will be necessary.

How would one construct such an account? How shall we shape our narrative once we discard the national framework and the inevitable story of settlement, development, and apparent progress? How do we transform an apparently inevitable narrative into a contingent one? What themes and conceptual tools are useful? Here I will draw together the suggestions of the previous pages and see where they lead us.[19]

First, we must empty the concept of region of all of its pre-existing meaning. If the Pacific Northwest is genuinely the creation of its inhabitants, then *they* must decide its meanings and boundaries. It must be recognized that these boundaries changed over time, from the north- south trade and kinship links of coastal native peoples to eventually the present-day U.S.- Canadian and state boundaries. Yet, even today, regional borders are constantly breached by inhabitants whose primary loyalties lie elsewhere. Trans-national migrants like the Irish miners who came to Butte and Anaconda in the 19th century, those from Japan early in the 20th century, and those from Mexico since the 1940s (to name just a few) all have links to their homelands that stretch far beyond conventional demarcations. The idea of flexible and permeable boundaries seems one valuable way to acknowledge all the region's residents who do not claim a regional identity. Otherwise the concept of region is exclusive rather than inclusive.

Now to return to Donald Worster's deceptively simple instructions about "how a people or peoples acquired a place and, then, how they perceived and tried to make use of it."[20] First, we begin with what is known about the lives of the generations of native people who first occupied the region and attempt to draw a full, rich portrait of the ways they lived on the land and how they regarded outsiders. Seen from the native perspective, most of the well-known explorers, including Lewis and Clark, were rather inconsequential because the contact was so brief. The first real outside agents of change, because of their profound effect on the native people's livelihood, were the sea-borne and land-based fur traders of the late-18th and early-19th centuries. Next, chronologically, came the white American pioneers of the 1830s and 1840s and the successful U.S. diplomatic claim to the Pacific Northwest. And so forth. Various groups came to the Pacific Northwest, often in waves of migration that can be differentiated by time and ethnic group, and each in turn interacted with those already present in the region.

The changing demography of the Pacific Northwest is an important part of our reconceptualization of region, but by itself it does not lend itself to a compelling narrative. To make these ongoing encounters meaningful, we need to rediscover precisely the sources of conflict that earlier regional textbooks strove to ignore. Not all confrontations were about land alone. In an example of gender system conflict, native women did hard physical work that European women usually did not perform. As a result, white observers assumed that Indian women were degraded and subordinated to their men. This incorrect presumption, which ignored the equality that Indian women possessed, became an important source of the cultural misunderstanding that led to a feeling of Euro-American superiority. Such interrelated analytic categories of race, class, and gender provide valuable tools to examine the conflicts that shaped the region, and should be employed in the writing of the future.

Some readers may object that I put too much stress on race and ethnicity, rather than on individuals. That is a valid point, in the sense that the use of racial/ethnic categories commits the same error as older notions of region by assuming an internal homogeneity. The use of these categories need not create racial stereotypes or imply homogeneity, but simply provide aggregations of individuals in large enough groups to make a manageable narrative. But neither is the use of race/ethnicity simply a narrative tool, because social conflicts do in fact arise from different cultural values, which usually originate in the racial/ethnic group itself. Although the organization of other societies may be based on homogeneity, the primary differentiator, in our nation of immigrants, has always been race. My deliberate use of racial/ethnic categories, then, is intended to counteract the persistent and pernicious emphasis on individualism that prevails in textbooks. Such accounts usually overlook the important ways connections tie our societies together.

By far the most important overlooked connector is kinship. Being part of a family (however that family is defined) has been the basic building block of societies throughout the world and throughout history. For example, the Oregon pioneers of the 1840s and 1850s put their trust in kinship. Famous families such as the Applegates of Oregon traveled the trail in a multigenerational group, but even more common was the pattern of chain migration exemplified by

Washington's Phoebe Judson. She and her husband migrated in 1852, joining her parents and a sister who had made the trip earlier. They were joined in subsequent years by her husband's parents and siblings.[21]

Similar connections have characterized migrations to the Pacific Northwest ever since, except where exclusion laws prevented it. This latter restriction is illustrated by an example from a cache of letters discovered in the Kam Wah Chung Mercantile Store in John Day, Oregon, in the 1970s. Chinese miners, who sent and received mail at the store, were forbidden by the Chinese Exclusion Act of 1882 from bringing their wives and families to the United States. Yet, the exclusion legislation failed to diminish the importance of trans-national kinship ties for one Chinese miner, who received the following letter from his mother in 1898:

> Chin-hain, my Son: I'm writing to tell you the whole family is fine; you don't need to worry too much. But because I'm your mother, I feel you've been away from home far too long… Save your money and come home no later than next year to get married. I probably won't live much longer. If you come home after I die you won't have a mother to depend on. How will you soothe your conscience then?[22]

Kinship not only connects people over distance, it is also the crucial underpinning of new communities. As migrants of every ethnic and racial group settled in the Pacific Northwest, their children intermarried, often with the offspring of neighbors of different ethnicities, thus forming new kin networks that provided vital stability. But when members of racial and ethnic minorities faced hostility and discrimination, as Monica Sone describes in the pre-World War II Japanese community in Seattle, out-marriage (marriage to members of other racial and ethnic groups) became uncommon. In fact, in many Western states it was illegal.[23] Formal restrictions on marriage may seem trivial, but they prevent underlying and ongoing connections that, in Sone's case, might have helped subvert racial barriers.

Kinship systems also are often an important part of community laboring structures, providing the connection between work and family. For instance, the Norwegian Lutheran farming community of La Crosse, founded in eastern Washington in the 1890s, was tied together by mutually reinforcing bonds of kinship, religion, and the common enterprise of farming.[24] The role of specific occupations as shapers of communities has long been acknowledged, but in the traditional versions, such as Frederick Jackson Turner's famous definition of the frontier, all the identified workers are male.

Work is more than a way of understanding how a population makes a living, since it has, in fact, always been gendered, raced, and (most obviously) classed. As Laurie Mercier has pointed out, the traditional Pacific Northwest occupations in agriculture, logging, mining, and fishing have historically been male-dominated, but communities composed of women as well as men have grown up around these industries. Women's many activities have probably been most fully recognized in mining towns, as Mercier demonstrates in her book *Anaconda,* where she shows the many ways women were involved in shaping the ethnic and working-class identity of that Montana smelter town throughout the 20th century.[25]

These few examples, roughly arranged in chronological order, illustrate the themes that can be used to drive the narrative of a new regional history. First there is the land, then the people who live on it, how they organize their communities around work and family, and how they struggle with other peoples to establish, maintain, or modify the values they place on specific systems of gender, race, and class. These are the basic principles that can be used to fashion a coherent narrative.

When a new regional history is written, it will be very different from our current versions. No longer will textbooks open with stirring tales of European exploration. They will begin with lengthy and vivid descriptions of what the land meant to the native inhabitants and how they made their living on it. The new text will give as much space to the Chinese, Scandinavian, Japanese, African American, and Chicano migrations as to the Oregon Trail pioneers. Politics will remain an important part of the text, but it will be discussed in the context of the different communities that shaped it. A stylistic change, but one with deep meaning, will be the use of particularistic rather than the unisex language that is so common in current textbooks. In other words, difference will be evident in the language itself.

The principles described here—gender, kinship, race/ethnicity, occupation, and class—shaped the lives of the migrants who came to the Pacific Northwest and formed the basis of new and growing communities. For a general public unaware of these shaping bonds—of the way we all have been affected by our regional experience—historians can promote a more complete and accurate Pacific Northwest history in the articles, books, and textbooks they write, in the talks they give, and in the classrooms where they teach. The new regionalism, in which race, gender, and other forms of difference are central, requires another kind of textbook, one that is still to be written. Until then, we need to remind ourselves to read existing textbooks with critical attention to what and who is missing.

Notes

1. Portions of this essay appeared previously in my article, "From the Inside Out: Rewriting Regional History," *Frontiers: A Journal of Women Studies* 22 (2001).
2. Patricia Nelson Limerick, *Legacy of Conquest: The Unbroken Past of the American West*, rev. ed. (New York: W.W. Norton, 1987), 2006.
3. For my first effort to add to the master narrative of Pacific Northwest history, see "The Challenge of Women's History," in David H. Stratton and George A. Frykman, eds., *The Changing Pacific Northwest: Interpreting Its Past* (Pullman: Washington State University Press, 1988), and in Karen J. Blair, ed., *Women in Pacific Northwest History* (Seattle: University of Washington Press, 1988). My second effort was "Tied to Other Lives: Women in Pacific Northwest History," in Karen J. Blair, ed., *Women in Pacific Northwest History*, 2nd ed. (Seattle: University of Washington Press, 2001).
4. Carlos A. Schwantes, *The Pacific Northwest: An Interpretive History*, 2nd ed. (Lincoln: University of Nebraska Press, 1996).
5. Joan Scott, "Gender: A Useful Category of Historical Analysis," *Feminism and History*, Joan Scott, ed., (New York: Oxford University Press, 1996).
6. Joel Garreau, *The Nine Nations of North America* (Boston: Houghton Mifflin, 1981); Ernest Callenbach, *Ecotopia: The Notebooks and Reports of William Weston* (Berkeley, California: Banyan Tree, 1975); William Riebsame, ed., *Atlas of the New West: Portrait of a Changing Region* (New York: W.W. Norton, 1997); Sheila McManus, *The Line which Separates: Race, Gender, and the Making of the Alberta-Montana Border* (Lincoln: University of Nebraska Press, 2005).
7. Donald Worster, "New West, True West: Interpreting the Region's History," *Western Historical Quarterly* 18, no. 2 (1987):149; Limerick, *Legacy of Conquest*, 27.
8. Worster, "New West, True West," 149; Patricia Nelson Limerick, "Region and Reason," in *All over the Map: Rethinking American Regions*, Edward Ayers, et al. (Baltimore: Johns Hopkins University Press, 1996), 84; Katherine Morissey, *Mental Territories: Mapping the Inland Empire* (Ithaca, New York: Cornell University Press, 1997).
9. John Mack Faragher, et al., *Out of Many: A History of the American People*, 5th ed. (New York: Prentice Hall, 2005).
10. Irving Stone, *Men to Match My Mountains: The Opening of the Far West. 1840–1900* (Garden City, New York: Doubleday, 1956); Brian Booth, ed., *Wildmen, Wobblies, and Whistle Punks: Stewart Holbrook's Lowbrow Northwest* (Corvallis: Oregon State University Press, 1992); Stephen E. Ambrose, *Undaunted Courage: Meriwether Lewis, Thomas Jefferson, and the Opening of the American West* (New York: Simon and Schuster, 1996).
11. Worster, "New West, True West," 149.
12. See for example, Ella E. Clark, *Indian Legends of the Pacific Northwest* (Berkeley: University of California Press, 1953); Jarold Ramsey, *Coyote Was Going There: Indian Literature of the Oregon Country* (Seattle: University of Washington Press, 1977); Zitkala-Sa, *American Indian Stories, Legends, and other Writings* (New York: Penguin Books, 2003); Donald M. Hines, *Ghost Voices: Yakima Indian Myths, Legend, Humor, and Hunting Stories* (Issaquah, Washington: Great Eagle, 1992).
13. Colin Calloway, *One Vast Winter Count: The Native American West before Lewis and Clark* (Lincoln: University of Nebraska Press, 2003), 21.
14. For other views of white-native relations, see Alexandra Harmon, *Indians in the Making* (Berkeley: University of California Press, 1999), and Elizabeth Vibert, *Traders' Tales: Narratives of Cultural Encounters in the Columbia Plateau, 1807–1846* (Norman: University of Oklahoma Press, 1997).

15. This is my view of the narrative strategy employed by Ronald Takaki in his widely acclaimed study, *A Different Mirror: A History of Multicultural America* (Boston: Little, Brown, 1993).

16. Phoebe Goodell Judson, *A Pioneer's Search for an Ideal Home* (1927; reprint, Lincoln: University of Nebraska Press, 1984).

17. For the experience of Mexican American migrants viewed in these terms, see Antonia Castaneda, "Que Se Pudieran Defender (So You Could Defend Yourselves): Chicanas, Regional History, and National Discourses," *Frontiers: A Journal of Women Studies* 22 (2001).

18. Carlos A. Schwantes, "The Case of the Missing Century, or Where Did the American West Go after 1900?" *Pacific Historical Review* 70, no. 1 (2001):2.

19. For the following discussion, I am indebted to the thoughts of five regional women's historians—Antonia Castaneda, Jeanne Eder, Laurie Mercier, Mary Murphy, and Gail Nomura—who met with me in 2000 to discuss these issues.

20. Worster, "New West, True West," 149.

21. Judson, *A Pioneer's Search for an Ideal Home.*

22. Letter to a son from his mother in China, February 2, 1898, in the Kam Wah Chung Collection, Oregon Historical Society, Portland.

23. Monica Sone, *Nisei Daughter* (Boston: Little, Brown, 1953).

24. Marvin G. Slind and Fred C. Bohm, *Norse to the Palouse: Sagas of the Selbu Norwegians* (Pullman, Washington: Norlys Press, 1990).

25. Laurie Mercier, *Anaconda: Labor, Community, and Culture in Montana's Smelter City* (Urbana: University of Illinois Press, 2001).